Bedside Seductions

Nursing and the Victorian Imagination, 1830-1880

Catherine Judd

Bedside Seductions

Nursing and the Victorian Imagination, 1830–1880

Catherine Judd

St. Martin's Press
New York

Library of Congress Cataloging-in-Publication Data

Judd, Catherine.
  Bedside seductions : nursing and the Victorian imagination, 1830-1880 / Catherine Judd.
       p.   cm.
  Includes bibliographical references and index.
  ISBN 0-312-17705-4
  1. English fiction—19th century—History and criticism.
2. Nurses in literature. 3. Literature and medicine—Great Britain-
-History—19th century. 4. Women and literature—Great Britain-
-History—19th century. 5. Nurses—Great Britain—History—19th
century. 6. Great Britain—History—Victoria, 1837-1901. 7. Social
conflict in literature. 8. Social classes in literature.   I. Title.
PR878.N8J83   1997
823'.809352613—dc21   97-32199
                                                                             CIP

Design by Acme Art, Inc.
First edition: January 1998
10 9 8 7 6 5 4 3 2 1

To Marc and Helena Bramble

Contents

Acknowledgments

I am grateful to the National Endowment for the Humanities, which provided a grant for the summer of 1994. I also thank the University of Miami for generous summer fellowships as well as leave time. I am indebted to the staff of the libraries at Stanford University, the University of California at Berkeley, the University of Washington, and the National Institute of Health library in Bethesda, Maryland. A version of chapter 5 appeared in *Nineteenth-Century Contexts*.

My work on this book benefited greatly from the early readings of D. A. Miller, Thomas Laqueur, and especially Catherine Gallagher. I owe much to their intelligent responses and to their encouragement from the inception of this project. I have also found invaluable the many conversations about narrative I have shared with Robert Tracy; John Bishop; Leslie Whitney; Teresa Faherty; Annie Morse; Juliet Musso; Andrea Liss; Ellen Lane; Nina Zaslove; Kimberly Latte O'Malley; Mia Baldwin; and Aliki Barnstone.

My colleagues at the University of Miami have provided much intellectual and emotional sustenance. Tassie Gwilliam, Russ Castronovo, and Sandra Pouchet Paquet have generously read and commented on parts of this work. I have also benefited from the advice and support of Benesha Fenster; Ruth Barron; Mary Hope Anderson; Mary Dulik; Kathryn Kruger; Frank Stringfellow; Mihoko Suzuki; Frank Palmeri; John Paul Russo; Kathryn Freeman; Shari Benstock; Leslie Bow; Patrick McCarthy; Teresa and Tom Prendergast; Thomas Goodman; Anthony Barthelemy; Peter J. Bellis; Thomas Pepper; Ross Murfin; Lindsey Tucker; Zack Bowen; Robert and Anna Antoni; Jeffrey Shoulson; and Margery Sokoloff. Further, my graduate students at the University of Miami have helped me to refine many of my readings of Victorian narrative.

My editor at St. Martin's Press, Maura E. Burnett, and the production manager, Alan Bradshaw, have extended invaluable advice in the preparation of this book for publication.

This work would not have been possible were it not for the support of my parents Lewis and Patricia Judd, and Anne Hoag Kennedy, and my sisters Allison Fee, Deirdre Kennedy, Stephanie Judd, Serena Kennedy, and Maura Kennedy, and brother Miles Kennedy. The advice and goodwill of Tony and Sylvie Roder, Paul Roder, Cliff Greenblatt, Frank Fee, the Nealy family, and Henry Lewis Greenblatt have also been crucial. Well remembered is Susan Hoag, and our dear friend Pam O'Connor and her daughter Caitlin whom we lost during the summer of 1996.

Finally, I dedicate this work to my husband Marc Roder, whose splendid paintings offer me continual creative inspiration, and to our beautiful baby daughter, Helena Bramble Roder.

Preface

"A nurse's tongue is privileged to talk"

—English proverb circa 1659

In 1744, the author of *The Midwife Rightly Instructed* published *The Nurse's Guide,* a "dialogue betwixt a SURGEON and a NURSE." Here the wise Surgeon imparts his expertise to Lucina, a "very handy, tractable, neat Woman" who wishes to "recommend herself to the People of better Fashion in Quality of a DRY-NURSE" (1).[1] At the start of the dialogue, the Surgeon declares that the "two grand Qualifications of a good Nurse" are "FIDELITY and TRACTABLENESS," and before instructing Lucina, he exacts a promise of obedience from her. Lucina assures him that she "shall be infinitely oblig'd to [him] and shall endeavour carefully to treasure up in [her] Mind whatever [he] shall be so good as to impart to [her]" (2).

Towards the end of the eighteenth century, James Humphreys published his popular *Nurse's Guide, or Companion for a Sick Chamber.* Here, too, the narrator emphasized the obedience and "tractableness" required of the professional nurse: "none should be nurses, unless they are possessed of the following qualities, viz. honesty and fidelity . . ." (48). It becomes clear in the course of reading Humphreys's guide that this "fidelity" refers most specifically to the nurse's allegiance to the instructions of the attending physician:

> if the nurse deviates from the above plan, it ought to be by the advice
> of the Physician (58); it behoves the patient therefore to regard [the
> doctor's] rules, the nurse to see them punctually observed, and both,
> to be cautious how they deviate from them (137); when you are
> obliged to act by yourselves, you are justifiable in acting to the best
> of your judgement; but, when a [Physician] is concerned, whom you
> see watchful of every step which nature takes, and ready to give the

necessary aid as soon as indicated, you may certainly rest satisfied
with only such [food and medicine] as he allows (141).

Although Humphreys can conceive of certain situations in which the
nurse might be called upon to act according to her own judgment,
those moments of independence must be quickly relinquished with
the reappearance of the "infallible" physician.

Less than one hundred and fifty years after *The Nurses's Guide*
appeared, Florence Nightingale composed her generically similar
Notes on Nursing: What it is, and What it is not (1859). Yet here the
compliance and submission of the nurse has been replaced by a
necessary self reliance: "I have often seen really good nurses distressed, because they could not impress the doctor with the real danger
of their patient. . . . The distress is very legitimate, but it generally
arises from the nurse not having the power of laying clearly and
shortly before the doctor the facts from which she derives her opinion,
or from the doctor being hasty and inexperienced, and not capable of
eliciting them. A man who really cares for his patients, will soon learn
to ask for and appreciate the information of a nurse, who is at once a
careful observer and a clear reporter" (123).

Between Humphreys, whose vision of the ideal nurse encompassed mute obedience and unthinking reliability, and Nightingale,
who represented the nurse as potentially in rebellion against the
authority of the doctor, there exists a gap that is both minuscule and
immense. It is minuscule in the sense that each one of these theorists
of nursing offered structurally comparable texts with their emphatic,
pragmatic instructions to those attending the sickroom. Nonetheless,
the breach between these two eighteenth-century doctors and
Florence Nightingale seems unnavigable despite the superficial correspondences between their projects (all are interested in professionalizing nursing, all believe in the miasmatic theory of contagion).[2] Within
the space of time that separates Humphreys from Nightingale, the
eighteenth-century ideal of an obedient, tractable nurse has been
supplanted by a sickroom attendant who has not only voice and
authority, but heroic, and even prophetic, stature. As we shall see,
through a series of complex maneuvers, the humble sickroom attendant of the late eighteenth century transmutes into a pivotal cultural
icon of the mid-Victorian era. In the following pages, I chart the
repercussions of this remarkable transformation.

Introduction: Nursing and the Victorian Imagination

DURING THE COURSE OF BRITAIN'S CRIMEAN WAR (1854-1856), Florence Nightingale emerged as one of the exalted heroes of the nineteenth century, her renown based on her ministrations to the working-class soldiers in Britain's military hospital at Scutari.[1] In his poem "Santa Filomena" (1856), Henry Wadsworth Longfellow pays tribute to Nightingale when he proclaims that

> A lady with a lamp shall stand
> In the great history of the land,
> A noble type of good,
> Heroic womanhood.

Longfellow's homage to Nightingale is only one of the thousands of accolades that poured forth for her during the mid nineteenth century, her role of national and international secular saint generating a hagiography that often obscured her actual goals, goals strongly aligned with Benthamic programs of public health and institutional reformation and the administration of the general health of the British army.[2]

Although the adulation that Nightingale garnered during the mid-nineteenth century derived in part from her force of character and the romantic situation surrounding her decision to become an army nurse, Nightingale's stupendous popularity more pointedly bespeaks a profound shift in the status and image of the nurse during the Victorian era. Due to the prodigious fame of "the Lady with a Lamp," nursing historians traditionally have dated the emergence of modern Anglo-American nursing from the time of Nightingale's labors during the Crimean War. Revisionists push the date back to the 1840s when reformers such as Elizabeth Fry, Lydia Sellon, Edward Pusey, and

William Gladstone founded Protestant nursing sisterhoods throughout Great Britain.[3] As we shall see, however, the terms for nursing reformation and the creation of the heroic nurse were in fact already set in motion by the 1820s, thus suggesting an investment in the trope of the nurse during the early nineteenth century that set the stage for the emergence of Nightingale in the 1850s. That Nightingale's popularity should attain such expansive dimensions indicates an ideological significance for mid-Victorians in the concept of the nurse that far transcends, although it is best exemplified by, the cult of Florence Nightingale.[4]

In this study I trace the remarkable shifts in the status and meaning of the Victorian nurse, and by extension, the nurse's seminal location in mid-Victorian literary and social history. By examining representations of the nurse in mid-nineteenth-century England, especially the ways in which the nurse became codified into a privileged object of knowledge for the mid-Victorians, I recover the events that the transmutation from Humphreys to Nightingale suggests: at the heart of this metamorphosis, I argue, is the convergence of Romantic notions of poetic responsibility, mid-Victorian concepts of domestic ideology, and positivist-inspired issues of social and public-health reforms.[5]

From the early to the mid-nineteenth century, the nurse develops as a category for perceptions about gender and class, consolidating for Victorian writers fundamental political and social anxieties—especially concerns over class conflict, public health, the Woman Question, female heroics, and the construction of middle-class sexuality. The overdetermined fascination nursing images generate points to the nurse's importance as a paradigm for imaginary resolutions to ideological problems faced by the mid-Victorians. Cultural theorists such as Michel Foucault have argued for the importance of decoding interpretive frameworks, of examining those "ideologemes" with which the narratives of ideology are constructed. Following this view, the central project of *Bedside Seductions* is to set in motion the hitherto inert and typologizing classifications of the Victorian nurse through their reinsertion into a concrete historical situation.[6]

BEDSIDE SEDUCTIONS

In 1872, Sir Lawrence Alma-Tadema completed his painting *The Nurse* (fig. A). Executed in the autumnal jewel-tones favored by the Pre-

Figure A: Alma-Tadema, "The Nurse," 1872

Raphaelites, *The Nurse* delineates a neurasthenic who stares from her sickbed with a look of despair or resignation. At her bedside, but screened from her view by a rich tapestry, sits the Nurse of the painting's title.[7] Alma-Tadema is known especially for his skill in rendering the textures of skin and fabric, and judging from the Nurse's lustrous and lavishly embroidered clothing, she seems not to be a working-class nurse but a genteel volunteer or a relative of the patient. However, the Nurse pays no heed to her distressed charge. Rather, enclosed by the chivalric figures woven into the sickbed's tapestry, she is lost in her perusal of what appears to be an illuminated manuscript. At this moment, the Nurse has either drifted into sleep or is in mid-blink. In any case, her eyes are downcast and she wears a beatific smile. In his painting, Alma-Tadema represents nursing as a retreat into a private, fanciful space—a space impenetrable by either the patient or the painting's audience. In this sense the Nurse symbolizes, like Alfred Tennyson's isolated Lady of Shalott, the seductions and solipsisms of the imagination itself.

Alma-Tadema's painting appears towards the end of the period that I explore in this study. By 1873, the world had grown used to

Nightingale's heroism, a heroism that threatened to become a cliché. By 1873, the idealism and reforming energies that helped to shape the novels of the 1840s had died down. By 1873, the French systems of public-health surveillance and notions of a "medical police" had gained a stronghold in England, as evidenced by the notorious Contagious Diseases Acts of the 1860s.[8] By 1873, Britain was turning its attention away from domestic problems and moving increasingly towards empire-building, as illustrated by Prime Minister Benjamin Disraeli's successful negotiations for England's control of the Suez Canal in 1875 and John Ruskin's famous lecture of 1870 where he asked his audience of Oxford students whether "you youths of England [will] make your country again a royal throne of kings, a sceptred isle, for all the world a source of light" by founding "colonies as fast and as far as she is able, formed of her most energetic and worthiest men."[9] By 1873, against the backdrop of the cataclysmic changes wrought by the Industrial Revolution, England had experienced the specific catastrophes of the Irish Famine (1845-49), the Crimean War, the Indian Mutiny (1857), the Eyre scandal (1865), and the ongoing cholera epidemics.[10] By 1873, the recently concluded Franco-Prussian War had helped to solidify the presence of English nurses on the battlefield, and the professionalization of nursing was well underway with the founding of the Nightingale School of Nursing in 1860 and the continuing incursion of trained nurses into England's homes, institutions, and neighborhoods.

None of these historic events seems evident in Alma-Tadema's painting—indeed, the clothing and furniture indicate *The Nurse's* medieval inflection.[11] Nonetheless some of the most crucial issues of Victorian nursing are bodied forth in his painting. First, as we have seen, the determining affiliation of nursing with the seductions of the imagination is foregrounded here. Further, Alma-Tadema's medieval setting signifies the inherent nostalgia surrounding the Victorian nurse. As an example of the Victorian cult of the household nun, the nurse participates in nineteenth-century Protestant England's paradoxical yearning for the long-banished Catholic institutions that could provide a coherent social faith.

Yet Alma-Tadema's nurse is far from a St. Theresa, a St. Elizabeth, or a Mary Magdalen, all of whom provided models for the heroic British nurse of the 1840s through the 1860s.[12] In his painting, Alma-

Figure B: "Old-style" nurse

Figure C: "New-style" nurse

Tadema breaks several of the Victorian conventions of what was known as "new-style," or professional, nursing. Indeed, representations of a sleeping nurse and a horribly alert, neglected patient are part of the cadre of the anti–working-class nursing reformation movement of the nineteenth century in which the neglectful "old-style" nurse was inevitably depicted as aged, corpulent, slovenly and unconscious due to drugs or alcohol (fig. B). The heroic new-style nurse, of whom Nightingale was the most famous example, was celebrated precisely for her erect, vigilant managerial competence and dedication to her patients (fig. C).[13] Here Alma-Tadema, fond of irony in his paintings, delineates a young, beautiful, apparently upper-class nurse, but aligns her with the negligence associated with old-style nursing. Although Alma-Tadema's inversion of the clichés of old- and new-style nursing is fairly atypical, this reversal nonetheless reflects the general motif of transposition present in the figure of the Victorian nurse. Reversals of class positions (old-style nurses "ruling" their middle- and upper-class patients; new-style nurses tending to the sick poor) and gender roles (military nurses saving the soldiers; the supine, sickly male patient and the powerful, healthy female nurse) inform the anxieties and charisma surrounding the mid-Victorian nurse.

In this work, I am claiming for the mid-nineteenth-century nurse a similar cultural resonance to that amply recognized in the figure of the fallen woman and the Victorian prostitute.[14] As we shall see, the Victorian nurse mobilized issues analogous to those raised by the fallen women in terms of class, gender, and sexuality. However, there are added complexities due to the nurse's specific association with the Victorian medical profession. Further, while the prostitute registered concerns about working-class sexuality, exploitation, and social control, the nurse functioned as a symbol whose class affiliations ranged from Nightingale to Charles Dickens's infamous working-class character Sairey Gamp—in this sense, she seems to be a figure that erased class. Yet, as I argue especially in chapter 2 on nursing and sexuality, class antagonisms remain at the heart of representations of the mid-nineteenth-century nurse.

In the Victorian nurse, I locate the invasiveness of middle-class reform and domestic ideology and I also map the ways that that aggression was connected with the pleasures of the imagination itself. To return to Alma-Tadema's painting, we need only to remark the apparent desperation in the patient's eyes to correlate this despair with the pleasures that the negligent nurse is experiencing. While ignoring her patient's distress, the nurse appears selfishly absorbed in the satisfactions of her illuminated text and her own imagination. This tension between the duties and the pleasures of the imagination embodied by Alma-Tadema's dreaming Nurse was one of the most salient controversies of mid-Victorian aesthetics.[15] However, Alma-Tadema represents the nursing imagination not as an unproblematic retreat of pleasure. Rather, cloaked and inaccessible, the striking darkness of the nurse's hood seems a tacit recognition of both the sinister and seductive qualities of this imaginative space. The menacing image of the hood in Alma-Tadema's painting signifies a hostility in the act of nursing: that this aggression is utterly passive underscores the subtleties of its manifestation. Alexander Welsh has pointed out that "personified death" in the nineteenth century "was not always seen as a masculine force or a robed and hooded skeleton" but was often portrayed as "a beckoning, welcoming, comforting figure," that is, as "an angel of the softer sex" (192).

NURSING AND THE VICTORIAN NOVEL

As is evident from Alma-Tadema's painting, as well as poems such as Alfred Tennyson's *The Princess* (1847) and Owen Meredith's *Lucile* (1860), the image of the nurse was a powerful symbol for many imaginative laborers, regardless of their medium. However, while the cultural impact of nursing was widespread, the nurse became a particularly crucial trope within the mid-nineteenth-century domestic novel. Starting from John Ruskin's contention in 1880 that detailed, clinical depictions of disease and death characterize the Victorian novel, I argue in the following chapter that the extreme pathology located in descriptions of suffering and illness that, in Ruskin's words, "mark the peculiar tone of the modern novel" derives not strictly from a Victorian fascination with morbidity, but further indicates the ideological significance of the image of nursing itself.

Although there has been much recent critical interest in nineteenth-century British and U.S. nursing, most of this scholarship concentrates on Florence Nightingale in particular or army nursing (during the Crimean and American Civil wars) and the reformation of hospital nursing in general.[16] In fact, sparse notice has been paid to images of nursing and nurses in Victorian literature per se. For example, in her important study of women's work in the Victorian novel, Helena Michie argues that "heroines of canonical Victorian novels [are] rarely depicted in the act of working. Like sex and eating, women's work is carried on in the lacunae of the text" (36). Michie cites in example Jane Eyre, Dorothea Brooke, Dinah Morris, Mary Garth, and Little Dorrit, all of whom she claims are seen working as infrequently as they are seen eating. Yet each one of these characters recurrently is depicted ministering to the sick, an activity that Victorians considered to be at once arduous and heroic labor. Similarly, Elizabeth Langland's otherwise exhaustive study of the motif of the "angel in the house," which focuses especially on the "angels" of the mid-Victorian novel, pays only slight attention to nurses or the act of nursing.

In his discussion of the Victorian "angel of death," Alexander Welsh writes that "Victorian novels would lead us to believe that it is the special office of young women to watch over the dying. . . . [The Victorian novel] dwell[s] on the subject, celebrating the heroine's loyalty and courage and even hinting of some special efficacy in her services. Agnes Wickfield, Jane Eyre, Mary Garth, Margaret Hale, Little Dorrit, Esther Summerson, [and Florence Dombey], all figure in deathbed scenes and in some cases death occurs in their embrace" (184).[17] Like Welsh, several recent scholars have recognized the importance of representations of nursing in the mid-nineteenth-century novel.[18] However, these studies have tended to foreground not the nurse, but the sickroom or the general theme of illness in the Victorian novel. While these explorations have engendered beneficial insights into patterns of nursing in the realist novel, none situates nursing or the nurse within a detailed historical framework.[19] In contrast, I am particularly interested in the bearing of political and institutional constructions on Victorian fiction.

NURSING AND SOCIAL REFORM

The representations of the nurse I scrutinize in this work were created primarily by middle-class writers. Although there are broad differences between these writers in terms of religious, political, and social beliefs, there nonetheless exists a shared set of assumptions about working-class morality, sexuality, and culture, and the perils that the working classes presented to middle- and upper-class security. As with most nineteenth-century social improvement projects, the mid-Victorian focus on nursing grew out of England's dissenting traditions and eighteenth-century reformation energies.[20] However, within the nineteenth century's ecumenical "age of reform," medical reforms held a special place. First, public-health issues seemed to possess a unique clarity compared to other nineteenth-century political topics such as abolition or enfranchisement. John Roach has argued that beginning in the late 1840s and well into the 1870s, public health displaced other reform issues because it was a topic that seemed nonpartisan and nonsectarian (172). Furthermore, public-health reform appealed to both utilitarian and evangelical reformers. To utilitarians such as Edwin Chadwick, public health seemed the most expedient way to offer the "greatest good to the greatest number."[21] For Christian reformers, the parable of Dives and Lazarus, the example of the Good Samaritan, and the healing activities of Christ pointed to a Christian mandate to assuage the suffering of the sick poor.[22]

Nonetheless, public-health reforms carried an ambivalent message of sympathy on the one hand, and disgust and castigation on the other. For utilitarian reformers, the working classes were increasingly seen as hopelessly degenerate and diseased—both the victims and the source of contagion.[23] Evangelical reformers faced the paradox that while they must mitigate the afflictions of the poor, these very afflictions were both the will of God, and more important, signs of God's displeasure. That the poor, especially the urban poor, bore the burden of this suffering intimated that they were at best God's scapegoats, at worst sinners who had incurred God's wrath.[24] In her study of the Contagious Diseases Acts of the 1860s, Judith R. Walkowitz has demonstrated the shift from the interclass dialogues of reform during the mid-1840s to an increasingly monologic middle-class voice of the 1850s and 1860s (41-44). Not surprisingly, with the diminishment of this dialogue, British humanitarianism and social reform became substantially more punitive. Many of these contradictions can be found in Victorian representations of the nurse. As I contend in chapter 2, working-class nurses were singled out as objects of disgust by middle-class reformers, while middle- and upper-class nurses were venerated as harbingers of social purification. Chapter 3 demonstrates that the claims for this purification stem in part from the new-style nurse's affiliation with heroic codes of domestic ideology.[25]

Nonetheless, the new-style nurse cannot wholly lay claim to the social harmony and refinement for which she is celebrated. Mary Poovey, for example, has argued that "the domestic ideal always contained an aggressive component," and she finds the image of Florence Nightingale to be one of the most important mid-Victorian examples of that domestic aggression. Poovey claims that the mingling of domesticity and aggression in Nightingale's representation derives from the amalgamation of domestic and martial tropes that were used to create Nightingale's heroic persona.[26] Alexander Welsh also recognizes the sinister quality of the heroic sick-nurse in his discussion of the "two angels of death" (Agnes Wickfield in *David Copperfield* and Florence Dombey in *Dombey and Son*) where he writes of the "ominous aspect of the heroine's power" (182). As we shall see, my focus on the Victorian nurse provides insight into the crucial ways in which domesticity and sentimentality connected up with middle-class hegemony.

LITERATURE AND MEDICINE

Bedside Seductions also addresses questions about the relationship between medicine and literature with the strong caveat that this distinction is a debatable one. The separation of the "arts and sciences" can, as critic Ludmilla Jordanova contends, "deter rather than enhance historical understanding."[27] Raymond Williams has argued that there are many historical reasons for the separation of "what we have learned to call 'disciplines,'" but that these differentiations are not timeless or absolute. Nonetheless, there are genuine difficulties involved in the question of how diverse disciplines "relate or should relate to each other, in assumptions, methods and results" (Williams 10, 1986). Williams suggests that one means of bridging the distances between discursive practices is to "look at the actual composition of ideas, arguments and theories in some of their hitherto least noticed conditions of production" (11). A critical practice that works to show the interrelatedness of categories heretofore seen as autonomous can take many forms. Williams cites among other potential approaches the analysis of the transfer, both "deliberate and unexamined," of concepts and models from science to literature or vice versa.[28]

In recent years, increasing numbers of scholars have begun to explore the strands that link the literary and the medical. To a great extent, discussions of medicine and literature have taken one of two paths. One strategy has been to juxtapose medicine and aesthetics and then to tabulate the correspondences. Thus numerous studies stress the analogies between literary and medical healing, or the similarities that exist between the work of the writer and the work of the doctor. These approaches generate many valuable insights, but can also result in the reproduction of myths about both medicine and literature. Rather than attempting to question such premises as the concept that literature is a "healing art," or the notion that doctors and poets have been endowed with "unusual sensibilities," some critics have been inclined to accept these ideas as self-evident truths.[29]

As a corrective to studies based on unexamined axioms, recent cultural historians have worked at once to scrutinize scientific and aesthetic myths while simultaneously claiming a dominance for the medical paradigm in modern culture that makes an analysis of the relationship between literature and medicine crucial for our under-standing not only of modern aesthetics, but modern subjectivity as well.[30] Thus the realization of what Foucault calls the general "medical-ization" of Western culture should compel many scholars of the nineteenth century to chart the impact of this medicalization on disparate discursive fields. As we shall see, there is a complex coales-cence between mid-Victorian aesthetics and the rise of the medical realm, and this coalescence can be elucidated in part by focusing on representations of the nurse—a figure crucial to the medicalization of Victorian England and consequently to the consolidation of middle-class power and the formation of middle-class subjectivity.

Current feminist rereadings of nineteenth-century medicine have tended to focus on the ways that women were objectified and controlled through medical discourse—indeed Jordanova notes that "much medical writing addressed itself to the nature of womanhood as a scientific and medical topic . . . because women were easily construed as objects in nature requiring explanation" (44). However, I want to complicate this notion by exploring the means by which nineteenth-century medicine was developed in part by middle-class women themselves through the deployment of domestic ideology. Correspondingly, I will also trace the shaping of domestic ideology through positivist and medical structures. Thus, as I argue in my final chapter, the boundaries between the public and the private realms, between the literary and the medical collapse in much the same way that distinctions between women of science such as Nightingale and women of letters such as George Eliot converge more than they differ. And so there is a balancing act, a crossing and recrossing, erasing and rebuilding of borders, dichotomies, and boundaries.

COUPLINGS AND UNCOUPLINGS

In my pairing of the categories of "medicine and literature," I am creating an artificial couple, and it is precisely such a dichotomous structure that invited much pernicious thinking in Victorian England: the binary concepts of mind/body; life/death; man/woman; black/white; God/man; human/animal; nature/culture; public/private were at the heart of much of mid-Victorian England's most deleterious ideologies. Nonetheless, dualisms can elucidate key issues. As Jordanova notes, by using two separate terms the "*difference* between them comes to the fore, while by pairing them together, the idea of a *kinship* between them is evoked" (Jordanova's emphasis, 44).

Another pivotal coupling that shapes the structure of this book is that of the generic and the thematic. Clearly, with my focus on the trope of the nurse, I am engaged on some level in the act of thematic criticism—and it is precisely a thematic focus that most expedites the collapse of boundaries among disciplines: this is both the strength and the weakness of thematic criticism.[31] Yet I do not want to wholly erase as arbitrary generic differences: the discourses of the realist novel, the parliamentary blue book, and the medical case history are not absolutely fungible. Part of my intent, then, is to develop ways of looking at correspondences between disparate genres while still respecting the divergences, and the distinct meanings, conveyed through those genres. For example, my chapter on Mary Seacole focuses on the generic heterogeneity of her narrative—a composite of male military adventure, heroic nursing discourse, and autobiography—and shows the ways that the trope of heroic nursing and the structure of Homeric epic helped Seacole to shape her self-representation.

There are occasions when my focus obliges me to deemphasize generic considerations in favor of thematic ones. For example in chapter 2 I look at the eroticism of heroic or "saintly" nursing as it is conveyed through a variety of genres: private letters, social treatises, pornography, hagiography, newspaper accounts, popular verse, short stories, novels, and memoirs. In many of my chapters, however, generic considerations are foregrounded. Indeed, the most persistent exploration of *Bedside Seductions* centers on the ways in which the mid-Victorian realist novel is shaped by the topic of nursing itself.

The following chapter concentrates on the connections between the mid-Victorian realist novel, a literary form particularly linked to medical discourse, and the medical climate that surrounded it.[32] Along with critics such as D. A. Miller, Nancy Armstrong, Jonathan Arac, Fredric Jameson, and Mary Poovey, I am reading the mid-Victorian novel as a genre essentially bound up not only with middle-class interests and sensibilities, but also as a literary form acutely concerned with issues of social reform and middle-class hegemony. In exploring the tangled interplay between the literary and the medical I want to avoid the notion, as Lawrence Rothfield has warned, that the history of the novel either "reduces to or merely reflects the history of medicine as a profession" (193, fn. 4). Rather, I contend that the affinities between medicine and realism share epistemological postulates in a way that is not confined to, although it is informed by, the concerns of Victorian positivism, social reform and domestic ideology.

For this study, I have selected authors and texts that raise the trope of Victorian nursing in pivotal or problematic ways. My first chapter, "'Infinite Nastiness': Social Healing and the Pathology of the Victorian Novel (1830-1880)," provides an overview of Victorian representations of the nurse. Here I delineate the origins of these representations, origins located especially in the growth of domestic and medical ideologies that resulted in the heightened authority of the nurse by the mid nineteenth century. Furthermore, this opening chapter describes the importance of Romantic notions of the vatic writer in shaping the heroic myth of the mid-Victorian nurse.

My second chapter, "'Thy Magic Touch': Nursing, Sexuality, and the 'Dangerous Classes' (1829-1880)" explores the class tensions that

existed at the core of the mid-Victorian nursing reformation movement. In this chapter I demonstrate the prevalent focus on working-
class female sexuality in the rhetoric of nursing reform and contend
that this focus on the working-class nurses' "dangerous" sexuality
functioned as a means of masking the sexual fantasies that were crucial
to the formation of the new-style or reformed nurse. Here I delineate
the ways in which the middle-class nursing reformers' insistence on
the sexual purity of new-style nursing gets undermined by the
contradictory eroticism of the "saintly" nurse figure.

"A 'Scrutinising and Conscious Eye': Nursing and the Carceral in
Jane Eyre (1847)" extends my concern with female literary authority and
class conflict as it is played out in the figure of the nurse. By focusing on
the persistent analogies between nursing and imprisonment in *Jane
Eyre*, I explore the oblique power of the new-style nurse, reading her
especially as a figure of middle-class female ressentiment. Here I link
this ressentiment with the disciplinary function of the Victorian realist
novel itself. In this chapter, I also establish the ways in which one of the
crucial analogies of realism, that is, the masculinist, scientific gaze of the
realist writer, finds a competing model in the scrutiny of disciplinary
individualism embodied in the eye of the nurse.[33]

"Scars, Stitches and Healing: Metaphors of Female Artistry in
Gaskell's *Ruth* (1853)" further elaborates the correspondences between realism and nursing. Here I juxtapose sewing and nursing in
Gaskell's *Ruth*, which I argue are competing metaphors for female
creative labor. Following Elaine Scarry's contention that representations of work in the nineteenth-century novel frequently illustrate
both the "external space of diurnal making and the internal space at
the hidden center of the artist's own dark act of making" (1983, 99), I
demonstrate the ways in which the rival analogies of nursing and
seamstressing in *Ruth* ultimately point to Gaskell's ambivalence concerning the didactic pressures placed on mid-Victorian realism by the
literary marketplace.

In "'A Female Ulysses': Mary Seacole, Homeric Epic, and the Trope
of Heroic Nursing (1854-1857)," I introduce the subject of race, imperialism, and nursing through my reading of the autobiography of Mary
Seacole, a Jamaican sick-nurse who garnered a measure of fame in
England during the 1850s and 1860s through her labors as a sick-nurse
during the Crimean War. Here I explore Seacole's transformation of the

Nightingale legend, a mythos especially associated with Nightingale's class standing and, correspondingly, her racial identity. Noting the arguments that claim for the Nightingale myth a crucial place in the creation of British imperialism's self-justification, chapter 5 charts the ways in which Seacole transmutes the heroic sick-nurse, especially through her introduction of Homeric epic, into an image of both personal power and general empowerment of the female colonial subject.

In the final chapter of this volume, "Nursing and Female Heroics: George Eliot and Florence Nightingale (1835-1873)," I continue my exploration of nursing's relationship to Victorian hero worship, especially the ways in which that worship was directed at the newly emerging female hero. Here I demonstrate that while the tenets of domestic ideology gave rise to new notions of female authority, there were competing models of that authority. By examining Florence Nightingale's vendetta against George Eliot over her representations of female heroic potentiality in *Middlemarch,* I investigate the intersection of science and sentiment conveyed by the figure of the nurse, and the ways that this convergence helped to create both parallel and competing theories concerning the possibilities of female social leadership.

"Infinite Nastiness": Social Healing and the Pathology of the Victorian Novel (1830-1880)

IN HIS VITRIOLIC ESSAY OF 1880, *Fiction—Fair and Foul,* John Ruskin meditates on the surfeit of death and illness in the Victorian novel, claiming that detailed, clinical depictions of morbidity are the hallmarks of the genre: "[the modern reader can] gather into one Caina of gelid putrescence the entire product of modern infidel imagination, amusing itself with destruction of the body, and busying itself with aberration of the mind . . ." (166). Finding Charles Dickens's *Bleak House* to be a salient representative of this "modern infidel imagination," Ruskin writes: "in the single novel of *Bleak House,* there are nine deaths . . . either by way of pleasing surprise, as the baby's at the brickmaker's, or finished in their threatenings and sufferings, with as much enjoyment as can be contrived in anticipation, and as much pathology as can be concentrated in the description" (159). Ruskin claims that it is not strictly the number of deaths that "marks the peculiar tone of the modern novel," rather, it is the fact that all of these deaths are "either violent or miserable" (159). In noting the distinctive focus on morbidity exhibited by mid-Victorian novelists, Ruskin anticipates twentieth-century critics such as Humphrey House and Alexander Welsh, who also point to the extraordinary abundance of death and disease in Victorian fiction.[1] Certainly the Victorian imagination is lavish in its depictions of the agonies of the consumptive, the fever of the typhus victim, and the pathology of the madwoman.

Some commentators have ascribed this mid-Victorian preoccupation with sickness to the myopic squint of realism, an aesthetic whose dedication to the chronicling of everyday life can turn a novel like George Eliot's *Mill on the Floss* into a "striking instance," as Ruskin asserts, of the "study of cutaneous disease" (Ruskin quoted in Levine 1981, 208). In other words, the abundance of disease and death in the novel can be ascribed to the nineteenth century's surfeit of afflictions. The realist novelists, as Welsh argues, were simply empirically recording daily events that now seem strange to us as we are much more removed from the details of dissolution (195-97).

Other critics attribute the prominence of death and disease in the Victorian novel to a counterphobic reaction to morbidity itself. No longer able to derive comfort or justification for suffering from religion, the argument goes, the Victorians were compelled to concentrate on that which they could not master, their preoccupation with death betraying a saturnine fascination with that which they most feared. As Humphrey House asserts concerning Victorian culture, "a religion in a state of transition from supernatural belief to humanism is very poorly equipped to face death, and must dwell on it for that very reason" (quoted in Welsh 195).

Ruskin himself is perplexed when it comes to accounting for the origins of the distinctive clinical tone apparent in Victorian depictions of death and disease, and he posits that this inflection stems from a combination of the upbringing of the modern writer and the appetites of the modern audience. Ruskin argues that both modern writers and modern readers are essentially products of urban blight, and "accustomed from the instant they are out of their cradles, to the sight of . . . infinite nastiness" (155), they crave the representation of their own misery and their own fate, which is to die like "rats in a drain" (1990, 159).[2]

Yet the most convincing explanation for the Victorian novel's morbid intonation might be one that Ruskin notes but does not develop. He sees the uniqueness of Victorian fictional death lying precisely in its *clinical* depiction of morbidity, and he calls this discourse the product of "modern infidel imagination" (156). Here

Ruskin hints at a phenomenon that Michel Foucault brings out more explicitly in his concept of the "medicalization" of modern culture—that is, the way the medical realm comes to replace the clerical realm during the nineteenth century, thus becoming a momentous, if insidious, channel of power.

HYGIENIC AESTHETICS

In "The Politics of Health in the Eighteenth Century," Foucault contends that during the eighteenth century a concentration on the health and physical well-being of the general population became one of the primary objectives of political power (170), and that a "medico-administrative" knowledge began to evolve with regard to "society, its health and sickness, its conditions of life, housing and habits," which serves as the basic core for the "'social economy' and sociology of the nineteenth century" (1980b, 176).

Foucault's earlier work, *The Birth of the Clinic*, describes the rise after the French Revolution of two great myths. The first is the myth of a "nationalized medical profession," organized like the clergy, and "invested, at the level of man's bodily health, with powers similar to those exercised by the clergy over men's souls." The second myth, at once utopic and edenic, envisions the "total disappearance of disease in an untroubled dispassionate society restored to its original state of health" (31-32). Although these two myths seem contradictory, they are in fact isomorphic, the former voicing in a positive way the "strict, militant, dogmatic medicalization of society, by way of a quasi-religious conversion, and the establishment of a therapeutic clergy," and the latter expressing the same medicalization, but in a "triumphant, negative way, that is to say, the volatilization of disease in a corrected, organized, and ceaselessly supervised environment" (32). Thus the pathology concentrated in the descriptions of suffering and death that "marks the peculiar tone of the modern novel" for Ruskin can be explained in terms of the general "medicalization" of society that influenced all realms of discourse in the nineteenth century (159).[3] Indeed, Ruskin asserts that this focus on disease, death, and contagion is not limited to fiction, but can be found even in "the most eagerly discussed texts of modern philosophy" (156).[4]

During the nineteenth century, the crucial route towards the medicalization of society lay in the proselytizing of a "therapeutic clergy": that is, those medical professionals who could spread the gospel of public health. For this reason, doctors were obviously key figures in the sanitary conversion of Western culture, and Foucault's *Birth of the Clinic* charts the deification of the doctor, showing especially how the ideological justification for the supremacy of the doctor was often borrowed from aesthetic and mystical domains. Foucault notes that the medicalization of society resulted in the bestowal of a "surplus of power" on the doctor: "the doctor becomes the great advisor and expert, if not in the art of governing, at least in that of observing, correcting and improving the social 'body' . . ." (1980b, 176-77).

However, Foucault points out that it is the doctor's role as hygienist rather than his prominence as a therapist that "assures him this politically privileged position" in the eighteenth century, prior to his accumulation of "economic and social privileges in the nineteenth century" (1980b, 177). This is because medicine, as a "general technique of health" even more than as a "service to the sick or an art of cures," assumes an "increasingly important place in the administrative system and the machinery of power" (1980b, 176-77). Conceivably the male doctor held sway over both the hygienic and the medical realms in France, but in England, as in the United States, hygiene was symbolically, and often literally, a female province.[5] Under the aegis of British domestic ideology, women were seen as the natural forwarders of a "general technique of health." In 1864, Florence Nightingale writes that "on women we must depend, first and last, for personal and household hygiene—for preventing the race from degenerating" (1864, 79). Indeed, Foucault observes that beginning in the eighteenth century, the family became "the most constant agent of medicalization" and was the target for a "great enterprise of medical acculturation" (1980b, 173), thereby implying a centrality to female agency in the medicalization of society, a centrality that he leaves unexplored. With the increasingly entrenched conception in the Victorian imagination of an innate split between male worldliness and female disinterestedness, male corruption and female purity, the nurse—who is gendered strictly female despite the fact that many nurses were male—comes to replace the doctor as the clerical figure of the medical realm.[6]

Ruskin and more recent commentators on the precision and pathology of description contained within Victorian literature have tended to focus on the figure of the doctor and the literary use of surgical and diagnostic images and metaphors.[7] Ironically, Ruskin uses surgical metaphors in his critique of the medicalized discourse of modern literature: "there is some excuse, indeed, for the pathologic labour of the modern novelist in the fact that he cannot easily, in a city population, find a healthy mind to vivisect: but the greater part of such amateur surgery is the struggle . . . to obtain novelty of material" (1990, 166).[8] However, accompanying this Hippocratic inflection was an equally developed set of tropes surrounding the sickroom, its patient, and its attendant nurse. In characterizing the shift from Romantic to Victorian fiction, for example, Ruskin specifies as crucial the modern use of detailed depictions of the sickroom. He argues that while Walter Scott may at times have succumbed to representing violent or bizarre deaths, he "never once withdrew the sacred curtain of the sick-chamber" (1900, 162). Thus it is the sickroom scenes above all that represent for Ruskin the hallmark of the "degenerate" Victorian novel: "in modern stories prepared for more refined or fastidious audiences than those of Dickens, the funereal excitement is obtained, for the most part, not by the infliction of violent or disgusting death; but in the suspense, the pathos, and the more or less by all felt, and recognized, mortal phenomena of the sick-room" (1900, 161).

Indeed, there is a marked increase in representations of nursing and the sickroom within Victorian narrative. Certainly following the Crimean War, professional nurses become the staples of popular fiction until well into the twentieth century. In *Notes on Nursing,* Nightingale objects to this convention when she complains that "popular novelists of recent days have invented ladies disappointed in love or fresh out of the drawing-room turning into the war-hospitals to find their wounded lovers, and when found, forthwith abandoning their sick-ward for their lover, as might be expected" (134). Yet the frequent presence in the Victorian novel of sickroom imagery began well before the Crimean conflict. Miriam Bailin, for example, notes a "discernible shift in the particular emphasis given to the sick-room itself" in the mid-nineteenth-century novel, and claims that "the nurse rather than the doctor is the primary caregiver in the sick-room scenes" (1994, 28).

"THE DEPTHS OF PAIN"

When in *Sesame and Lilies,* Ruskin states that "men are feeble in sympathy, and contracted in hope; it is [women] only who can feel the depths of pain, and conceive the way of its healing" (1871, 178), he is giving voice to a widespread Victorian view—what Walter Houghton calls "woman worship." In *Sesame and Lilies,* Ruskin advocates a female healing that transpires inside the home, enkindled by familial love. Home, as the Victorian poet Coventry Patmore wrote, is a "tent pitch'ed in a world not right" (11). From this viewpoint, the heroic nurse might seem to symbolize the restriction of possibilities imposed on women during the mid-nineteenth century, and indeed in the hands of Patmore, Ruskin, and the popular conduct manual writer Sarah Stickney Ellis she does. In their versions of domestic ideology, women, uniquely suited to tend to the sick, direct their talents to the care of their family, an activity that represented "the highest attainments . . . to which a woman can aspire" (Ellis 77).

The image of the homebound, healing woman became a strong subspecies of the angel in the house—what Bram Dijkstra has termed the "cult of the household nun," or John Reed has characterized as the "woman as saint." Yet there were many mid-Victorians who embraced the notion of women as possessed of special, even divine, healing powers, but who cast this healing in a much broader arena than the domestic sphere. For many social reformers, the heroic nurse best exemplified the ability of domestic morality and purification to move out of the home and into the tainted public domain. The example offered by Florence Nightingale's work during the Crimean War excited those interested in sweeping changes in public health in Britain and her colonies. Here the nurse was not a gentle mother or sister tending to her family, but a Joan of Arc, a Saint Elizabeth, or even a reincarnation of Christ.[9] Many mid-Victorians viewed the heroic nurse as a manifestation of God's goodness on Earth—like Christ, she was called into self-sacrificial service in order to redeem the world. Immune to moral pollution, the saintly nurse could traverse all geographic and social boundaries, and thereby purify the detritus of modern life. Indeed, many of the nurses in the Victorian novel are implicit or explicit Christ figures. For example, in discussing the nursing work of Amy Dorrit, the narrator in *Little Dorrit* asserts that "it is enough that she was inspired to be something which was not what the rest were, and to be that something, different and laborious, for the sake of the rest. Inspired? Yes. Shall we speak of the inspiration of a poet or a priest, and not of the heart impelled by love and self-devotion to the lowliest work in the lowliest way of life!" (111).

Although Nightingale dominated heroic nursing imagery, her decision to become a nurse and the public response to her nursing during the war had their roots in the examples set by the works of evangelical reformers like Elizabeth Fry, in the medieval and chivalric literary revivals instigated by Romanticism during the 1810s and 1820s, and in the growth of neo-Catholic nursing sisterhoods during the 1840s. Thus the model of the Victorian heroic nurse came to be shaped from an amalgamation of images of Christ, the Virgin Mary, Mary Magdalen, and Catholic saints (especially St. Elizabeth of Hungary), coupled with notions of Christian charity and aristocratic gentilesse. As early as 1829, for example, Robert Southey championed a scheme for purifying medicine through the introduction of saintly Protestant nursing sisters. In words that anticipate George Eliot's prelude to *Middlemarch*, Southey asks "where is the woman who shall be the Clara or Teresa of Protestant England, labouring for the certain benefit of her sex with their ardour, but without their delusion and fatal superstition" (305).[10] However, Southey locates the possibility of a modern Teresa in the woman or women who would found nursing sisterhoods, not in mystical orders removed from the world. Southey asserts that there is "work enough for all (it is of women that I am now speaking) who feel in themselves the strength of heroic virtue, and aspire to its rewards, and shrink not from the scenes into which in its exercise it would carry them. . . . Why then have you no Beguines, no Sisters of Charity? why in the most needful, the most merciful form that charity can take, have you not yet followed the example of the French and the Netherlanders? . . . Piety has found its way into your prisons; your hospitals are imploring it in vain" (2:318). As Southey imagines the nurse in this institutional capacity, she is transformed from a cloistered, domestic "nun," into a model for female activism and selfless dedication to public charity.[11]

Accompanying the power granted to the figure of the nurse through her association with religious imagery, the heroic nurse was further elevated through her affiliation with notions of preventative medicine and sanitary reform. In Britain, the infectionist (miasmic) versus contagionist (germ) schism split the medical community.[12] As we shall see, this debate became gendered, with the doctor standing for the contagionist theory response to disease and the nurse representing an infectionist response. Indeed S. E. Finer notes that after the Crimean War, "the national figure in sanitation was no longer [Edwin] Chadwick, but Florence Nightingale, a far more genial figure" (490).

Contagionists believed that the great nineteenth-century epidemics—typhus, typhoid and scarlet fevers, tuberculosis, and especially cholera—were brought about by germs spread through bodily contact. Infectionists maintained that disease and epidemics derived from poisoned air. They theorized that rotting matter in the ground or in damp, dark, closed spaces or crowded rooms transmuted into toxic effluvia. Darkness and heat aided the formation of this lethal miasma, while light and fresh air inhibited it. Epidemics were believed to occur when tainted vapor was inhaled, and the only means of stopping the spread of disease environmental control. In *Notes on Nursing,* for example, Nightingale longs for the invention of an "air test," similar to a thermometer, which would indicate the levels of "organic matter of the air," because the

> senses of nurses and mothers become so dulled to foul air that they are perfectly unconscious of what an atmosphere they have let their children, patients, or charges, sleep in. . . . And oh; the crowded national school! where so many children's epidemics have their origin, what a tale its air-test would tell! We should have parents saying, and saying rightly, "I will not send my child to that school, the air-test stands at 'Horrid.'" And the dormitories of our great boarding schools! Scarlet fever would be no more ascribed to contagion, but to its right cause, the air-test standing at "Foul." We should hear no longer of "Mysterious Dispensation," and of "Plague and Pestilence," being "in God's hands," when . . . He put them into our own. The little air-test would both betray the cause of these "mysterious pestilences," and call upon us to remedy it. (16-17)

In England, the nurse represented both prevention and attention to the entire circumstances of the patient, while the doctor represented the failure of prevention or the lack of prevention accompanied by a shortsighted focus only on the sick body of the patient, not on the surrounding elements that could cure or kill the ill (especially fresh air and cleanliness).[13] If one held a belief in contagion, then quarantine was the most effective response to epidemics. This solution was seen by infectionists as a mistaken approach to health because they believed that prevention in the form of hygienic measures was the true solution to disease. As Nightingale wrote:

> it is often thought that medicine is the curative process. It is no such thing . . . Nature alone cures and what nursing has to do . . . is to put the patient in the best condition for nature to act upon him. . . . You think fresh air, and quiet and cleanliness extravagance[s] . . . and medicine the *sine qua non,* the panacea. If I have succeeded in any measure in dispelling this illusion . . . [then] my object will have been answered (1864, 133).

With the advent of cholera, as Francois Delaporte points out, quarantine was proven to be ineffective, thus giving the infectionists greater political power during the nineteenth century.[14] In Britain, the infectionist policies of hygienic prevention were embodied in the heroic nurse, whether she was a living example such as Nightingale, Lydia Sellon, and Mary Stanley, or a literary character such as Grace Harvey in Charles Kingsley's novel *Two Years Ago*. This affiliation of the nurse and the sanitary reform movement had the effect of elevating the nurse to an unprecedented stature. Much has been made, for example, of Nightingale's conflicts with the physicians at Scutari during the Crimean War, and her battle with the medical profession was aimed precisely at the lack of prevention and attention to environmental details on the part of the army doctors. Nightingale herself once wrote that "experience teaches me that nursing and medicine must never be mixed up. It spoils both . . . I would say that the less knowledge of medicine a hospital matron has the better (1) because it does not improve her sanitary practice, (2) because it would make her miserable and intolerable to the doctors" (quoted in Cope 121).

For Nightingale, as for other public health reformers, national hygiene was a moral imperative, a direct message from God to cleanse and heal, thereby creating a new order of things. As Nightingale writes in a letter to Benjamin Jowett, "it is a religious act to clean out a gutter and to prevent cholera" (quoted in Jowett 23). Thus despite the potential subservience and subordination of the nurse, she was actually a figure of immense power. And while the heroic nurse had a wide popular appeal, she was, as we shall see, an especially resonant image for certain Victorian visionaries—writers such as Dickens, Nightingale, Charles Kingsley, George Eliot, Elizabeth Gaskell, Arthur Hugh Clough, Edwin Chadwick, and Christina Rossetti—who saw the nurse as a symbol for the possibility of social reform and social redemption.[15] For the novelists of this group, the heroic Nurse aptly embodied many of the elements the earnest Victorian writer saw inherent in his or her own work as social healer.

"THE GIANT AGONY OF THE WORLD"

In 1816, John Keats proclaimed that the sacred duty of the poet was to be a "sage; / A humanist, Physician to all men," and declared that the writer must feel "the giant agony of the world" in order to turn that realization into a healing spirit that could save the world (483). This Romantic secularization of the Passion of Christ turns the poet into both vatic seer and Everyman, and turns the realm of culture into the new realm of spiritual and political salvation.[16] In 1820 Percy Bysshe Shelley wrote his "Song of Apollo," which ends with the declaration that

> I am the eye with which the Universe
> Beholds itself and knows itself divine;
> All harmony of instrument or verse,
> All prophecy, all medicine is mine,
> All light of art or nature;—to my song
> Victory and praise in its own right belong. (613) [17]

As Shelley's poem implies, the lineage of the doctor-writer analogy dates back at least as far as the Greeks who deemed Apollo the patron saint of both writing and healing. In his ode "Pythia III: For Heiron of Syracuse," Pindar specifically equates his art with that of the physician's skill and posits his poetry as a relief from suffering and a form of curative medicine. In the following centuries a number of literary conventions developed around the figure of the "doctor of Physic," but the two predominant images were either a heroic equation of the writer and doctor as social healers, or a comic condemnation of doctors as greedy, evil, or incompetent. In England, cynical representations of doctors reached great heights during the Renaissance where they were stock figures of jestbooks, treatises, poetry, commedia dell'arte–influenced comedies, and Elizabethan tragedies.[18] Although the positive analogy between the writer and the physician was occasionally evident during the Renaissance,[19] this equation reblossomed in the eighteenth century when writers such as John Dryden and George Crabbe revised the Pindaric notion of the writer-physician as potential healer of a wounded or diseased readership.[20]

Yet, as the metaphor of the writer-as-healer gained urgency through Romanticism's assertion of the moral duties of creative labor, the equation of the doctor-as-healer became increasingly attenuated. Thus by the mid-nineteenth century, there was an assertion, akin to that seen in the Renaissance, of the doctor's association with callousness, incompetence, corruption, and evil. Alfred Tennyson's poem of 1880 "In the Children's Hospital" presents a stereotypical image of the successful doctor. Here the speaker is a hospital nurse who describes a new surgeon at the hospital: "I never had seen him before, / But he sent a chill to my heart when I saw him come in at the door" (1971, 447). As the poem continues, the nurse explains the reason for this "chill":

> Fresh from the surgery-schools of France and of other lands—
> Harsh red hair, big voice, big chest, big merciless hands!
> Wonderful cures he had done, O, yes, but they said too of him
> He was happier using the knife than in trying to save the limb,
> And that I can well believe, for he look'd so coarse and so red,
> I could think he was one of those who would break their jests on the dead,
> And mangle the living dog that had loved him and fawn'd at his knee—
> Drench'd with the hellish oorali—that ever such things should be!
> (1971, 448)[21]

By the mid-nineteenth century, surgery, heroic doses of medication, blistering, purging, bleeding, dissection, and vivisection resulted in the association of British doctors with invasive, corrupt, and fatal practices.[22] Doctors were further mistrusted on the basis of their prescribing drugs incompetently, their approaching medicine as self-interested businessmen, their eagerness to perform surgery, and their general incompetence or callousness.[23] For example, when J. Ruther-furd Russell came to write his *History and Heroes of Medicine* in 1861, his characterization of Francis Bacon as a "hero with feet of clay" would fit nearly all of the doctor-"heroes" he includes in his study. A few of the doctors in his book are represented as great men with mistaken notions (Hippocrates, Galen, and Bacon). Some are quacks with a smattering of good ideas (especially Jerome Cardan and Paracelsus). Still others are figures of selfishness, corruption, callous-ness, or utter evil.[24] Even Russell's most unequivocal portraits of famous doctors (those of William Jenner and Samuel Hahnemann) emphasize the human frailty of his subjects and are in no way hagiographical. We see Jenner, for example, testing out his experimental vaccines on the local children in his village and squabbling with London doctors over his status and fortune.

Although there are many sympathetic or even heroic doctors in nineteenth-century literature (such as Allen Woodcourt in *Bleak House* and Tertius Lydgate in *Middlemarch*), they never achieve the idealized status of the saintly nurses that they are typically paired with and obliquely compared to. Woodcourt, often considered one of the most unambiguously heroic doctors in the Victorian novel, was a surgeon and would have performed many dissections, and thus would have been associated with the ethically suspect nature of dissection and autopsy. Furthermore, Woodcourt not only supplies Nemo with his fatal dose of opium, but is also affiliated with the other "unmoved professionals" who attend Nemo's deathbed. Here Woodcourt displays a "professional interest in death" (107), thereby aligning himself with the callous Scottish doctor (who returns home to finish his dinner after coarsely affirming Nemo's demise), Tulkinghorn who addresses Woodcourt in his "unmoved, professional way" (107), and the "unmoved policeman" (110) who also attend the deathbed and inquest of Esther's father. These "unmoved professionals" provide a strong contrast to Esther's sympathetic reaction to the death of Jenny's baby three chapters earlier. Although *Bleak House* ultimately aligns the "good nurse" with the "good doctor" through the marriage of Esther and Woodcourt, Esther proves to be the more powerful moral force of the two.[25]

Despite the discrediting of the doctor however, the notion of the writer speaking in a prophetic and universal voice continued to be important to the Victorians. Those writers interested in claiming a special authority for the cultural realm drew on the Apollonic association of writing and healing to bolster their claims of access to humanistic and universal truths. Yet within the mid-nineteenth-century Victorian novel, the affiliation of the healing writer and the noble physician is largely displaced by the conception of the writer as heroic nurse. This is because the nurse embodied both the disinterestedness so crucial to the claims of the cultural realm, and the empathetic suffering needed to speak with a universal voice. Thus for some writers, especially mid-Victorian realist novelists, the professional, "encarnalized," and self-interested physician of the nineteenth century could no longer represent the cultural realm's assertion to speak in a ubiquitous voice. Conversely, the heroic nurse aptly personified both the healing spirit and the universality that the cultural realm was supposed to embody.

F. R. and Q. D. Leavis note that the doctor was seen as "a modern figure concerned not for private practice among the well-to-do but for public health and the scientific advancement of medicine, a figure as disinterested as the cleric and visibly more important in the new social conditions" (180), while Rothfield comments that the doctor "serves as a potent symbol for English novelists during the 1850s as it had for Balzac in the new, professionalising social conditions of France in the 1830s" (87). Yet what Woodcourt, Tom Thurnall, and the Physician in *Little Dorrit* symbolize is less a "medical-scientific consciousness than a reforming impulse" (Rothfield 87). And for the mid-Victorians, this reforming and healing impulse, especially in any claims made to noble or self-sacrificial healing, was best conveyed through the figure of the nurse.

"THEIR SACRED OFFICE OF HEALER"

Rooted in Greco-Roman, biblical, and Catholic literary traditions, the image of the saintly or magical female healer bears a lengthy genealogy. During the English Renaissance, images of healing women abounded. In comparing the representation of male and female healers in Shakespeare's plays, for example, Marjorie Garber has argued that it is inevitably the women who perform the real healing—the male doctors (amateur or professional) are consistently baffled or helpless in the face of mortality (with the exception of Edward the Confessor who is described in *Macbeth* as being able to cure scrofula). Garber points out that through their art, the healing women of Shakespeare's later plays successfully cure the sick: Lear is restored from madness by Cordelia's kiss, Pericles from grief by Marina's music, Leontes from jealousy and guilt through Paulina's reawakening of Hermione, and the King of France is saved from physical illness, melancholy, and despair by Helena (whose nickname is "Doctor She"). Garber contends that these healing women offer a contrast to the helpless male healers such as the Scottish doctor in *Macbeth*, Friar Lawrence in *Romeo and Juliet*, and Lord Cerimon in *Pericles*: "these doctors are associated . . . with a sense of their own limitation as healers. There are some cures they cannot effect, some knowledge they lack. Above all they lack a miraculous power over life and death" (106).

In *Sesame and Lilies*, Ruskin anticipates Garber's argument by also positing that women in Shakespeare save (he specifies Rosalind, Cordelia, Desdemona, Isabella, Hermione, Imogen, Queen Katherine, Perdita, Sylvia, Viola, Helena, and Virgilia) while the male characters destroy: "the catastrophe of every play is caused always by the folly or fault of man; the redemption, if there be any, is by the wisdom and virtue of woman; and failing that, there is none . . . [Shakespeare] represents [women] as infallibly faithful and wise counsellors . . . strong always to sanctify even when they cannot save" (1871, 137-39).[26] That Ruskin should be so attuned to the possibility of social redemption and purification through the feminine intervention that exists in many of Shakespeare's plays (though this motif is markedly absent in the sonnets) points to the appeal that female redemption held for the Victorians.[27]

Accompanying this messianic analogy between nursing and social healing was a more pragmatic affiliation, one that emphasized the professional parallels between nursing and writing. In Jane Austen's *Persuasion*, for example, the heroine Anne Elliot's moral worth consistently is displayed through her caretaking of her sick family and friends. However, it is the sole professional woman in the novel—nurse Rooke—who provides the most explicit connections between nursing and writing. Towards the end of *Persuasion*, Anne renews her acquaintance with her former governess Mrs. Smith, who is living widowed, paralyzed, and impoverished in Bath after a roisterous marriage. During one visit, Mrs. Smith extols the virtues of her sole attendant, nurse Rooke: "she is a shrewd, intelligent, sensible woman. Hers is a line for seeing human nature; and she has a fund of good sense and observation. . . . Call it gossip if you will; but when nurse Rooke has half an hour's leisure to bestow on me, she is sure to have something to relate that is entertaining and profitable, something that makes one know one's species better. . . . To me, who live[s] so much alone, her conversation I assure you is a treat" (136).

Anne agrees with Mrs. Smith's evaluation of nurse Rooke and elaborates upon the potential of the "sick chamber" to "furnish the worth of volumes" and of the nurse to become an invaluable storyteller (136):

> [Nurses] have great opportunities, and if they are intelligent may be well worth listening to. Such varieties of human nature as they are in the habit of witnessing [in the sick chamber]! And it is not merely in its follies, that they are well read: for they see it occasionally under every circumstance that can be most interesting or affecting. What instances must pass before them of ardent, disinterested, self-denying attachment, of heroism, fortitude, patience, resignation—of all the conflicts and all the sacrifices that ennoble us most. A sick chamber may often furnish the worth of volumes. (136)

Here Austen anticipates many of the themes of the persona of the realist writer in her description of nurse Rooke—her association with gossip, good sense, and observation, and her shrewd and entertaining observations of human nature demarcate the stance and interests of the mid-Victorian realist narrator. Further, Austen's description of nurse Rooke points to an arresting relationship between the novel and its readers. The novel-as-nurse amuses the reader-as-invalid with anecdotes of human nature. However, during the narrative act, the nurse-novel not only diverts, but further instructs the invalid-reader in lessons of patience, fortitude, and heroism. These didactic and professional analogies between the nurse and the writer can be traced from Austen into the Victorian novel, where the work of the nurse frequently offered a compelling parallel for the detailed particularity of the realist writer, an association I explore especially in my chapters on George Eliot, Elizabeth Gaskell, and Charlotte Brontë.

Thus far, this chapter has charted the epistemological history of the myth of the heroic nurse. Here I have been particularly interested in the ways in which the heroic nurse myth becomes an important conveyance of mid-Victorian, middle-class ideology and, by extension, influences the formation of mid-nineteenth-century British culture itself. I have offered an outline of the crucial shaping forces at work in the creation of the Victorian nurse—forces that include the Romantic myth of the vatic writer and the growing importance of both the public-health movement and mid-Victorian domestic ideology. In the following chapters, I continue to focus on the issue of nursing and writing as healing arts. As we have seen, over the course of the early to mid-nineteenth century, the Romantic secularization of the Passion of Christ, which claimed for the male poet the vatic knowledge of human nature and hence the ability to speak in a universal voice, transmuted through domestic ideology into the important analogy of the writer-as-nurse. In creating this parallel between the writer and the nurse, the novelist derived authority from the power connected to the nurse through both domestic ideology and the Victorian discourses of medical and sanitary reform. Indeed, George Levine points to the way that the "vacumn created by a dying religion" was being filled in mid-century by "a mythology of science," and that the "surface of realism is informed by [this] mythic energy" (1980, 152 and 153). Yet this compelling metaphor cannot ultimately subsume the novelist: he or she is not simply a propagandist for sanitary or nursing reform. Finally, the Victorian novelist was interested in making the writer the paramount authority in the struggle for claims to a prophetic voice.

In the following chapter, I depart from my focus on the mid-Victorian novel in order to further elaborate on the construction, and contradictions, of the saintly nurse. Here I am especially interested in the ways in which class struggle—conflicts over economic and social power—transmutes into controversies over working-class sexuality. Indeed, as we shall see, the middle class discrediting of the working-class "old-style" nurse is predicated upon her status as a sexually vulnerable, or predatory, being. However, rather than erasing sexuality from the mid-Victorian discourse over nursing reform, discussions of the "new-style" nurse replicate the sexual fantasies aroused by her working-class predecessor.

CHAPTER TWO

"Thy Magic Touch": Nursing, Sexuality, and the "Dangerous Classes" (1829-1880)

ON MARCH 15, 1989, the *San Francisco Chronicle* reported on "Nightingales," a short-lived Aaron Spelling television series about student nurses: "[It] is an offensive tale about 'little sex kittens' running around in their underwear, a group of angry real nurses said yesterday. . . . 'We do not want this type of image on TV. You're reducing nurses to a bunch of sluts,' said Dorothy Luniewski, an instructor at Framingham Union Hospital School of Nursing. . . . In the show, Suzanne Pleshette stars as den mother to five young nursing students who often are scantily clad and occasionally are caught in compromising positions with male doctors and patients" (1E).

This article points to the facile association of nurses with lax morality and the banal ease with which nursing generates erotic fantasies. Yet an irony exists in naming Spelling's show "Nightingales," for "Nightingale" or "new-style" nurses were created in the mid-nineteenth century in part to counteract what was seen as the renegade sexual transgressions of the "old-style" pauper or working-class nurses. Thus for Victorian reformers, being "caught in compromising positions with male doctors and patients" would be antithetical to the fundamentally chaste and asexual identity of a "Nightingale" nurse.

Much recent writing by British and American historians on nineteenth-century nursing reform in England has paid special attention to the antagonism reformers created and highlighted between the "new-style" nurse and her rival and predecessor, the "old-style" working-class nurse. Indeed, there is not much doubt that a uniform distrust of the working-class nurse lay at the heart of England's nursing reform campaign. Yet what is being overlooked in current discussions of the struggle between old- and new-style nursing is the way that this battle was often implicitly and explicitly fought over what was seen as the old-style nurses' transgressive sexuality. In this chapter, I will argue that due to the focus on the working-class nurses' supposedly "danger-ous" sexuality, claims about the ostensible purity and asexuality for the new-style or "saintly" nurse were crucial elements within the mid-Victorian nursing reform movement. However, as I contend in the following pages, the saintly nurse was in and of herself a highly eroticized figure, and Victorian writers and reformers remained at least tacitly aware of the inherent eroticism contained in representations of the "saintly" new-style nurse.

"THE MOST SLIPPERY RACE IN EXISTENCE" (Nightingale 1856)

After Charles Dickens published *Martin Chuzzlewit* in 1843, the image of Sairey Gamp became the common stereotype of the unreformed working-class nurse. Elderly, corpulent, disrespectful and predisposed to drunken-ness, Sairey Gamp was at once a well-loved caricature and a universal representative of what needed to be driven out of the medical profession. However, Sairey Gamp serves both to obscure and elucidate the nursing reformers' aims, for she is a domiciliary and not a hospital nurse—and the Victorian nursing reforms were directed mostly at institutional nursing.[1] Vincent Quinn and John Prest, for example, write that "the nurses trained in the Nightingale School at St Thomas's were not expected to take private work. Instead, they were sent out as missionaries for cleanliness to the great London teaching hospitals and to workhouse infirmaries in the big cities" (xxii). Similarly, in her chapter on nursing reform, Martha Vicinus explains this focus on the large urban hospitals that served the poor and the working class and had attached medical schools: "Nightingale and her followers believed that if they concentrated their reforming efforts upon the most influential hospitals they would ultimately have a wider impact than if they started with the most retrograde or smallest" (85).

Currently, nursing historians seem to assume that Dickens's caricature of Gamp generated the nursing reform movement in Britain. Mary Poovey, for example, states that "it is difficult to tell whether Dickens's *Martin Chuzzlewit* created or capitalized on a cultural stereotype, but it is certain that Sairey Gamp galvanized the prejudices and anxieties of a large sector of the English public" (1988, 173). In an even stronger claim for the impact of Gamp on the nursing reform movement, Anne Summers implies that the British nursing reform movement itself dates from the publication of *Martin Chuzzlewit* (see Summers, 1989, 365 and 385). Yet despite the fact that castigating working-class nurses might seem peculiarly Victorian, this loathing of "Gamp-like" nurses originated well before the nineteenth century. For example, writings about London's "great plague" of 1665 anticipate the Victorian attack on nurses. Thomas Vincent, a Londoner who witnessed the plague, imagines the mental anguish of the pestilence victims "when their doors have been shut up . . . and none suffered to come in but a Nurse, whom they have been more afraid of, than the Plague itself" (32). In Daniel Defoe's *Journal of the Plague Year,* written in 1721, the narrator recounts the "many frightful stories told us of . . . hired nurses, who attended infected people, using them barbarously, starving them, smothering them, or by other wicked means, hastening their end [and] murdering [the sick in order to rob them]" (87).[2]

Nonetheless, Sairey Gamp's age accurately represents the dominant presence of older women within institutional nursing. The 1851 census records that of the 25,466 institutional nurses working in Great Britain, 19,325 were beyond their mid-forties (quoted in Nightingale, 1969, 138, see fig. 1). In wishing to rid themselves of the "Gamps," nursing reformers wanted to open up hospital and workhouse nursing to a relatively young female workforce. During the nineteenth century, the population of England and Wales "nearly trebled," creating a large pool of fairly young workers who were typically under- or unemployed (Perkin 4). This population boom coupled with the working class's low life expectancy resulted in a relatively youthful, regularly underemployed workforce.[3] For this reason, middle-class nursing reformers usually aimed their recruitment, their rules, and their anxieties about hospital nursing at women from ages twenty to forty. For example, in 1873 the Central London Sick Asylum District was authorized "to receive single women or widows between 25 and 35 years of age as [nursing] probationers" (quoted in Abel-Smith 98). In 1858, Florence Nightingale recommends that "except in emergencies [war] Nurses should not be taken under 30, or above 40." The probationers admitted to the Nightingale School for training ranged in age from twenty-five to thirty-five and were expected to retire at sixty, while the *Regulations as to the Training of Probationer Nurses Under the Nightingale Fund* states that the "age considered desirable for Probationers is from 25 to 35" (Nightingale 1954, 237).[4] However, in wanting to replace "incompetent hags" with younger workers, Victorian reformers encountered a new set of anxieties—their fear of sexually corruptible and corrupting workers.

Considering the relatively low number of young women who worked as institutional nurses (6,141 between the ages of twenty and forty compared to 19,325 above the age of forty according to the 1851 census), the nineteenth-century nursing reform movement focused a great deal of attention on the supposed promiscuity of youthful pauper nurses who were seen as either seducing or being seduced by patients, doctors, and medical students. There was an anxiety about the ongoing sexual corruption of the old-style nurse that seemed to assume a young, sexually active, and seductive, or sexually vulnerable, worker. For example, in a rare defense of old-style nurses, an anonymous London physician writes to the London *Times* in 1857 that English hospital nurses are "insulted, if old and ill-favoured; talked flippantly to, if middle-aged and good humoured; tempted and seduced, if young and well-looking" ("One Who Has Walked a Good Many Hospitals"). Similarly, Florence Nightingale's concern with "an unnameable (sexual) indulgence" that she suspected "in every unlit hospital corner" has been noted (Poovey 1988, 181). At the inception of her nursing career in 1845, Florence Nightingale writes to Dr. and Mrs. Samuel Gridley Howe: "Oh if we could but live to see Protestant Sisterhoods of Charity without vows, for women of education—but the difficulties of the first step are so great in England—I do not mean the physically-revolting parts of a hospital, but *things about the surgeons and the nurses . . . which you may guess*" (1934, 332, my emphasis).

When she took her band of mostly working-class hospital nurses to tend the wounded during the Crimean War, Nightingale drew up a strict code of discipline: "Nurses might not go out alone or even in pairs; they must be accompanied by the housekeeper or by three other nurses;

misbehaviour with soldiers would bring instant dismissal. . . . No coloured ribbons on their attire, and liquor to be strictly rationed . . ." (quoted in Huxley 72). Similarly, in a letter to Charlotte Canning from Scutari, Nightingale describes the lack of privacy for her nurses and claims that these "are the things which deaden women's feeling of morality & make them take to drinking & worse—if the Superintendent is not continually on the alert" (Nightingale 1990, 123).

Thirteen years later, Nightingale revealed her continued distrust of the morals of patients, orderlies and nurses alike: "All provision, &c., &c., should be as much as possible brought into the wards. . . . Nothing should be fetched by the nurses. . . . [This] above all, would obviate the great demoralization consequent on the nurses, patients, and men-servants congregating in numbers several times daily. The orderly must never enter the Nurse's room. . . . Do not let Nurses "congregate" with the orderlies or each other, [as] associating the nurses in large dormitories tends to corrupt the good, and make the bad worse. . . . Give the Nurse plenty to do so that mischief will not tempt her" (1858, 110, 11, 81).

The Victorian nursing reform movement consistently expressed the desire to replace old-style nurses with either morally groomed pauper girls or "naturally" asexual, indigent gentlewomen. For example, in a typical description of the morally purifying new-style nurse, E. J. R. Landale writes in 1896 that they should "be chosen not only for their excellence in ward work, but for that higher moral force and excellence which will fit them to rule and influence their subordinates wisely, and for their highest good" (quoted in Vicinus, 109).[5] In her *Subsidiary Notes* on female nursing in military hospitals, Nightingale asserts that: "none but women of unblemished character should be suffered to enter the work [of hospital nursing], and any departure from chastity should be visited with instant final dismission" (1858, 7). This focus on the nurses' sexuality sets the nineteenth-century nursing reform movement apart from traditional British anxieties concerning working-class nurses.

In part, this new emphasis on working-class nurses' sexuality derives from the nursing reformers' focus on hospital nursing. Like other sites of nineteenth-century reformation, nursing reform points to urban middle-class fears of a working-class revolution and the subsequent need for a policed society. This policing is seen especially in the close connection between the creation of the nursing profession and the birth of the modern hospital. Anne Summers notes that "it was . . . through the establishment of hospital-based training programmes that the professionalisation of nursing was ultimately achieved" (1989, 366-67). Revisionist historians such as Michel Foucault, Judith Walkowitz, E. P. Thompson, and Eric Hobsbawm argue that the nineteenth-century development of institutionalized asylums was motivated not only by humanitarianism but also by a need to reestablish a sense of discipline, obedience, and hard work in a "disintegrating" society. Within the nursing reform movement, the old-style nurse was an emblem of underlying social pathology, and like the prostitute, she came to symbolize the undisciplined and possibly rebellious character of the working class in general. Hence hospitals, like prisons or lock hospitals for prostitutes, became "disciplinary institutes of confinement, subjecting . . . working-class [women] to lessons in deference, respectability and personal cleanliness" (Walkowitz 60).

Another crucial reason for this new focus on the nurses' sexuality lies in the nineteenth century's ecumenical preoccupation with human sexuality. In *The History of Sexuality,* Michel Foucault persuasively debunks the "repressive hypothesis": that is, the widely held belief that repressive bourgeois morality inhibited human sexual expression during the Victorian era. Indeed, recent post-Foucauldian scholars have shorn up his assertion that nineteenth-century Western culture is in fact characterized by a "veritable discursive explosion" of and about sex (Foucault 17). Foucault attributes this explosion to the emergence at the end of the eighteenth century of a completely new technology of sex, a technology that he terms *scientia sexualis* (53-73). *Scientia sexualis* denotes a technique of insidious power characterized by the voluntary surrender of personal freedoms coupled with self-surveillance. Through pedagogy, medicine, and economics, this technique pervades modern life and makes sex "a matter that required the social body as a whole, and virtually all of its individuals, to place themselves under surveillance" (116).

Foucault posits that *scientia sexualis* was brought about by the ruling class's concern with the "vigor, longevity, progeniture, and descent" of their own bodies. Hence the working classes managed for a long time to escape the "deployment of 'sexuality'" (121).[6] Yet when the working class did encounter this "garrulous sexuality," they found it was imposed upon them by the ruling class "for the purpose of subjugation" (127). Two pivotal examples of this subjugation can be found in the Victorian Contagious Disease Act campaign of the 1860s and in the nursing reform movement under discussion here.[7] Frank Mort, for example, notes that working-class women were simultaneously eroticized and condemned as "immoral pollutants, the cause of the decline of whole communities" (47). Thus it is not surprising to find excessive, repressive concern with the working-class nurses' sexuality among the discourse of nineteenth-century nursing reformation.

In his essay "The Eye of Power," Foucault recounts how his studies of eighteenth-century hospital architecture in France led him to notice that the "whole problem of the visibility of bodies, individuals and things, under a system of centralized observation, was one of [the reformers] most constant directing principles" (146). This desire to create "the dream of a transparent society," to "eliminate the shadowy areas of society" led to "control over sexuality becom[ing] inscribed in architecture" (150). With Nightingale, Britain's foremost nursing reformer *and* hospital architect, we see the same attention to moral discipline and surveillance of sexuality noted by Foucault among French reformers. Nightingale's architectural plans, inextricably linked to her nursing reforms, emphasized the nurses' sexuality and created a program for confining them in the hospitals, surveying their activities, and morally reforming them through their work. In her *Subsidiary Notes as to the Introduction of Female Nursing into Military Hospitals* Nightingale's discussions of the need for the well-ventilated, light, and airy "pavilion" design for Britain's hospitals consistently slips between eliminating "holes and corners" for the sake of controlling infectious disease and for the sake of overseeing both workers and patients. Poovey claims that Nightingale's description of this system "suggests that her supervisors were involved in an elaborate counterespionage scheme rather than the work of healing" (Poovey 1988, 181). This supervision and surveillance within the hospital is linked not only to keeping general order on the wards, but also to guarding against sexual transgressions: "Guard against too many closets, sinks, &c., &c., &c. . . . [E]ndeavour to prevent the system of holes and corners. It is best that the [Head] Nurse's door should command the view of those who come in or out of the lavatory, and in and out of the water-closet. This whole section is both ugly and important" (Nightingale 1858, 92 & 94).

Ironically, Nightingale envisions the hospital as at once the site of, and the solution to, transgressive eroticism. Thus to guard against unnameable sexual activity, she incorporates the vigilant patrolling and supervision of patients and workers into many of her hospital and nursing reforms. Indeed, the two main principles of Nightingale's nursing school, established at St. Thomas's Hospital in 1860, were first that "nurses should have their training in hospitals specially organized" and second that they should "live in a home fit to form the moral life and discipline" (quoted in Austin 264).

"THY MAGIC TOUCH DID EACH DEAD MUSCLE CHARM!"
(John Davies 1856)

To a great extent, hospital reformers invented "Nightingale" or "new-style" nurses to counteract the supposed renegade sexual offenses of the pauper nurses. As substitutes for their "lascivious" predecessors, the new-style nurses were "new" precisely in their embodiment of chastity and asexuality. We have seen, for example, Robert Southey's location of the source of institutional purification in British Beguines: "Why then have you no Beguines, no Sisters of Charity? . . . how different would be the moral effect which these medical schools produce upon the pupils educated there, if this lamentable deficiency were supplied! . . . many are the young hearts which would be preserved, by [the Sisters'] purifying and ennobling presence, from an infection worse than any evil influence which affects the life alone" (R. Southey 2:318-19). Southey's faith in the sanitizing force of the pious Beguine stems from the nineteenth-century's tacit assumption that saintly nursing erased female sexuality. Yet, as we shall see, saintly nursing in and of itself conveyed a distinct eroticism that undermined claims for the new-style nurse's function as a means of sexual purification.

Thomas De Quincey's *Confessions of An English Opium Eater* (1821) offers a striking example of the claim that saintly nursing purges tarnished female sexuality. With Ann of Oxford Street, the fallen heroine of his memoirs, De Quincey desexualizes the prostitute through her nursing.[8] Drawing on the image of the purification of Mary Magdalene through her tending of Christ, Ann's succoring of De

Quincey when he falls ill on the streets of London obliterates her tainted sexuality: "let me not class thee, oh noble-minded Ann——, with [street-walkers]; let me find, if it be possible, some gentler name to designate the condition of her to whose bounty and compassion, ministering to my necessities when all the world had forsaken me, I owe it that I am at this time alive" (50).

For De Quincey, Ann's "ministering to [his] necessities" dispels her identity as a prostitute, and his own ill-health absolves him of the possibility of being a prostitute's customer. In fact, De Quincey is very anxious to reassure the reader that his passion for Ann was not based on lust—that he was too poor (and too ill) to feel sexual desire: "I feel no shame, nor have any reason to feel it, in avowing that I was then on familiar and friendly terms with [prostitutes] . . . it may well be supposed that in the existing state of my purse, my connexion with such women could not have been an impure one" (49).

De Quincey continues to transform his potential erotic partners into nurses by characterizing his wife as his "Electra" who watches over him through the nights: "thou thoughtest not much to stoop to humble offices of kindness, and to servile ministrations of tenderest affection;— to wipe away for years the unwholesome dews upon the forehead, or to refresh the lips when parched and baked with fever . . . not even then, didst thou utter a complaint or any murmur, nor . . . shrink from thy service of love" (68). Playing patient to his wife's role of nurse, De Quincey presents his marriage as free from conjugal pleasure. He brings the reader to the marriage bed and shows it to be a place of infantilism, wifely martyrdom, and husbandly impotence. Thus for De Quincey, saintly, selfless nursing seems to be the perfect activity with which to erase female sexuality.[9]

Nonetheless, pious nursing conveyed its own eroticism, and the sexual elements of saintly nursing consistently accompanied the naïve assumption of its ability to purify as seen in De Quincey's *Confessions*, as well as in most nineteenth century discussions of the saintly nurse. Southey, for example, writes to Robert Gooch in 1825 that "the Beguines are much esteemed in the Low Countries as the Sœurs de la Charité in France, but I have incidentally learnt from books that scandal used to be busy with them" (quoted in C. Southey 4:156).

Although we cannot ascertain precisely the nature of the "books" from which Southey gleaned his awareness of the cloistered women's "busy scandals," it is highly possible that Southey derived this comprehension of taboo associations connected with images of saintly nursing in part from some form of the important subgenre that existed within libertine literature—that is, the convention of the erotic convent.[10] Roger Thompson, for example, has argued for the cultural importance of the European tradition of anti-Catholic, specifically anti-papistical, pornography that often featured cloistered women as objects of erotic fascination. Anti-papistical pornography became an influential literary form in England during the late seventeenth century when such works as *The Adamite, or The Loves of Father Rock and His Intrigues with the Nuns* (1683), *Vénus dans le cloître ou la religieuse en chemise* (circa 1680), *Romes Rarities, or, The Popes Cabinet Unlock'd* (1684), and *An Anatomy of the English Nunnery in Lisbon* (1685) were published and widely distributed throughout Europe, especially in England and France. These are a very few titles of the immense quantity of anticlerical pornography written in late-seventeenth-century England or translated into English, usually from the French. In his chapter on anti-papistical pornography, Thompson states that "the English had contributed a steady stream of sexual mud-flinging against Roman Catholicism in the sixty years before the Restoration. Its volume is such that only a few examples can be mentioned here" (135). Similarly, Christopher Rivers notes that in a corpus of "two hundred libertine titles taken from the Enfer collection of the Bibliothèque Nationale, there are more clerical references than references to prostitution or brothels . . . even a cursory knowledge of the French libertine tradition informs us that many of these clerical titles are more specifically allusions to nuns and/or the convent" (382-83).[11]

This legacy of clerical erotica survived and flourished in the eighteenth century in both clandestine literature and more mainstream works such as Denis Diderot's *La Religieuse* (1796), Donatien-Alphonse de Sade's *Juliette ou les Prospérités du vice* (1797), Matthew Lewis's *The Monk* (1796), or Laurence Sterne's *Tristram Shandy* (1760-67). Indeed, Sterne's depiction of the Beguine in *Tristram Shandy* anticipatorily mocks the nineteenth century's sentimental glorification of the saintly nurse and its attempted obfuscation of the eroticism associated with pious nursing.

In the story of Corporal Trim's love affair with a young Beguine, Sterne emphasizes the latent concupiscence of the saintly nursing scene. Playing on the metaphor of love as war and falling in love as receiving a wound, Sterne sets Trim's love affair on the fields of Flanders where, as a wounded soldier, he falls in love with his nurse. After being wounded in battle, Trim and other injured soldiers being conveyed to the army hospital stop at a peasant's house. Here Trim faints, and a young Beguine insists that Trim stay at the house under her care. She "foments" Trim's knee "soundly for a couple of hours" and then tends him throughout the night. Trim's narrative emphasizes the saintliness of the Beguine's nursing ("She often told me . . . she did it for the love of Christ . . . the fair Beguine [was] like an angel" [461]), but it also mingles this saintliness with sensuality.

At the beginning of the narrative, Trim's knee is confused with his groin, thus setting the stage for the double entendre of a wounded groin and its suggestion of male impotence with every mention of the Beguine's tending to Trim's wounded knee.[12] Trim finds himself "falling in love" with the Beguine when she kneels down to rub his "itching wound." Here Sterne mingles the piety of nursing as a heroic vocation with the overt eroticism of the job itself:

> The fair Beguine, said the corporal, continued rubbing with her whole hand under my knee—till I fear'd her zeal would weary her— "I would do a thousand times more," said she, "for the love of Christ." . . . As she continued rub-rub-rubbing—I felt [my love] spread from under her hand . . . to every part of my frame. . . . The more she rubb'd, and the longer strokes she took—the more the fire kindled in my veins——till at length, by two or three strokes longer than the rest—my passion rose to the highest pitch. (463)

This image of the resuscitation of the "wounded" groin exposes one central nurse-patient sexual fantasy, that is, the cure of male impotence through the ministrations of the nurse. Wounded and near death, Trim at first feels no desire for the Beguine, just reverence and gratitude. Under her gentle care he begins to recover his strength and, without any pressure from the nurse, he finally "responds" to her nursing. In this fantasy of curing impotence, the nurse doesn't want any reciprocal physical satisfaction, in fact she is "in love" with Christ. Thus the Beguine facilitates Trim's cure by eliding the strain of his responsibility for her sexual pleasure. These examples from Sterne and

De Quincey illustrate the futility of the Victorian attempt to supplant the eroticized working-class nurse with the supposedly asexual, genteel new-style nurse. This attempted replacement does not hold because the "purity" of the pious, middle-class nurse is undermined continually by a variety of conventional erotic associations.

Yet De Quincey's and Sterne's representations of saintly nurses reveal characteristically male sexual fantasies that are markedly different from the fantasies that inspired middle- and upper-class women to daydream about becoming nurses. Indeed, we can chart two distinct erotic motifs associated with the mid-nineteenth-century debates over new-style nursing. One fiction, a vision expressed most often by middle-class male writers, emphasizes the position of the patient. In this scenario, the new-style nurse was a maternal figure who often represented both a cure for impotence and an expression of a longed-for release from social responsibilities. From this viewpoint, the saintly nurse fantasy tended above all to encompass a refusal of an "active" masculine role. The nurse is an object of desire, but not one that the male patient has to pursue: the pious nurse comes to him willingly, and through her disinterested attention, she cures him of sexual trauma—especially impotence. The masculine saintly nurse fantasy is one of regression and infantilization. Here the nurse simultaneously titillates and nurtures the coddled male patient, while on his part, the patient has no responsibility for the sexual fulfillment of his partner. As we have seen from the examples of Sterne and De Quincey, the saintly nurse wants simply to serve and to heal. This dynamic is similar to the configuration of sex with a prostitute in that a prostitute's client is not expected to sexually please the prostitute. However, unlike prostitution, in the saintly nurse fantasy there exists no overt economic taint.[13]

We can infer a second important cultural fantasy located around the topos of the saintly nurse, an erotic imagining in which the role of the nurse predominates. As we shall see, it is this second fantasy that appears as a frequent motif in the writings of mid-Victorian middle-class women. Here the writer's and the reader's identification shifts from the patient to the nurse, and with this shift comes a metamorphosis of the emphasis of the fantasy. Rather than regression, passivity, infantilization, and escape, the saintly nurse fantasy for middle- and upper-class women customarily foregrounds issues of overt social power and control. In this predominately female fantasy of saintly nursing, the patient frequently is a working-class male—either a soldier or an injured worker. Thus the locus of power typically is directed towards control over working-class men. From this perspective, we could argue that not only is the hostility aimed at working-class nurses an attempt to control working-class female sexuality, but further, that with the eroticization of the working-class male patient, the "asexual" saintly nurse signified a usurpation or replacement of working-class female sexuality.

"SPIRITUAL FLIRTATION WITH THE PATIENTS"
(Nightingale 1865)

In her essay "Cassandra," Nightingale specifies romantic or erotic daydreaming as a reason for nursing being a potent fantasy for bored middle-class women who otherwise occupied their time with "the endless tweedling of nose-gays in jugs" (quoted in Woodham-Smith 25): "We fast mentally, scourge ourselves morally, use the intellectual hair-shirt, in order to subdue the perpetual daydreaming, which is so dangerous! . . . What are the thoughts of these young girls while one is singing Schubert, another is reading the Review, and a third is busy embroidering? Is not one fancying herself the nurse of some new friend in sickness; another engaging in romantic dangers with him etc." (Nightingale 1979, 27).

Nightingale claims that female daydreams are dangerous, and she characterizes a typical female fantasy as nursing "some new friend in sickness." Similarly, in 1865 Nightingale complained about the "lady" nurses who tended to be given to "spiritual flirtation with the patients" (quoted in Cook 1:252). Indeed, the fantasy of nursing was widespread among Victorian middle-class women. Nightingale was fairly atypical in that she acted out her fantasy, but many of her contemporaries shared her dreams of "nursing some new friend in sickness." Christina Rossetti, for example, begged to accompany Nightingale to Scutari but was forbidden to go by her mother (cf. Marsh 130). Dorothy Pattison ("Sister Dora") became a nurse around the same time as Nightingale (see below). Similarly, in one of her letters, Elizabeth Gaskell recounts her response to her adolescent daughter Meta's wish to become a nurse: "I have told Meta she may begin to prepare herself for entering upon a nurse's life of devotion when she is thirty or so, by going about among sick now, and that all the help I can give in letting her see hospitals, etc., if she wishes she may have. I doubt if she has purpose enough to do all this; but I have taken great care not to damp her—and if she has purpose, I will help her, as I propose, to lead such a life; tho' it is not everyone who can be Miss N[ightingale]" (Gaskell 1967, 320). Indeed, a large measure of Nightingale's overwhelming fame stemmed from her tapping into, not inventing, a national fantasy.

What, then, is "dangerous" about this nursing daydream? In part the danger of the fantasy of becoming a saintly nurse lies in its evocation of sexual freedoms and sexual debasements. Submerged in the saintly nurse fantasy, "respectable" women could indulge in prostitution fantasies without overstepping the bounds of propriety. Much of the iconography surrounding Nightingale's nursing in Scutari, for example, conveys a subtext of prostitution imagery, especially in her most famous posture of the "lady with the lamp," a lady in possession of a "kissable shadow":

> Lo! in that house of misery
> A lady with a lamp I see
> Pass through the glimmering gloom,
> And flit from room to room.
> And slow, as in a dream of bliss,
> The speechless sufferer turns to kiss
> Her shadow, as it falls
> Upon the darkening walls. (Longfellow 23)

As the Lady with the Lamp, Nightingale walks through corridors of bedded men, exciting "dreams of bliss" as they kiss her passing shadow. The connection between the shadowy Lady with the Lamp and contemporaneous depictions of urban streetwalkers is striking. For example, William Acton's 1869 preface to his report on prostitution characterizes the prostitute problem as a "fear that starts at shadows," the prostitutes being "fair creatures, neither chaperons nor chaperoned" who "[flaunt] along the streets" (7). Nightingale is also a creature of the shadows, an unchaperoned "slender form" gliding alone through the hospital corridors at Scutari. Harriet Martineau describes Nightingale "carrying the lamp through miles of sick soldiers in the middle of the night, noting every face, & answering the appeal of every eye as she passed" (quoted in Poovey 1988, 164-65), a description that echoes French socialist feminist Flora Tristan's description of a London gin-palace as a "stage where the prostitutes . . . entice the men with their glances" (quoted in Hellerstein et al. 419).

Not only does the Lady with the Lamp mimetically evoke the urban streetwalker as she "flits" alone past miles of bedded men, Nightingale's iconography also echoes that of the gin-palace prostitutes and the madams of established houses of prostitution. Images of procuring, purveying, and scavenging occur frequently in Nightingale's letters written during the war.[14] In January 1855, she writes that she is "a kind of General Dealer" in dry goods, and that her storeroom was a "Caravanserai into which beasts come in and out" (quoted in Huxley 101). On February 1, 1855, she writes to her mother: "Can you suppose that such a Scavenger as I am have not a sack of Chlor[ide] of Lime at the corner of every Corridor. . . . Alas! I am Purveyor, Scavenger, everything to these colossal calamities, as the Hospitals of Scutari will come to be called in History" (1987b, 81). In her self-appointed role of "scavenger," Nightingale aligns herself with purveying and shopkeeping. Indeed, a crucial part of her reforming plans in Scutari included catering to the recovering soldiers' needs for pleasure. In her premature obituary for Nightingale written in 1856, Harriet Martineau describes Nightingale "spending precious hours in selecting books to please the men's individual wish or want; & stocking her coffee-house with luxuries and innocent pleasures" (quoted in Poovey 1988, 164). Here Martineau places Nightingale in direct opposition to the prostitutes of the gin-palaces; Nightingale's coffeehouse exists "to draw the soldiers away from poisonous drinks and mischief." Similarly, the *Punch* poem "Florence Nightingale" (1855) declares that Nightingale and her band of "gentle lady" nurses "check[ed] the foul word on the tongue, calm[ed] the fierce thought in the brain; / Till all about those crowded wards a gradual gracious change befell, / Some holy influence bringing guards of Heaven, where, till they came, was Hell" (32-34).

The oblique prostitution imagery within the saintly nurse fantasy expressed a fantasy of debasement as the figure of the prostitute evoked an image of enthrallment to male desire. Both gin-palace prostitutes and Nightingale in her twin manifestation as coffeehouse mistress and the Lady with the Lamp cater to the their clientele's need for pleasure and bodily comfort. Nightingale must "answer the appeal of every eye" while Tristan characterizes the prostitute as one who has "surrender[ed] herself! annihilating both her will and her bodily feelings; sacrific[ed] her body to brutality and suffering" (quoted in Hellerstein 420). Yet in *Cassandra*, Nightingale claims nursing as a realm of freedom beyond the desires of men, especially beyond their sexual appetites: "Jesus Christ raised women above the condition of mere slaves, mere ministers to the passions of man, raised them by this sympathy, to be ministers of God" (1977, 31). Thus mingled with the debasement fantasy is an accompanying fantasy of indifference to, and power over, the male patients that are under the nurse's care. At the same time that the saintly nurse is an Iphigenia, a self-sacrificial martyr to the male body, she also has immense sexual power over the patient either through sexual insouciance or through the use of the patient for her own pleasures. This is seen both in a claimed indifference to pleasure (as in Nightingale's statement quoted above) or in the recurrent coupling of the genteel nurse with the working-class patient.

Lack of sexual desire affirmed either through images of the asexual, saintly nurse or in the undercurrent of the sexually apathetic prostitute results in power over those who possess sexual desire. The scenario of male desire versus female indifference is played out in the juxtaposition of the patient and the nurse. Here the crippled, bedridden patient represents complete enslavement to his bodily needs and an obviously inferior position to the ambulatory, unfettered nurse who can give or withhold her physical attentions as she wishes. Thus through her apparent enslavement to the physical needs of men, the nurse ironically transcends male desire by having no somatic wants or desires herself.

Furthermore, the saintly nurse gains power over her patients not only through sexual indifference, but also through sexual untouchability. For example in "The Hospital Nurse.—An Episode of the War: Founded on Fact," a propagandistic short story published during the Crimean War, the heroine Mary Vaughan discusses her plans to nurse the wounded at Scutari. Her brother-in-law warns her of the dangers of the hospital wards in an attempt to dissuade her from going: "you have failed to make me see the propriety of an English lady . . . carefully guarded from the sight and sound of everything which . . .

might shock a woman's delicacy or refined taste, voluntarily exposing herself to the . . . certainty of witnessing scenes which ought never to pass before her eyes, and hearing expressions which ought never to enter her ears. You do not know what soldiers are, Mary . . . you cannot possibly form any idea of the wickednesses and ribald conversation of their camps and their barracks" (96-97).

Of course neither Mary nor the reader worry about Mary's unprotected girlish modesty, for there is a tacit belief that the potentially sexually threatening working-class soldiers will be awed and tamed by Mary's innate, untouchable upper-class purity. It is this purity that keeps saintly, middle-class heroines such as Nightingale and Mary Vaughan safe from male contamination. Like the prostitutes Tristan writes of, the saintly nurse "sacrifices her body to brutality and suffering" (Mary states that "it was proposed to me to offer myself" to nursing), but unlike the prostitute, the new-style nurse triumphs over the self-annihilation and physical humiliation of her vocation.

The physicality of both nursing and prostitution perhaps explains one crucial appeal of the nursing fantasy for middle- and upper-class women. As the rhetoric of domestic ideology attempted to render leisure-class women increasingly "disembodied," nursing became an important way for these women to imagine themselves reconnected to physical life. Alain Corbin notes that "the lower-class woman, at the heart of the bourgeois household, is entrusted with all that is organic, the management of the body's needs," while the "young girl of good family and the wife show a growing disgust for the practice and the transmission of this somatic culture" (213). With the fantasy or actual activity of nursing, women like Nightingale could express rebellion against the pressure for middle-class women to distance themselves from somatic life.

Accompanying this general reconnection with the body, the image of the saintly nurse expresses a sexual fantasy comparable to the middle-class male's libidinal focus on working-class women. The imaginary coupling of working-class women and upper-class men was a dominant Victorian image.[15] Corbin notes that the servant girl's body "serves as an object of obsession in the master's house," and that the upper-class male's "recourse to the prostitute" can be accounted for by the working-class female taking over more and more of the "instinctive [bodily] needs" of the bourgeois family. Middle- and upper-class Victorian men fantasized and acted on fantasies about the seduction of household servants, while most Victorian prostitutes were recruited from the ranks of working-class women.

One recurrent image of the upper-class male and the working-class woman is that of the male in a position of physical superiority to the female. For example, in their reading of the diaries of Hannah Cullwick, a servant clandestinely married to a Victorian gentleman, Peter Stallybrass and Allon White note that the "opposition between the erect bourgeois and the kneeling maid" recurs incessantly. They see this conjunction as a major motif in the sexual preoccupation masters directed at their servants. Here the juxtaposition of the working-class maid and the upper-class male depended upon a "physical and social separation which was constitutive of desire," the "'lowness' of the maid reinforc[ing] antithetically the status of the gentleman" (155-56).

The conjunction of the upper-class nurse and the working-class male patient replays the gentleman/maid combination with a reverse in gender, but not in class. Here the genteel nurse replaces the "erect gentleman," and the kneeling but active maid is supplanted by a supine, incapacitated working-class male. Thus through nursing, the upper-class female expresses both sexual fascination with and domination over the working-class male that echoes upper-class male fantasies about working-class women. For example, Nightingale's popularity derived particularly from the fact that she nursed working-class soldiers. This supreme instance of noblesse oblige rendered Nightingale the "Iphigenia" of her class, an Iphigenia whose self-sacrifice would result in a reconciliation between the "two nations." Yet accompanying this heroic account of Nightingale's involvement with the working-class soldiers at Scutari was the sexually intriguing image of Nightingale alone with all those helpless, adoring, working-class men.

SISTER DORA

Sister Dora Pattison, an Anglican nurse and a contemporary of Nightingale's, evokes a similarly sexualized discourse. Like Nightingale, the pious, upper-class, beautiful heiress (Margaret Lonsdale's epigraph for the second chapter of Pattison's biography states "'But then, you see, she was a real princess'") gives up her privileges to dedicate her body to the bodies of the poor (27).[16] In her biography of Pattison, *Sister Dora* (1880), Lonsdale characterizes Pattison's vocational dedication in sexual metaphors: *"spending and being spent for them* [that is, her patients] was a delight to her" (25) and "[Sister Dora] was surrounded by hundreds of people, whose needs, physical and moral, she supplied out of her own large store. She was always giving out, *spending and being spent for others"* (my emphasis, Lonsdale 85).[17]

Although Pattison nursed men, women, and children, Lonsdale emphasizes the mutual devotion of Pattison and her male working-class patients. For example, Lonsdale represents Pattison's primal nursing encounter as a schoolboy crush turned tragic. Lonsdale claims that "the only instance of Sister Dora having shown in early youth any aptitude for nursing sick people" occurs when a working-class "school-boy" from her village falls ill of rheumatic fever while Pattison is abroad (20). As he lay dying, the boy's one wish was to see "Miss Dora" before he perished. Upon her return, Pattison immediately went to the boy and "stayed with him, nursing him till he died" (20). Lonsdale intimates that this romantically tragic encounter sets the scene for Pattison's later dedication to nursing. Indeed, Lonsdale claims that a broken engagement led Pattison into her nursing career.

Once Pattison becomes a nurse, the original image of the working-class male yearning for Pattison and demanding her attention continues: "The ward resounded with, 'Sister, come and look at my leg;' 'Sister, my back do ache;' 'Sister, I wish you would give me another pillow;' or, 'I'm sure the bandage is come undone on my knee' (This for the sake of getting some attention probably)" (Lonsdale 87). Yet this devotion and longing is not simply one-sided; Lonsdale depicts Pattison as encouraging the romanticization of her nursing and likewise treating her working-class patients as wayward but cherished lovers. For example, the letter Pattison writes "For the Patients" at her regular ward when she is quarantined at a smallpox hospital is characterized by a scolding, maternal, but also sexual voice: "'Delicate man' is to tell me how he sleeps, and if he does not miss me to arrange his leg and look after him. Tell my Irishman I miss his blessing. . . . I will soon come and starch [his leg]. . . . What shall I say to my beloved Sam? I wish I had my boy here. I send him twenty kisses, and hope he has been in church to-day. . . . He must not sulk all the time I am away" (170-71).

This playful flirtation between Pattison and her "boys" takes a severe turn when Pattison's usual role of gentle comforter of the ill and wounded is exchanged for a policing guise at the Epidemic Hospital during Walsall's smallpox epidemic of 1875. Here the relationship between Pattison and her patients is still covertly eroticized, but the nature of the erotic exchange shifts from the romantic and flirtatious to a more dangerous mode—one of domination and even rape. Yet it isn't the male patients that pose a sexual threat to Pattison, rather she menaces her charges.

To set the mood for this shift from romantic to sadistic sexuality, Lonsdale recounts Pattison's craving for sensation novels as she undertakes her new occupation of nurse/jailer during the smallpox epidemic: "she wrote to some friends, begging them to send her all the old railway novels they could find; for she said she was so weary at night that nothing but a *real sensation novel* would keep her awake while she was not actually employed with her patients" (181, Lonsdale's emphasis).[18] Pattison's "employment" with her patients and the necessity of her sitting up all night (hence the need for the sensation novel "amphetamine") was not only or primarily to nurse the smallpox patients, but rather to guard them and ensure that they did not escape the hospital. Lonsdale recounts one late night errand where Pattison "ran all the way" because of her "terror at leaving the hospital unguarded" (184).

Pattison not only guards the patients, "nearly all of the lowest and most ignorant class" (180), but "arrests" and conveys them to the smallpox hospital as well. Lonsdale fondly describes "Sister Dora's . . . jolly face, smiling out at the window" of the "little small-pox ambulance" that collected the stricken in Walsall: "When people refused to send their patients to the hospital, [Pattison] would go in the ambulance, and announce that she had 'come to fetch So-and-so;' and if further difficulty was made, she would take up the man or woman in her arms, as easily as if the burden had been a baby, and lift it into her omnibus" (186). In this passage, Lonsdale both infantilizes ("as if the burden had been a baby") and dehumanizes ("the burden . . . and lift it") Walsall's working-class sick. Although Lonsdale minimizes the conflicts between Pattison and her patients, she unwittingly indicates working-class resistance to incarceration in the Epidemic Hospital. Indeed, Guy Williams asserts that "going to hospital in the . . .

nineteenth century was an experience to be avoided at all costs" (89), while F. B. Smith notes the "justified reputation as death-traps" possessed by Victorian fever or epidemic hospitals, and that the poor "hated being forced" to enter them (1979, 242).

Pattison's most dramatic struggle with a recalcitrant smallpox patient occurs on a Saturday night, and it is in this encounter that sick-nursing as an expression of sexual domination gets most clearly expressed. Since Saturday night is the traditional night of pleasure, the hospital porter is off drinking, leaving Pattison to guard the hospital alone. She is finding her own gratification in "quietly reading her yellow-backed [sensation] novel," when suddenly "a delirious patient, a tall, heavy man, in the worst stage of confluent small-pox, threw himself out of bed . . . and rushed to the door" (184). Pattison "grappled" with him, "all covered as he was with the loathsome disease." Finally, she dragged him back to his bed where she "held him there by main force until the doctor arrived in the morning" (185). Pattison's "hand-to-hand struggle" with the delirious patient evokes an ambivalent image of at once merging with and triumphing over the working-class male. Considering that smallpox was a disease of "confluence," Pattison's intense physical contact with her patient implies a coalescence with him. Yet at the same time, despite the threat of contagion, Pattison remains immune to his sickness.

In her biography of Pattison, Lonsdale summons up much of the recurrent erotic imagery connected with saintly nursing. As with Nightingale's mythic persona, Sister Dora's experiences play out fantasies of romance, adventure, noble self-sacrifice, and heroism for Lonsdale's readers. Yet not the least of these fantasies is one of mergence with, and domination over, working-class men. The erotic component of this domination gets displayed in a variety of subtle images surrounding the hospital bed and the bodies of the sick or injured working-class male patients. Thus far from creating or retaining a strong position of moral purity from which middle- and upper-class women could claim the right to rule the "dangerous classes," a close look at one of the most powerful icons of Victorian middle-class female purity, the saintly nurse, in fact reveals a reinscription of the very transgressive sexuality that the gentlewoman-nurse was meant to erase. Nor was the tacit awareness of the erotics of saintly nursing limited to women: middle-class male interest in the image of the gentlewoman-nurse evoked an equally powerful, but quite different, set of erotic fantasies. Thus not surprisingly, the immense anxieties exhibited by male and female nursing reformers over working-class nurses' supposed immorality tells us more about the desires of the reformers themselves than it reveals about the "nature" of the old-style nurses. Their story is still waiting to be told.

In the following chapter, I continue to explore the surveillance and "guarding" of new-style nursing exemplified by Sister Dora in the smallpox hospital through a reading of images of nursing in Charlotte Brontë's *Jane Eyre*. Here I link the powerful surveillance embodied in the nurse figures in *Jane Eyre* with Brontë's conception of her own political role as a domestic novelist. Through a consideration of the discourses surrounding nursing in mid-nineteenth-century England, the following chapter contends that Brontë's novel expresses the belief that the ability to keenly control through surveillance is a particularly feminine attribute.[19] Further, I argue that Brontë's depiction of the "controlling eye" of the nurse metaphorically enacts the burgeoning authority of the Victorian domestic novelist. As we shall see, the figure of the nurse best expresses this rising authority due to the ways in which her image fuses the rhetoric of humanitarian sympathy with the normalizing and policing projects of middle-class morality.

A "Scrutinising and Conscious Eye": Nursing and the Carceral in *Jane Eyre* (1847)

> "[T]he book is interesting—only I wish the characters would talk a little less like the heroes and heroines of police reports."
>
> —George Eliot on *Jane Eyre,* 1848

JUST BEFORE HER ILL-FATED ENGAGEMENT TO EDWARD ROCHESTER, Jane Eyre leaves Thornfield to nurse her dying aunt, Mrs. Reed: "I had taken a journey of a hundred miles to see my aunt, and I must stay with her till she was better—or dead" (202). On her first night at Gateshead Hall, Eyre visits her aunt's sickbed to fulfill her nursing goal. Yet Mrs. Reed resists Eyre's nursing and banishes her from the sickroom. On the night Mrs. Reed dies, however, Eyre returns to the sickroom and reappropriates the role of nurse:

> I bethought myself to go upstairs and see how the dying woman sped, who lay there almost unheeded. . . . [T]he hired nurse, being little looked after, would slip out of the room whenever she could. . . . I found the sick-room unwatched . . . no nurse was there; the patient lay still. . . . I renewed the fuel, re-arranged the bedclothes [and] gazed awhile on her who could not now gaze on me. (208)

This passage emphasizes the connections between nursing and surveillance in *Jane Eyre.* Eyre will "see how the dying woman sped."

The hired nurse is "little looked after," and because no one watches her, the sickroom itself is "unwatched." Perhaps most remarkable is Eyre's "gazing on her who could not now gaze on me." Eyre's stare bespeaks her powerful, unsettling, and usurping eye. On her sickbed, Mrs. Reed recalls the young Eyre's "continual, unnatural watchings of one's movements" (203), and by the end of the novel Eyre is not only the injured Rochester's faithful nurse, but also his "vision . . . he saw nature—he saw books through me; and never did I weary of gazing for his behalf" (397). Brontë often links Eyre's "unnatural watching" to her caretaking of the sick. Similarly, the professional nurse in the novel, Grace Poole, shares Eyre's alert gaze. When they first meet, Poole examines Eyre "warily" with "the same scrutinising and conscious eye" (135).

In an essay, Peter J. Bellis aligns the "social and sexual power" of *Jane Eyre* with a "visual power," yet he does not associate this visual power with the scrutinizing eye of the nurse. Bellis critiques both the precepts of the specifically masculine Lacanian gaze and the extensive feminist reassessment of Lacan, with its postulation of a feminine discourse built upon "fluidity and contiguity instead of univocality and hierarchy" and hence embodied in "the touch and the voice instead of the gaze and the written word," for their failure to account for a powerful female gaze (639). Yet although Bellis recognizes the importance of the female gaze in general, and in Brontë's novel specifically, he nonetheless reads Eyre's powerful and usurping eye as a product of "the masculine structures of power" and an emblem of Brontë's appropriation of a masculine gaze. However, I will argue in this chapter that Eyre's powerful gaze draws its authority from a specifically feminine realm of power, a realm closely connected with nursing itself. As we have seen, the authority of this controlling female gaze derived from an amalgamation of domestic and medical ideologies: by the mid-nineteenth century, domestic ideology firmly claimed not only an innate feminine moral authority, but also a uniquely feminine ability to discern, control, and manage environmental details. Female moral and domestic authority combined with the medical discourse of nursing to grant mid-nineteenth-century women a unique claim to authoritarian prerogatives—prerogatives that include precisely what has come to be seen as "masculine" patterns of hierarchy and univocality.

Brontë affiliates both Grace Poole's and Jane Eyre's nursing with incarceration, guarding, and a generally authoritarian spirit. Obviously Brontë closely aligns Poole's caretaking of Bertha with a "carceral spirit." Yet Eyre's nursing also reveals her penchant for dominating and supervising her own metaphoric and literal patients. For example, Eyre associates her longing to nurse her dying aunt (and surrogate mother) Mrs. Reed with "a determination to subdue her—to be her mistress in spite both of her nature and her will" (203). Tellingly, when Eyre sits on Mrs. Reed's bed, her elbow "rest[s] on a corner of the quilt, fix[ing] it down," thus imprisoning Mrs. Reed in her deathbed. Concomitantly, Eyre believes her impulse to nurse Rochester when he tumbles from his horse derives from her "mood for being useful, *or at least officious*" (99, my emphasis). Rochester also locates Eyre's initial nursing of him in an authoritarian proclivity when he recalls this introductory meeting and claims that Eyre "stood by [him] with strange perseverance, and looked and spoke with a sort of authority" (275). This authority, however, derives not from a usurpation of a masculine gaze. Rather, as we shall see, Brontë unobtrusively establishes Eyre's powerful gaze, a gaze that echoes the authority of the domestic novelist, through oblique linkings of Eyre's medical function in the novel with the kinds of claims to power being made for the nurse in the late 1840s.

THE FEMALE CARCERAL

In part, Brontë's stress on the affinities between policing and nursing stems from the fundamental paradigm of incarceration in *Jane Eyre*. Like many Victorian novels, *Jane Eyre* takes imprisonment as a basic theme. As Sandra Gilbert and Susan Gubar note: "[Jane's] story, providing a pattern for countless others, is . . . a story of enclosure and escape" (338-39). Gilbert and Gubar assert that incarceration is a subject generally characteristic of the female bildungsroman: the carceral appears in so many women's texts because it reflects the claustrophobic experiences of middle-class Victorian women trapped in the domestic sphere. In *The Novel and the Police*, D. A. Miller expands Gilbert and Gubar's thesis to recognize the ecumenical presence of the theme of the carceral in Victorian literature.[1] For Miller, the Victorian novel's extensive representation of the carceral points to the novel's own identity as an instrument of disciplinary power and institutional control. The novel enacts its disciplinary function through a playing out in the plot of the notion of self-policing as a way to circumvent the carceral's menace. Oliver Twist, for example, escapes both the workhouse and the prison, but the disciplinary functions of both sites of incarceration are taken on by his adoptive, "rescuing" family. Yet Rose Maylie and Mr. Brownlow don't simply patrol and monitor Oliver; he can sustain his position in the domestic realm only through his own self-policing.

Miller notes that the Victorian novel frequently depicts the rescuing domestic circle as a domain that is ironically maintained through a "domestic self-discipline that internalizes the institutional controls it thereby forestalls" (167). Typically, the Victorian novel signals the internalizing of institutional controls and the mingling of the domestic and the carceral through the troubling of the boundaries between the asylum-as-confinement and asylum-as-refuge. In *Jane Eyre,* we witness this confusion between the perimeters of the imprisoning "asylum" and the desirable sanctuary of domestic space. Gateshead Hall, Eyre's first home, sets the pattern of Brontë's conflation of domesticity and imprisonment. This mingling is seen, for example, in the contrast between the haven Eyre finds in the window seat in the novel's opening scene, and its swift displacement by "the red room" as a site of traumatic incarceration. The nursery, the primary setting of Eyre's childhood, correspondingly blends the carceral and the domestic: it is at once a refuge from the Reeds' cruelty, a site of maternal nurturance in Bessie's caretaking of little Jane, and a prison cell where a solitary Jane gazes out through barred windows upon a frozen landscape.

This confusion between home-as-prison and home-as-refuge continues at both Lowood and Thornfield. Eyre's first impression of Lowood—the most overtly carceral site in the novel and Eyre's first introduction to an institutional world—is of "a wall before me and a door open in it; through this door I passed with my new guide: she shut and locked it behind her" (36). With his rules of "silence" and "order," and his insistence upon drab uniforms, starvation rations, and corporal punishment, Brocklehurst manages Lowood Institution as if it were a prison. The typhus epidemic that "transform[s] the seminary into a hospital" in the novel's ninth chapter also heightens Lowood's carceral associations since typhus, passed in the fecal dust of lice, was commonly known as "gaol fever" (66). Yet even within the primarily penal space of Lowood, pockets of domesticity exist. The first room Eyre sees at Lowood has "papered walls, carpet, curtains, shining mahogany furniture: it was a parlour, not so spacious or splendid as the drawing-room at Gateshead, but comfortable enough" (36). Eyre also finds domestic comfort in Maria Temple's "cheerful" apartment where she is given tea, seedcake, and conversation.

Eyre's next abode, Thornfield, also blends domesticity and incarceration in its dual identity of "splendid mansion" and lunatic asylum. Poole's brooding presence and Bertha's escapes trouble the boundaries that cordon off the "wild beast's den" on the third floor from the elegance and comfort of the civilized spaces of the mansion (272). Eyre describes Thornfield as both "cozy and agreeable . . . the beau ideal of domestic comfort" (83) and as a "grey hollow filled with rayless cells" (102), anticipating Rochester's statement that the house "is a mere dungeon" (189). After Rochester's secret is disclosed, he announces his intention of giving over the whole of Thornfield to its carceral function and turning the mansion into a "Grimsby Retreat"— that is, the local lunatic asylum from whence Rochester has hired Grace Poole: "I'll nail up the front door, and board the lower windows: I'll give Mrs. Poole two hundred a year to live here with *my wife* . . . Poole shall have her son, the keeper at Grimsby Retreat, to bear her company" (264, Brontë's emphasis).[2]

By the novel's end, Eyre seems to have finally circumvented her consistent imprisonment in her escape from St. John Rivers and her marriage to Rochester. Indeed, Gilbert and Gubar claim that Eyre is at last "freed from the burden of her past" (362 and 368). However, we can read Ferndean as Eyre's final site of both domesticity and incarceration. Located, like Lowood, in an "ineligible and insalubrious site," Ferndean is enclosed in a thick, gloomy wood: "iron gates between granite pillars" mark the entrance to the manor, while the forest leading to the house is all "interwoven stem, columnar trunk, dense, summer foliage—*no opening anywhere*" (379, my emphasis). Like Lowood's apertures, Ferndean's doors and windows are "latticed and narrow." Thus in her depiction of Ferndean as both a love-cottage and a prison, Brontë underscores the novel's persistent confusion of domesticity and imprisonment.[3]

Eyre lives uneasily amid the shifting sands of home-as-refuge and home-as-prison, largely because she faces the constant specter of her own incarceration due to her potential insanity. This menacing incarceration is an example of what Miller calls the "feminine carceral," a concept he uses to describe the ways in which errant, transgressive, or undesirable Victorian women were classified as "madwomen." Hence the feminine carceral is characterized by an image of the alienated madwoman imprisoned in an insane asylum or its metaphoric equivalent. The feminine carceral exists in contradistinction to a masculine carceral that permits male transgressive characters to be not mad, but criminal, and thus incarcerated in actual or symbolic prisons rather than lunatic asylums (167).[4]

In *Jane Eyre,* Bertha Mason classically illustrates the workings of the feminine carceral. Her "insanity" during her early years of marriage manifests itself as strong, rank "vices" and a "pigmy intellect . . . [with] giant propensities" (269). The diagnosis of Bertha's madness originates in her contaminating crimes of intemperance and promiscuity, and her imprisonment for lunacy stems from Rochester's sense of being abused and blighted by her unlawful offenses: "What a pigmy intellect she had—and what giant propensities! . . . Bertha Mason,—the true daughter of an infamous mother,—dragged me through all the hideous and degrading agonies which must attend a man bound to a wife at once intemperate and unchaste" (269-71). The logic at work here claims that women can't be criminals: if they indulge in vices then they must be lunatics. This notion emanates from a domestic ideology that asserted an innately pure morality for women. A transgressive woman must de facto be mentally ill since deliberate criminality would be a violation of the "laws" governing female subjectivity.

Like Bertha, Eyre faces a constant threat of incarceration for a malfeasance that is conflated with madness. When she is locked up in the red room, Mrs. Reed and the maids view this imprisonment as righteous punishment for her transgressive behavior, yet Eyre's subsequent "species of fit" in the room troubles her criminal identity (15). With her temporary madness and its accompanying mysterious seizure, Eyre becomes both invalid and outlaw—as the adult narrator, Eyre hides her childhood transgressions behind this excuse of infirmity. Her "illness," euphemistic for her temporary insanity, absolves Eyre from a justifiable but potentially "criminal" act—that is, wounding John Reed. When John Reed attacks her, Eyre recounts that she "received him in frantic sort," and that she did not "know very well what I did with my hands," because, "the fact is, I was a trifle beside myself; or rather *out* of myself, as the French would say" (9, Brontë's emphasis). Thus in her own eyes and the eyes of the Reader, her madness pardons Eyre for any injuries she inflicts on John.

At Lowood, Eyre is once more labeled a criminal when Brocklehurst exhorts the students and teachers to "be on your guard against [Jane] . . . this girl is—a liar!" (58). Yet Brocklehurst also sees her "criminality" as an illness: "she has [been] sent here to be healed, even as the Jews of old sent their diseased to the troubled pool of Bethesda" (58). After her move to Thornfield, Eyre once again struggles against her own impulses towards a criminality that is conflated with madness and the incarceration that accompanies it. Here Bertha Mason acts as both agent for Eyre's subjugated hostility and an exemplar of the dangers of allowing madness to take over. As Gilbert and Gubar note, Bertha "is Jane's truest and darkest double: she is the angry aspect of the orphan child, the ferocious secret self Jane has been trying to repress" (360).

AGORAPHOBIA, HOMELESSNESS, AND PRISON GUARDS

With the continual menace of the feminine carceral and the profound inability of the "rescuing" domestic space to remain stable, not to shift from haven to dungeon, Eyre logically should long to escape the domestic/carceral realm. And indeed, she recurrently proclaims a yearning for freedom and liberty. Yet as much as Eyre voices a desire for freedom, it is this very emancipation that frightens her more than her life within the institution. The famous opening lines of the novel seem to register Eyre's protest against her confinement: "there was no possibility of taking a walk that day." However, Eyre immediately undermines that very protest with her declaration that she was "glad" to stay inside (5). Towards the novel's end, Eyre describes her rejection of St. John Rivers as producing "a shock of feeling [that] had come like the earthquake which shook the foundations of Paul and Silas' prison; it had opened the doors of the soul's cell, and loosed its band" (371), thereby implying that her refusal of Rivers has led to her spiritual, sexual, and physical liberation. Yet the image of an "earthquake" opening "the soul's cell doors" indicates the trauma involved for Eyre in quitting literal and metaphoric confinement. Her reference to the

Paul and Silas prison story from Acts also underscores her reticence to leave confinement. When the earthquake shakes the prison's foundation, "immediately all the doors were opened, and everyone's bands were loosed" (Acts 16:26). However, Paul and Silas do *not* escape the prison. Given the opportunity to flee their cell, they choose to stay and work from within the Thyatirian prison.[5] Likewise, in gaining her inheritance and breaking free from River's potential tyranny, Eyre's "soul's cell" doors are unlocked, her fetters are "loosed," yet she does not quit her confines, rather, she returns to Rochester and a final incarceration at Ferndean.

Although Eyre daydreams of exploration, adventure, and travel, this professed desire for expansion and freedom is only ostensible. Part of the threat posed by Eyre's first two suitors, for example, is that they menace Eyre's comfortable sequestration. After their illegal wedding, Rochester plans to take Eyre: "to regions nearer the sun: to French vineyards and Italian plains" (228). Similarly, Rivers will take Eyre from England to India where she "would not live [beyond] three months" (365). Eyre's nightmares further underscore her agoraphobia as they typically portray her traveling alone on an open road. Before her Thornfield wedding, Eyre has two nightmares. In the first dream, Eyre is "following the windings of an unknown road," and in the second she is once again a homeless wanderer. In this second dream, Thornfield, symbolic of both protection and imprisonment, is a "dreary ruin," and the climax of her nightmare occurs when she climbs Thornfield's "thin wall." Here the "ivy branches" she grasps "give way," "stones roll from under [her] feet," and the thin wall "crumbles" under her weight (247-49). Because this is a "nightmare," the implication here is that Eyre needs to be immured by thick, sturdy walls that won't cave in and ivy branches that won't give way, and she finds these walls and branches at Ferndean with its granite pillars, iron gates, and "close-ranked" trees.[6] Eyre's agoraphobia causes her to fear existence outside the carceral more than she fears incarceration itself.

Eyre's fascination with open spaces can be read as counterphobic, and her one journey outside the asylum provides her with the opportunity to reaffirm her desire for enclosure. After fleeing Thornfield, Eyre experiences complete "freedom" and "liberty," the sort of picaresque wandering typical of the male bildungsroman. Indeed, she leaves Thornfield on a "lovely summer morning," setting out with the "rising sun," the "smiling sky," and "wakening nature" on a beckoning road that promises much adventure (282). Yet Eyre perceives this journey as a "drear flight and homeless wandering," comparing herself to a condemned prisoner going to his execution: "he who is taken out to pass through a fair scene to the scaffold thinks not of the flowers that smile on his road, but of the block and axe-edge; of the disseverment of bone and vein; of the grave gaping at the end" (282). While Eyre's immediate anguish derives from her "disseverment" from Rochester, her misery also stems from her more primary fear of her own homelessness.

When she arrives at her cousins' house, Eyre is near death from starvation and despair. As the outcast wanderer, she can gaze longingly in through the window on the rescuing space of the Rivers' cottage, hence reconfirming the bliss of domestic confinement. At first denied admission into the "rosy peace and warmth" of Marsh End, Eyre sinks down on the doorstep with the "specter of death" before her: "alas, this isolation—this banishment from my kind . . . the anchor of home . . . was gone" (295). St. John Rivers saves her from "certain death" by inviting her in: "now that I had once crossed the threshold of this house . . . I felt no longer outcast, vagrant, and disowned by the wide world" (297). Like Eyre's other homes, Marsh End combines elements of imprisonment with comforting domesticity. While the house's interior is all "rosy peace and warmth" (292), it is in a "sequestered" location, and Eyre's subsequent bondage to Rivers once again turns the rescuing domestic space into a prison cell.[7]

Eyre's experience of homelessness reaffirms her belief that her survival depends upon her confinement within the domestic-carceral realm. Hence she must adapt a strategy that will enable her to eliminate the threat of the feminine carceral that haunts these "asylums." Her solution is to take on the role of those who live in a prison but *do not* become prisoners: Eyre circumvents the possibility of becoming a captive by appropriating the role of keeper or warden of the institution.

Eyre's habitual identification with the guards of the carceral-domestic spaces she inhabits is conspicuous. After her nervous fit at Gateshead, she grows closer to the servants—especially Bessie Leaven—the very people who imprisoned her under orders from Mrs. Reed: "'If you don't sit still, you must be tied down,' said Bessie" (9). Lowood's teachers also act as metaphoric prison guards. Brocklehurst, for example, instructs them to "watch [Eyre]: keep your eyes on her movements, weigh well her words, scrutinise her actions" (58). As a crucial part of her maturation, Eyre emulates the policing spirit of her teachers and ends her time at Lowood by being "invested with the office of teacher," a job she performs "with zeal" for two years (73).[8]

When she arrives at Thornfield, Eyre becomes fascinated with Grace Poole, the most overt prison guard in the novel. Eyre sees her as "enigmatical," the "mystery of mysteries," and "absolutely impenetrable" (134). Of course Poole's enigmatic mysteriousness stems from her acting as a cover for Bertha Mason. Yet the substitution of Poole for Bertha camouflages more than Bertha's existence: this exchange also serves to disguise Eyre's affinities with the madwoman's nurse. Hence, once Poole's false identity is revealed, the reader can easily dismiss Eyre's speculations about Poole, thus leaving the parallels between Eyre and Poole unexamined.[9]

GRACE POOLE, JANE EYRE, AND THEIR PATIENTS

During a drawing lesson, Eyre's charge Adèle asks her: "Qu'avez-vous, mademoiselle? . . . Vos doigts tremblent comme la feuille, et vos joues sont rouges . . . comme des cerises!" (137). What causes Eyre's remarkable flush and tremble is her disturbing meditation on Grace Poole. The night before the drawing lesson, Bertha Mason had escaped from Poole and set Rochester's bed on fire. Eyre discovered and extinguished the fire, and by way of an explanation, Rochester had intimated that Poole had started the conflagration. Stating that she had heard a laugh just before the fire, Eyre said to Rochester: "there is a woman who sews here, called Grace Poole—she laughs in that way," and Rochester replied: "Just so. Grace Poole—you have guessed it" (132). When Eyre attempts to leave Rochester, he tries to detain her: "Strange energy was in his voice, strange fire in his look . . . I was going. 'What! You *will* go?' 'I am cold, sir.' 'Cold? Yes,—and standing in a pool! Go, then, Jane; go!'" (133, Brontë's emphasis).

The "pool" Eyre stands in tellingly stems from the water she has thrown on Rochester's bed, evoking her possible descent into immoral sexuality: Rochester's bed is "on fire," and Jane must try to control or extinguish Rochester's passions. But the puddle in Rochester's bedroom also recalls Grace "Poole," the person Rochester has just blamed for the fire.[10] By pointing out that Eyre is "standing in *a* pool," Rochester also invites Eyre to consider that she might be "standing in *for* Poole."

The next day, Eyre ceaselessly contemplates the relationship between Poole and Rochester: "I hardly heard Mrs. Fairfax . . . so much was I occupied in puzzling my brains over the enigmatical character of Grace Poole, and still more in pondering the problem of her position at Thornfield" (136). Bound up in Eyre's speculations over Poole is a concurrent musing over her own position at Thornfield, her own relationship to Rochester, and a comparison between herself and Poole. Eyre resists equating herself with Poole, yet she broods over the possibility of correspondences between them: "I hastened to drive from my mind the hateful notion I had been conceiving respecting Grace Poole: it disgusted me. I compared myself with her, and found we were different. Bessie Leaven had said I was quite a lady; and she spoke truth; I was a lady" (137). Eyre's assertion of difference between herself and Poole rests on the premise of their class divergence. The irony is that Eyre can only establish this class difference based on the authority of a working-class woman and another carceral-nurse figure: Bessie Leaven.

One of the first correlations Eyre draws between herself and Poole is that they are both "plain." Eyre wonders if Poole is kept on at Thornfield because she is Rochester's discarded mistress, but Poole's "square, flat figure, and uncomely, dry, even coarse face" seems to make a former romantic connection with Rochester an impossibility. Yet, thinks Eyre "*you* are not beautiful either, and perhaps Mr. Rochester approves you" (137, Brontë's emphasis). Indeed, Rochester later declares his love for Eyre despite the fact that she is "small and plain" (223). Eyre also identifies Poole as someone who shares her marginality, solitude, and the lack of pity or notice received from others. At Thornfield, Eyre states that: "The strangest thing of all was, that not a soul in the house, except me, noticed [Poole's] habits, or seemed to marvel at them; no one discussed her position or employment; no one pitied her solitude or isolation" (144). From the beginning of the narrative, Eyre establishes her own identity as an outcast, "a little, roving, solitary thing" (33), who receives no sympathy or attention from the people around her. On the other hand, both women seem to relish isolation and seek out solitude: Poole's "private solace in her own gloomy upper haunt" (144) corresponds with Eyre's "sanctum of the schoolroom" (145).

Yet the most significant connection between the two women emanates from their work. More than the other characters in the novel, Eyre and Poole seem "formed for labour, not for love" (354). They are constantly occupied: if Poole isn't watching Bertha Mason or Eyre isn't teaching Adèle, they sit and sew. They also share an immutable capability. The other servants describe Poole as "extremely good at what she does—she is a good hand, I daresay . . . ah! she understands what she has to do,—nobody better" (136). Likewise, Eyre's identity is interwoven with her invariable proficiency. St. John Rivers declares to Eyre that "I do not speak to the feeble . . . I address only such as are worthy of the work, and competent to accomplish it" (353).

But Eyre and Poole aren't connected just in their competence, they actually have the same occupation: they are nurses. Obviously Poole's major or sole identity in the novel is that of Bertha Mason's caretaker. Eyre's own identity of nurse, however, is less conspicuous. At Lowood, Eyre cries out for a "new servitude," and by the novel's end she turns away from her former occupations of teacher and governess to become Rochester's nurse: "I meant to become [Adèle's] governess once more; but I soon found this impracticable; my time and cares were now required by another—my husband needed them all" (396).[11]

Rochester's and Eyre's marriage is indeed that of nurse and patient. When Eyre rediscovers Rochester at Ferndean, she declares: "I will be . . . your nurse" (383), and their marriage proposal and acceptance is predicated on Eyre's caretaking role: Rochester posits that Eyre "could make up [her] mind . . . to wait on [him] as a kind little nurse," to which Eyre replies that she is "content to be only your nurse" (383). At the novel's end, Eyre's summary of her ten-year-old marriage underscores the nurse/patient alliance between herself and Rochester: "I was then his vision, as I am still his right hand. . . . Never did I weary of conducting him where he wished to go: of doing for him what he wished to be done . . . he knew no reluctance in profiting by my attendance" (397). Indeed, Brontë consistently connects Eyre's and Rochester's marital sexuality to Eyre's nursing of her husband: "there was a pleasure in my services, most full, most exquisite . . . he felt I loved him so fondly that to yield that attendance was to indulge my sweetest wishes" (397). It is important to note, however, that this intensely pleasurable attachment through nursing occurs between them well before Rochester's final maiming. From start to finish, Rochester's attraction to Eyre derives from her caretaking of him.[12]

Indeed, viewing the couple in terms of their roles as nurse and patient helps to clarify the origins of Rochester's perplexing desire for Eyre, a desire that Nancy Armstrong, for example, characterizes as "so highly personalized that it . . . defies explanation in terms of any rational and worldly motive" (194). Eyre's first words to Rochester are: "are you injured, sir? . . . can I do anything?" (99), and their earliest physical contact consists of Eyre helping the wounded Rochester onto his horse: "He laid a heavy hand on my shoulder, and leaning on me with some stress, limped to his horse" (101). Rochester experiences this leaning on Eyre as an acutely blissful sensation: "when once I had pressed the frail shoulder, something new—a fresh sap and sense— stole into my frame" (275). He explicitly dates his romantic, sexual, and spiritual connections with Eyre from this succoring beginning: "the arbitress of my life . . . waited there in humble guise . . . it came up and gravely offered me help . . . I must be aided, and by that hand: and aided I was" (275).

Brontë repeats this primary image of Rochester leaning on Eyre's shoulder at crucial moments in their courtship. When Richard Mason arrives at Thornfield, Rochester receives the news as "a blow" and Eyre nurses him:

> "Jane, I've got a blow;—I've got a blow" . . . he staggered. "Oh!—lean on me, sir." "Jane, you offered me your shoulder once before; let me have it now." . . . "Can I help you sir?—I'd give my life to serve you." . . . "Fetch me now, Jane, a glass of wine. . . ." Mr. Rochester's extreme pallor had disappeared . . . He took the glass from my hand. . . . "Here is to your health, ministrant spirit!" he said. (179)

Well before his final actual illness, Rochester sees himself as an invalid whose cure rests in Eyre's caretaking: "I have . . . been a worldly, dissipated, restless man; and I believe I have found the instrument for my cure" (192), and "I know [you are] one not liable to take infection . . . for while I cannot blight you, you may refresh me" (126). Yet Rochester only toys with the role of patient, and as long as he remains vigorous and healthy, he cannot achieve a perfect union with Eyre.

This is due to Rochester's outrageous and intentional, that is, masculine, criminality. The healthy Rochester has deliberately lied, married for money, hidden away his legal wife, fathered illegitimate children, seduced and abandoned numerous women, and attempted bigamy and rape with Eyre herself.

Many readers remark on Rochester's "feminization" at the end of the novel, usually through a study of his symbolic castration. Yet as John Maynard and other critics argue, it is not Rochester's sexuality per se that becomes feminized since Brontë carefully emphasizes the fecund sexuality of Eyre's and Rochester's marriage (cf. Maynard 138-43). What does get feminized at Ferndean is Rochester's criminality. Rochester replaces his mad wife as patient in the asylum, and through this exchange, he enters into the feminine carceral. Eyre can only live with Rochester once his criminality is pathologized. His menacing, "masculine" criminality causes Eyre to flee Thornfield. However, once criminality transmutes into illness, Eyre can thoroughly forgive and manage Rochester.

By the novel's end, Brontë signals Rochester's move into the feminine carceral through the accretion of similarities between Rochester and his dead wife. Rochester had originally thought of incarcerating Bertha at Ferndean since it was a more natural site for imprisonment: "I possess an old house, Ferndean Manor, even more retired and hidden than [Thornfield], where I could have lodged Bertha safely enough, had not a scruple about the unhealthiness of the situation, in the heart of the wood, made my conscience recoil from the arrangement" (264). Ultimately, Rochester unwittingly realizes his plans for transforming Ferndean into an asylum with Eyre and himself supplanting Poole and Bertha. When Eyre first sees Rochester at Ferndean, he has a "desperate and brooding" countenance that reminds her of "some wronged and fettered wild beast or bird, dangerous to approach in his sullen woe" (379). This imagery echoes Eyre's earlier description of Bertha: "what it was, whether beast or human being, one could not, at first sight, tell . . . it snatched and growled like some strange wild animal" (258). Everyone, except Poole, is terrified of Bertha. Only Poole knows how to manage her: "We're tolerable, sir, I thank you . . . rather snappish, but not 'rageous" (258).[13] Like Poole, Eyre is not afraid of her beastly charge: "do you think I feared him in his blind ferocity?" (379). Yet unlike Poole, Eyre is able to "rehumanize" her patient.

Brontë indicates this regeneration by Eyre's "taming" of Rochester's wild hair: "'it is time some one undertook to rehumanise you,' said I, parting his thick and long uncut locks; 'for I see you are being metamorphosed into a lion'" (384). Like Bertha, Rochester's "shaggy black mane" (385) signifies his degeneration from human to beast. His "long uncut locks" (384) correspond with Bertha's "shaggy locks," her "quantity of dark, grizzled hair, wild as a mane" (258). Yet Bertha's locks are never untangled. Conversely, Eyre combs out Rochester's mane. Thus despite the parallels between the two nurses in the novel, Brontë wants to emphasize the distinctions between Eyre's and Poole's nursing styles.

OLD- AND NEW-STYLE NURSING

Jane Eyre emphasizes Poole's strictly mercenary interest in her work: "Grace will do much for money" (264). Poole displays no compassion towards her charge and seems incapable of rehabilitating the madwoman. Conversely, Brontë equates Eyre's nursing of Rochester with their sexual and emotional affinities, and aligns Eyre's other acts of nursing with similar self- sacrificial and humane motivations. The novel's emphasis on Eyre's benevolent and rehabilitating nursing points to the nineteenth century's ongoing debate between "old-" and "new-style" nursing. As we have seen, "old-style" or working-class nurses were soundly vilified during the nineteenth century by a male medical profession insecure about its own respectability and anxious to sever itself from its working-class origins. Old-style nurses were also discredited by middle- and upper-class female reformers such as Florence Nightingale who were looking for an occupation that could be "cleaned up" and made into either a respectable career for gentlewomen or a field where working-class women could find genteel employment. Thus reformers portrayed old-style nurses as drunkards, former or current prostitutes, thieves, incompetents, and criminals who nursed because they were fit for no other labor. Antithetically, reformers depicted new-style nurses as "clean, intelligent, well-spoken

Christian[s]" (Summers 1989, 365) who nursed out of a sense of Samaritan duty and divine inspiration.

Poole is a particularly frightening version of the greedy, drunken working-class hireling. Much anxiety over old-style nurses stemmed from the potential economic interest nurses had in their patients' illness. As Sairey Gamp says to Betsy Prig in Dickens's *Martin Chuzzlewit:* "Wishin you lots of sickness, my darlin creetur . . . and may our next meetin' be at a large family's, where they all takes it reg'lar, one from another, turn and turn about, and has it business-like" (1968, 538). Correspondingly, Poole is quite happy with Thornfield and her large salary, and hence has an economic interest in *not* curing Bertha even if she were capable of helping the madwoman: "'She gets good wages, I guess?' 'Yes . . . I wish I had as good . . . they're not one-fifth of the sum Mrs. Poole receives. And she is laying by: she goes every quarter to the bank at Millcote. I should not wonder but she has saved enough to keep her independent if she liked to leave; but . . . it is too soon for her to give up business'" (144). Eyre, on the other hand, represents the noble new-style nurse who works out of pity, and not for pay. When Rochester tells Eyre that "your pity, my darling, is the suffering mother of love: its anguish is the very natal pang of the divine passion" (270), he invokes the conventional correlation, as we have seen, between saintly nursing and Christ's divine compassion.

Brocklehurst also anticipates the novel's opposition between the old-style nurse represented by Poole and Eyre's new-style nursing when he compares Lowood to the "troubled pool at Bethesda." Here Brocklehurst notes that "the Jews of old sent their diseased" to the Bethesda pool. Ironically for Brocklehurst, the Bethesda pool is precisely an inadequate form of healing that precedes Christ's miraculous curative powers. In John 5:2-9, Christ visits the Bethesda pool in Jerusalem, finds a sick man who has been sitting by the pool for thirty-eight years with no results, and orders the man to walk—which of course he does.[14] Just as Brocklehurst's unregenerate Lowood echoes the Bethesda pool in that it houses the orphaned girls but never "heals" them, so Poole, the old-style nurse, imprisons Bertha but makes no attempt to cure her. The parallels between Lowood, Bethesda pool, and Grace Poole seem deliberate on Brontë's part for "Bethesda" means "grace" or "house of grace." In contrast to Grace Poole, Eyre can, like Christ, regenerate or "rehumanize" Rochester through her "divine pity."

Like the unregenerate Lowood, that is, Lowood before the typhus scandal, Poole has an overtly carceral function in the novel, and it is this more than anything that brands her as a sinister character. Eyre mistakenly compares Poole to "a prisoner in her dungeon" (144) as Poole is not the prisoner but the guard. In *Shirley*, Brontë creates a comic version of Poole and reiterates the image of nursing as a form of evil imprisonment when Robert Moore is nursed by Zillah Horsfall, "the best nurse on [Dr. MacTurk's] staff" (525). Horsfall is "no woman, but a dragon," who holds Moore in "captivity": "Moore used feebly to resist Mrs Horsfall . . . but she taught him docility in a trice . . . When he was good, she addressed him as 'my dear,' and 'honey'; and when he was bad, she sometimes shook him" (526). Later, Martin Yorke describes Horsfall's nursing of Moore: "she leads him a rich life: nobody else is let near him: he is chiefly in the dark. It is my belief she knocks him about terribly in that chamber. I listen at the wall sometimes . . . and I think I hear her thumping him. You should see her fist . . . I wish she may not be starving him" (532).

Poole and Horsfall are associated with dragons and dungeons because Brontë correlates old-style nursing with "old-style" inquisitional imprisonment; that is, guarding without "rehumanizing," using harsh discipline to control the patient or prisoner and otherwise resorting to what the eighteenth-century prison reformer John Howard termed the "gothic mode of correction."[15] In 1770, for example, he writes that "we have too much adopted the gothic mode of correction, *viz.* by *rigorous severity*, which often *hardens* the heart; while many foreigners pursue the more *rational* plan of *softening* the mind in order to [encourage] its amendment" (quoted in Bender 22, Howard's emphasis).

In the nineteenth century, reformers often accused working-class nurses of ruthlessly disciplining their patients. In an 1865 Lancet Sanitary Commission report on workhouse infirmaries, the investigators write: "We have no wish to make 'sensation' statements against the pauper nurses. But . . . testimony asserts that, in the great majority of cases, pauper nurses can only manage their patients by inspiring fear, and that their conduct is consequently often brutal" (170). In 1866, the *Saturday Review* writes of pauper nurses in the Paddington Workhouse who "took bribes, got drunk, and were occasionally cruel" to the patients (quoted in Austin 184). In 1875, Sister Dora Pattison writes of "the old Irish-woman, sixty-seven! who shouts at the patients, and is a regular old Sarah Gamp" (quoted in Lonsdale 168).

Private or domiciliary nurses were also often affiliated with cruel nursing that was performed under the guise of "managing" the patient. In *Martin Chuzzlewit,* for example, Charles Dickens depicts Betsy Prig's nursing of Mr. Lewsome:

> "[W]e're as cross as two sticks. I never see sich a man. He wouldn't have been washed, if he'd had his own way."
>
> "She put the soap in my mouth," said the unfortunate patient feebly . . .
>
> Here Mrs. Prig seized the patient by the chin, and began to rasp his unhappy head with a hair-brush.
>
> "I suppose you don't like that neither!" she observed. . . .
>
> It was just possible that he didn't, for the brush was a specimen of the hardest kind of instrument producible by modern art, and his eyelids were red with the friction. (535-36)

Rather than being cruel workers in corrupt asylums, workhouses, or jails, domiciliary nurses like Prig, Horsfall, and Poole bring the taint of degenerate institutions into the domestic realm, thereby transforming private homes into metaphoric prisons.

NURSING, SURVEILLANCE, AND DISCIPLINE

Yet carceral or disciplinary aspects of old-style nursing received as much praise as condemnation. In fact, the core notions of desirable old-style nursing during the nineteenth century connect up with images of guarding and watching. In 1857, Dr. J. F. South writes of the nursing at St. Thomas' Hospital in London. Here he praises the surgical nurse who is "constantly with the patient, day and night—often for many together . . . [and] whose duty is to be on watch at the bedside" (quoted in Austin 165). In 1885, Sir James Paget describes the nursing at St. Bartholomew's Hospital during the 1830s: "old Sister Rahere was the chief among [the nurses], stout, ruddy, positive, *very watchful.* . . . And there was her neighbor, Sister Colston, rough-tongued, scolding, not seldom rather tipsy; and yet *very watchful*" (quoted in Austin 165, my emphasis).

Not only are the skillful old-style nurses "very watchful," they are also quite officious. Lord Lister's nephew recalls Lister telling of a "Mrs Porter. . . . She was head nurse in his wards. . . . She kept [all the medical students] in order, and, it was said, her chiefs also. She acted as if all the responsibility rested on her shoulders, and was in fact an important and efficient personage" (quoted in Austin 167). In a letter written in 1872, Nightingale deems Sara Wardroper, the Matron of St. Thomas' Hospital, a "real Hospital genius [who] manages St. T.'s better than any one" (Nightingale 1990, 331). In an 1892 eulogy written for Wardroper, Nightingale notes that her "force of character was extraordinary; her word was law. . . . She was a strict disciplinarian" (quoted in Austin 265).

Nightingale's praise of Wardroper points to a crucial conflict in the discrediting of the old-style nurse and the nineteenth-century reformers' attempts to distance new-style nursing from its working-class origins. Wardroper was an "old-style" nurse, yet far from being an alcoholic or an incompetent worker, she was a skilled, respected, highly qualified matron who, ironically, was in charge of training the new-style nurses who were to be so different from their old-style forerunners. Monica Baly, noting the "absolute power" possessed by Wardroper, states that "it was she who selected the nurses, and she who dismissed them. . . . Probationers were now accountable to the matron and to no one else" at St. Thomas's nursing school (Baly 1984, 56).

The myth of Nightingale's reformation of the nursing profession consistently emphasizes the changes wrought through the introduction into hospitals of "educated, trained, refined women" (Lavinia Dock quoted in Baly 1984, 55), yet old- and new-style nursing conjoined on many levels. Perhaps most fundamentally, the tenets of new-style nursing emphasized developing the nurse's policing talents, thereby retaining the carceral skills old-style nurses were both praised and condemned for possessing. Of supreme importance was a nurse's ability to control or "rule" either the patients in her care, or the nurses that worked under her if she was in a managerial position. In an 1871 letter, Nightingale repeats gossip told to her about Jane Deeble, Superintendent of Nurses for the British army and a woman from an upper-middle-class family. Here Nightingale implies that Deeble is unfit for her position due to her "absolute incapacity for ruling." Because Deeble "had been ruled all her life" by her mother, husband,

and "even the maids," she had "little or no influence or control" over the nursing sisters in her charge (1990, 317-18).

For Nightingale, this "influence or control" was intricately connected to surveillance.[16] Virtually everywhere in her letters, reports, tomes, or architectural plans, there is an intense concern with visibility and hierarchical watching: the nurses watch the patients, the head nurses police the nurses, the matrons oversee the head nurses, and Nightingale governs the matrons.[17] However, it is important to note that Nightingale envisioned this schema of hierarchical watching taking place in a feminine world. She wanted to elide the supervision of male medical authorities, and it was this omission that lay at the heart of her battles with the medical world.[18]

Nightingale believed that the female eye was a superior instrument for the observation and guarding of the sick. For example, in *Notes on Nursing,* she complains that the lack of hierarchical watching in the military hospitals, hospitals traditionally staffed entirely by men, brings about "suicides in *delirium tremens,* bleedings to death, dying patients dragged out of bed by drunken Medical Staff Corps men" (23). In these cases, the medical officers aren't to blame as "how can a medical officer mount guard all day and all night over a patient?" What is needed in the military hospitals, and in all nursing situations, is "an organized system of attendance" with a "trustworthy *man* in charge of each ward, or set of wards, not as officer clerk, but as a head nurse." Nightingale emphasizes the word "man" here because with a trustworthy male head nurse overseeing the wards, fatal hospital accidents "would not, in all probability, have happened." Yet with a trustworthy *woman* in charge, ward accidents "would not, in all certainty, have happened. In other words, it does not happen where a trustworthy woman is really in charge" (1864, 23).

Nightingale's faith in the innate superiority of the female eye stems from her particular vision of domestic ideology, a vision that granted women immensely superior powers when it came to household management.[19] In Victorian England, as we have seen, the miasmic policies of hygienic prevention personified in the image of the nurse elevated her to an unprecedented stature. For England, it was the nurse and not the doctor that represented both prevention and attention to the entire environment of the patient. In fact, the doctor represented the failure of prevention or the lack of prevention accompanied by a shortsighted focus only on the sick body of the patient, not upon the surrounding elements that could cure or kill the ill—that is, fresh air, wholesome food, warmth, and general hygiene.

Rather than being a usurpation of the male medical gaze, the policing eye of the nurse derives its authority from sources separate from, and often in opposition to, male medical authority. As we have seen, Nightingale recounted that she had often seen talented nurses distressed because they "could not impress the doctor with the real danger of their patient. . . . A man who really cares for his patients, will soon learn to ask for and appreciate the information of a nurse, who is at once a careful observer an a clear reporter" (1860, 69). Similarly, Nightingale insisted that "nursing and medicine must never be mixed up. It spoils both. . . . If I were not afraid of being misunderstood I would almost say—the less knowledge of medicine a hospital matron has the better . . ." (quoted in Cope 121).

Nightingale ascribes the superiority of the female gaze in part to circumstance, arguing that because the nurse provides constant care to the patient, there are "facts the nurse alone can observe" (Nightingale 1860, 68). Yet she couples this nurture narrative with one of nature in her assertion that women, particularly English women, have a distinctive capacity for observation: "In countries where women (with average intelligence certainly not superior to that of Englishwomen) are employed, e.g., in dispensing, men responsible for what these women do . . . have stated that they preferred the service of women to that of men, as being more exact, more careful, and incurring fewer mistakes of inadvertence. Now certainly Englishwomen are peculiarly capable of attaining to this" (1860, 64).[20]

Brontë also connects the proficiency and worth of both old- and new-style nursing with the guarding gaze of the nurse. Grace Poole's managerial efficiency, for example, depends upon her ability to stay sober and hence vigilant—her lapses in supervision occur only when she gives in to her craving for gin. Similarly, Brontë obliquely attributes the trauma young Eyre undergoes by sleeping with the dead Helen Burns, and Burns' death itself, to the slumbering, unvigilant hired nurse whose apathy towards her patient echoes Poole's drunken lapses and the unreliability of the hired nurse who watches at Mrs. Reed's deathbed. In this scene, the insomnious Eyre creeps into Burns's sickroom around eleven o'clock to "embrace [Burns] before she died"

(70). Eyre is "fearful lest the nurse who sat up all night should hear me," but when she gets to the sickroom, "the nurse . . . sat in an easy-chair, asleep" (70). Without waking the nurse, Eyre and Burns hold a lengthy whispered conversation about Burns's imminent journey to the "mighty, universal Parent" (71). From eleven at night until dawn, the hired nurse never wakes up or checks on her gravely ill patient. Eyre sleeps undisturbed with the dead Burns until Maria Temple discovers her when she returns at dawn from nursing a delirious fever patient. Temple, an institutional goddess who purifies the otherwise corrupt establishment of Lowood, provides a model for Eyre of selfless, dedicated, and attentive nursing. When the typhus epidemic strikes, "Miss Temple's whole attention was absorbed by the patients: she lived in the sick-room, never quitting it except to snatch a few hours' rest at night" (66-67).

When called upon to function as a nurse, Eyre imitates Temple's watchfulness—and it is only this attentiveness that can keep Richard Mason from death: "I must watch [his] ghastly countenance . . . I must dip my hand again and again in the basin of blood and water, and wipe away the trickling gore. I must see the light of the unsnuffed candle wane on my employment . . . I had, again and again, held the water to Mason's white lips; again and again offered him the stimulating salts" (184-85). Brontë implies in this scene that Eyre's nursing of Richard Mason transmutes her into a Christlike figure. During her vigil, Eyre becomes mesmerized by "the doors of a great cabinet" whose twelve front panels "bore in grim design the heads of the twelve apostles . . . while above them at the top rose an ebon crucifix and a dying Christ" (184). Here although Richard Mason is literally bleeding to death from his knife wound and in that sense echoes the crucified Christ, it is Eyre's martyred nursing of Mason that is more an imitation of Christ's deeds.[21] In this scene, as in the other images of heroic nursing in *Jane Eyre*, Brontë implies her possession of the ability to heal through her writing, and she can lay claim to these special powers based both upon her experiences of deprivation and suffering as well as her innate feminine sympathy.

In her preface to the second edition of *Jane Eyre*, Brontë depicts the novel as a modern prophetic form. She dedicates *Jane Eyre* to William Thackeray whom she hails as the "first social regenerator of the day" (2). Brontë implies that through his novels, Thackeray has achieved a voice akin to the utterances of Christ and the biblical prophets: "There is a man of our own days whose words are not framed to tickle delicate ears: who, to my thinking, comes before the great ones of society, much as the son of Imlah came before the throned Kings of Judah and Israel; and who speaks truth as deep, with a power as prophet-like and as vital—a mien as dauntless and as daring" (2). Brontë, in her "claim to the title of novelist," has a need to join her authorial identity with the weighty company of Thackeray, Christ, and the Old Testament prophets, and she quite unabashedly declares her shared role with them as a "social regenerator" who "speaks truth" with a "vital" and "prophet-like" power. In this sense, Brontë appears to align her art with a very masculine voice.

However, Brontë's seemingly masculinized authority contradicts a critical tradition that has read *Jane Eyre* as a revolutionary book in terms of the history of the British novel precisely because it articulated the passions and desire of women.[22] Thus what seemed so thrilling or threatening to many readers of the late 1840s was *Jane Eyre*'s giving voice to a new realm of specifically feminine experience, and it was this voice that opened the door for the establishment of a new kind of female authority.[23] Virginia Woolf characterized Brontë's narrative authority in this way: "the writer has us by the hand, forces us along her road, makes us see what she sees, never leaves us for a moment or allows us to forget her. At the end we are steeped through and through with the genius, the vehemence, the indignation of Charlotte Brontë . . . It is the red and fitful glow of the heart's fire which illumines her page" (quoted in Brontë 1977, 455-56). In asserting that Brontë "makes us see what she sees," Woolf evokes Brontë's own metaphor for her art.

In her preface to *Jane Eyre*, Brontë writes that the public "may hate him who dares to scrutinise and expose" (2), thereby metaphorically connecting her own art with the observing gaze, a gaze, as I have argued, that is particularly correlated in *Jane Eyre* with the act of nursing. The visual metaphors that authorize Brontë's expertise are an important means for Brontë to align herself with the prophetic masculine voice delineated in her preface. However, by aligning visual power in *Jane Eyre* specifically with nursing, I would contend that Brontë structures a feminine voice that ultimately overrules those masculine models evoked in her preface. Thus the "scrutinising eye" of the novelist in Brontë's preface is transmuted into the scrutinizing eye of the nurse, in both her elevated (Jane Eyre, Maria Temple) and degraded (Grace Poole) manifestations.

Yet the eye of the novelist and the eye of the nurse are not indelibly connected for Brontë, and by *Villette* she has ceased to insist on the correlation. Rather, Brontë shifts the authority of the observing eye of the novelist from the nursing gaze to the critical scrutiny of the connoisseur, a paradigm for female authority present in *Jane Eyre* but subordinated there to the nursing gaze. Rather than maintaining a heroic and redemptive status in Brontë's oeuvre, by *Villette* nursing instead becomes equated with degradation and self-immolation. For example, Lucy Snowe's sojourn as nurse and companion to the invalid Maria Marchmont carries none of the moral weight and heroism of Jane's nursing activities, inciting degeneration and hysteria in Lucy rather than redemption or enlightenment. Similarly, Lucy's hysterical breakdown at the end of "The Long Vacation" is triggered to a great extent by the role of nurse that she is forced to play to Madame Beck's "crétin" boarder Marie Broc:

> The hapless creature had been at times a heavy charge; I could not take her out beyond the garden, and I could not leave her a minute alone; for her poor mind, like her body, was warped: its propensity was to evil. A vague bent to mischief, an aimless malevolence made constant vigilance indispensable. . . . it was more like being prisoned with some strange tameless animal, than associating with a human being. Then there were personal attentions to be rendered which required the nerve of a hospital nurse; my resolution was so tried, it sometimes fell dead-sick. These duties should not have fallen on me. . . . Attendance on the crétin deprived me often of the power and inclination to swallow a meal, and sent me faint to the fresh air . . . (229).

Unlike the spiritualized and uncomplaining nursing of Maria Temple and Jane Eyre, Brontë infuses Lucy's nursing with a gritty realism.

When Lucy is compelled by Dr. John to become Paulina's nurse after the theater fire, Lucy transforms the act of nursing into a space of aesthetic judgement, a continuation of the scrutiny and opinions she had been imparting during "Vashti's" performance.[24] As Lucy undresses the injured Paulina she turns that disrobing into a striptease for the readers, scrutinizing the little Countess in much the same way she herself had been critiqued by Madame Beck upon her arrival in Villette:

> making the women stand apart, I undressed their mistress, without their well-meaning but clumsy aid. I was not in a sufficiently collected mood to note with separate distinctness every detail of the attire I removed, but I received a general impression of refinement, delicacy, and perfect personal cultivation. . . . This girl was herself a small, delicate creature, but made like a model. As I folded back her plentiful yet fine hair, so shining and soft, and so exquisitely tended, I had under my observation a young, pale, weary, but high-bred face. (345-46)

Here the emphasis is not on the physical suffering of the patient and the spiritual healing of the nurse. Rather, the patient has become a "model" whose personal attributes are carefully catalogued and evaluated by the cool discernment of Lucy's discriminating, aesthetic eye.

This dramatic shift in the image of nursing from *Jane Eyre* to *Villette* can be explained in part by Brontë's decreased interest in predicating her narrative authority on the role of "social regenerator." By 1853, Brontë had moved away from the social concerns present in both *Jane Eyre* and *Shirley* to create a narrative of individual fulfillment, and with this move there is a concomitant diminishment in her metaphoric use of the saintly nurse as an emblem for her persona of social healer. In the following chapter, I look closely at the image of heroic nursing in Elizabeth Gaskell's *Ruth*. Like Brontë, Gaskell exhibits through her use of the nurse both the establishment of her narrative authority, and a rebellion against her self-proclaimed role of social healer.

Scars, Stitches, and Healing: Metaphors of Female Artistry in Gaskell's *Ruth* (1853)

SEWING AND NURSING IN *RUTH*

ELIZABETH GASKELL'S NOVEL *RUTH* (1853) ends with the heroine's death; a death the narrator characterizes with a line from Shakespeare's *Cymbeline*. Upon her death Ruth "home must go and take her wages" (447). Since Ruth is a fallen woman and an unwed mother, a cursory reading of this quotation might connect Ruth's "wages" with the "wages of sin." Indeed, because Ruth dies from a fever she contracts while nursing her seducer, commentators generally interpret Ruth's premature demise as an authorial punishment for youthful transgressions.[1] Yet this passage from *Cymbeline* points to one of the most salient issues in Gaskell's novel: that is, the question of labor in general and woman's work in particular. Indeed, Martha Vicinus writes that the "passion for meaningful work, so often underestimated and misunderstood, was the sacred center of nineteenth-century single women's lives and communities. It was the means out of the garden, out of idleness, out of ignorance, and into wisdom, service and adventure" (1).

In *Ruth*, the occupations of sewing and nursing bracket the plot's trajectory. The novel opens with an extended description of Ruth's work as a dressmaker's apprentice, and it is this distressing occupation that ostensibly smoothes the path for her seduction. After her seduction, impregnation, and abandonment by the callow Henry Bellingham, the balance of Gaskell's novel follows Ruth's quest for suitable work. By the story's end, Ruth finds redemptive labor in her vocation of village nurse, an occupation that leads directly to her death, but also to her social and spiritual salvation.

Like many popular writers of the 1840s and 1850s, Gaskell infuses her domestic tale with didactic purport, focusing especially on a critique of, and solution to, the crisis of labor brought about by England's Industrial Revolution. From this perspective, Ruth-the-oppressed-seamstress corresponds with other conventional representations of tormented "white slaves" depicted in mid-Victorian condition-of-England novels. Catherine Gallagher, for example, has argued that the popular reforming rhetorics of both paternalism and domestic ideology found in the exploited seamstress a powerful emblem for all working-class suffering and abuse: "seamstresses were even more appealing sufferers than other working women because their trade was unmistakably feminine. . . . Because almost all women sewed, the seamstress seemed at least as much woman as worker" (1985, 130).

However, *Ruth* does not technically fit into the "industrial novel" genre, set as it is in, respectively, a provincial market town, a Welsh mountain retreat, a village, and a seaside resort—nowhere in *Ruth* do we see the urban blight and the troubled factory workers as we do in such novels as Gaskell's *Mary Barton* and *North and South* or Dickens's *Hard Times*. Rather, *Ruth* is an important example of the "fallen woman" genre—a genre that includes such novels as Nathaniel Hawthorne's *The Scarlet Letter,* George Eliot's *Adam Bede,* and Thomas Hardy's *Tess of the D'Urbervilles.*[2] Nonetheless, in *Ruth* Gaskell evokes many similar issues of causality and exploitation that form the nucleus of the social questions that she explores in her industrial novels *Mary Barton* and *North and South*. The echo of the industrial novel within the fallen woman genre occurs in *Ruth* largely due to Gaskell's profound association of female fallenness with woman's work: paradoxically, women fall both because they are exposed to the workplace and because they are denied fair access to the workplace. Gaskell's ambivalence about female labor, an uncertainty shared by many of her contemporaries, finds expression in her rejection of the rhetoric of paternalism and her endorsement of domestic ideology as the most compelling solution to the crisis of female labor created by England's Industrial Revolution.

The ideology of paternal reform rests on the principle that social problems are brought about through the failure of the father—thus the solution to social crisis is insured by the reinstatement of paternal authority. Social reformers who adhered to this belief frequently represented members of the working class as "orphans" in need of a rescuing, benevolent father figure. Correspondingly, Ruth's presence in the workplace occurs precisely through the failure of her father, both as an inept man of business and through his premature demise: as an impoverished female orphan, Ruth must pay for the crimes of her parents', especially her father's, blunders. However, Ruth's rescue from her onerous labor as a seamstress is mock-paternal in that her "fairy-tale" release from Mrs. Mason's sweatshop by the wealthy Henry Bellingham turns out to be a gesture of exploitation, not deliverance. Finally, it is Ruth's own maternity, coupled with the Bensons' rescuing domesticity, that redeems her.

In Gaskell's novels of domestic realism, she was delineating her political and ethical theories of domestic ideology, theories she shared with writers such as Sarah Stickney Ellis and George Eliot. For Gaskell, Ellis, and other proponents of domestic ideology, solutions to social issues depended on private ethics, especially ethics guided by female influence—domestic ideology places the source of social redemption within the hands of the "good mother." Correspondingly, solutions to social conflict are then to be found within the regenerative force of symbolic or literal maternal influences. In her novels, Gaskell typically searches for an ethical center in a morally complex world, and inevitably she finds that center in women, especially in the frequently symbolically maternal women who comprise the majority of her heroines.[3] In *Ruth*, the eponymous heroine constitutes the ethical center of the novel. Yet perversely, although she is a mother, one of the few literal mothers to represent an ethical focus in Gaskell's oeuvre, she is an *unwed* mother—a tainted version of motherhood. By incongruously choosing an unwed mother as the moral nucleus of her novel, Gaskell intends to demonstrate that maternity, and the sympathies awakened by maternity, counteract the social circumstances of impregnation. Rather than destroying her, maternity redeems Ruth as it does Hester Prynne: her seduction is paradoxically a fortunate fall.[4]

In *Ruth*, a return to the domestic realm precedes the heroine's reinstallment in the working world. As a metaphoric solution to the crisis of industrialism, Ruth's vocation as a village nurse embodies the self-redemption of the working class through the introduction of morally pure labor into the work-world. Here the exploited worker returns to the ethically purifying domestic sphere, imbibes the elixir of domestic rejuvenation, and then returns to the public realm to spread the gospel of domestic salvation through her role as community nurse. Ruth's former occupation as a seamstress, then, not only represents the helplessness and exploitation of the working-class woman, but sewing itself becomes a metonymy for all morally dangerous forms of female labor. Conversely, the work of nursing occupies an exalted position within this moral schema. As we shall see, just as Gaskell presents dressmaking as sharing a large part of the blame in Ruth's fall, so does she align nursing with Ruth's redemption. In the following pages of this chapter, I will concentrate on the conventional qualities of sewing that Gaskell emphasizes in *Ruth* in order to align sewing and female fallenness. Like many mid-Victorian writers, Gaskell depicts the occupation of sewing as especially jeopardizing to the moral development of young women; a moral peril derived through the intermingling of four basic dangers: the working conditions of "sweated" labor; the work's excitation of treacherous female vanity; the sexual exploitation of the seamstresses by their employers; and the opportunities presented by dressmaking for working-class women and wealthy men to meet.

The softening of the seamstresses' morals begins in the crisis of the workroom. The long hours, the dismal sweatshops, the lack of proper nourishment, and the absence of supervision during the employees' spare moments of leisure all combine to destroy the spirit, health, and judgment of the apprentices. In *Ruth,* the young women regard "most events" with "sullen indifference" due to a "deadened sense of life, consequent upon their unnatural mode of existence, their sedentary days, and their frequent nights of late watching" (9-10). The narrator also emphasizes the "monotonous idleness" of Sundays when Ruth is left without friends or supervision. It is during one of these Sundays that Bellingham seduces Ruth.

The second danger of the work of sewing is the dangerous vanity that dressmaking seemed to invite. Dressmaking was seen as "fallen" labor, work that catered to female vainglory. Exposure to fashion and wealth was believed to incite both greed and envy in the vulnerable apprentices. Indeed, Gaskell emphasizes Ruth's immunity to this particular corruption of dressmaking: it is her utter lack of vanity, despite her great beauty, that marks Ruth as the story's heroine. In strong contrast is the more vulnerable character of Esther, the fallen woman figure in Gaskell's *Mary Barton*. As with Ruth, Esther's beauty is a "sad snare," but she hastens her downfall through her love of fashion. At the novel's beginning, Esther's brother-in-law John Barton recounts how "Esther spent her money in dress, thinking to set off her pretty face. . . . Says I, 'Esther, I see what you'll end at with your artificials, and your fly-away veils'" (43). Similarly, in *Ruth,* one of Mrs. Mason's "greatest foibles" is to "pay an extreme regard to appearances," a failing characterized by the narrator as "very natural to her calling" (8).[5]

The attention paid by seamstresses such as Mrs. Mason to fashion and female beauty was seen to invite the third danger of dressmaking, that is, either the unwitting or the deliberate sexual exploitation of their apprentices. Dressmakers were believed to capitalize on the beauty of their apprentices, usually by using the young women as models or as attractive bait with which to lure new customers into the shop. In Dickens's *Nicholas Nickleby,* Kate Nickleby's employment at Madame Mantalini's dress-shop heightens the aura of sexual menace that follows Kate throughout the novel. At the shop, Kate's beauty attracts much unwanted attention: "Pray have up that pretty young creature we saw yesterday. . . . Everybody is talking about her . . . and my lord, being a great admirer of beauty, must positively see her" (295). Similarly, Mrs. Mason selects Ruth to mend customers' gowns during the hunt-ball because of the "remarkable beauty which Ruth possessed," a beauty Mrs. Mason regards as "such a credit to the house," thereby underscoring her role as a species of procuress (11).

It is during this ball that Bellingham first encounters Ruth, a meeting that introduces the fourth conventional danger of dressmaking: the opportunity for wealthy men to meet working-class women. This intermingling was seen to provide an opening for acquaintanceships that would lead to the vulnerable woman's seduction and inevitable betrayal. In George Eliot's *Adam Bede,* for example, Hetty Sorrel encounters Arthur Donnithorne when she goes to his estate to learn "fancy" sewing, while Ruth fatefully meets Bellingham while she is repairing his fiancée's torn ballgown. Although other occupations placed wealthy men and impoverished women in close proximity, like governesses, seamstresses were seen as particularly enticing and hence in greater danger of seducing or being seduced.[6] This allure existed because seamstresses were seen as performing genteel, feminine labor. Consequently, they were servants whose sexuality was heightened, rather than diminished, by their work. Indeed, Gaskell implicitly compares the feminine appeal of Mrs. Mason's apprentices with the "one or two char-women" working to prepare the ballroom for the party: "[they presented a] strange contrast with their dirty, loose attire [to the elegance of the ballroom]" (13).

Just as the etiology of Ruth's fall is bound up in her occupation as seamstress, so is nursing aligned with Ruth's redemption. After Bellingham abandons Ruth, she is sheltered by Thurston Benson, a nonconformist minister, and his sister Faith. This gentle couple commit a "pious fraud" by telling their neighbors that Ruth is a distant, recently widowed, relative. In this way they hope to spare Ruth and her unborn child the social ostracism that is the conventional destiny of the Victorian novel's fallen woman. Following the birth of her son Leonard, Ruth remains with the Bensons for many years, eventually finding work as a nursery governess. After fourteen years of loyal service, Ruth's past is revealed, and she is fired by her philistine employer Mr. Bradshaw. During this period of discovery and repudiation, Ruth's greatest anguish stems from her loss of vocation—above all, Gaskell presents the dilemma of the fallen woman as one in which the erring female is forever doomed to be an exile from "useful" labor. Indeed, Ruth states that she asks only "to be one of His instruments, and not thrown aside as useless—or worse than useless" (186). After Bradshaw dismisses her, Thurston Benson advises Ruth that "perhaps you will have to find your work in the world very low . . . [perhaps] you may have to stand and wait for some time; no one may be willing to use the services you would gladly render" (357). In arguing with Bradshaw about Ruth, Thurston Benson voices Gaskell's central belief about fallen women: "not every woman who has fallen is depraved . . . many, many crave and hunger after a chance for virtue—the help which no man gives to them— help—that gentle tender help which Jesus gave once to Mary Magdalen. . . . [T]o every woman, who, like Ruth, has sinned, should be given a chance of self-redemption" (350-51). This "self-redemption" comes not through mere repentance or contrition, but through work.

As Eliza Meteyard writes in 1850 in *Lucy Dean; the Noble Needlewoman:* "it is only through labour—honest self-help" that the fallen can rise (quoted in Mitchell 29).

But what sort of labor leads most expediently to "self-redemption"? For Gaskell and other Victorian writers, the fallen woman needed to redeem herself through labor that echoed the repentance of Mary Magdalen. Gaskell's epigraph for *Ruth,* a poem by Phineas Fletcher, refers explicitly to the repentance of Mary Magdalen:

> Drop, drop, slow tears! / And bathe those beauteous feet. . . . Cease
> not, wet eyes, / For mercy to entreat. . . . In your deep floods / Drown
> all my faults and fears; / Nor let His eye / See sin, but through my tears.

Atonement requires a labor that could evoke repentant, cleansing tears with which to wash away a fallen woman's sins. Although, as we have seen, many of her contemporaries reserved "new-style" nursing for morally pure women, Gaskell believed that nursing, more than any other occupation, both symbolized and offered the opportunity for the fallen woman to imitate Mary Magdalen's contrition. In her short story "Lizzie Leigh," written three years before *Ruth,* Gaskell has the erring Lizzie—another unwed mother—live out her repentant life as the village nurse: "every sound of sorrow in the whole upland is heard there—every call of suffering or of sickness for help is listened to by a sad, gentle-looking woman . . . who comes out of her seclusion whenever there's a shadow in any household. Many hearts bless Lizzie Leigh, but she—she prays always and ever for forgiveness" (31). When the parish doctor Mr. Wynn asks Ruth to become a nurse after he sees her devoted nursing of an impoverished widow, Ruth responds with the belief that through this occupation "the errors of my youth may be washed away by my tears—it was so once when the gentle, blessed Christ was upon earth" (301).

NURSING, SEWING, AND SELF REFLECTIVITY

Yet accompanying these conventions of sewing as a deleterious occupation leading to damnation and nursing as redemptive labor, there exists a subtext of self-reflectivity in the making of the novel itself. Gaskell's focus on work in *Ruth* points to her own pleasures and anxieties concerning her work as a woman writer. Elaine Scarry has argued that "factory, field, forge, or mine—comes again and again to represent both the external space of diurnal making and the internal space at the hidden center of the artist's own dark act of making, [they are] visual explanations of the human powers responsible" for artistic creation (1983, 99). Thus along with Gaskell's condemnation of sewing as morally dangerous labor, she builds up an analogy between sewing, creativity, and the art of writing. Similarly, within the occupation of nursing, Gaskell also embeds statements about female creativity.[7] Scarry notes that in the Victorian novel "different forms of work [are] explicitly presented as competing models of the imagination" (1983, 100). What, then, are the two models of the imagination being offered by sewing and nursing respectively?[8]

It is not surprising to find intricate analogies between "tailoring" and "tales," for whether spinning thread, weaving, or fashioning cloth into clothes as in *Ruth*, "the making of textiles . . . is in all of its phases, one of the most elaborated of analogues" between physical and imaginative labor (Scarry 1983, 102). One has only to think of Penelope, Arachne, Philomela or the spinning, measuring, and cutting of the three Fates to recall the venerable analogy between textiles and imaginative labor, especially female creativity.[9] Gaskell, who began her writing career under the pseudonym "Cotton Mather Mills," seems consciously to use the parallels between writing and sewing, assembling a garment and assembling a plot, trimming a gown and embellishing a story, textiles and text, to embed in *Ruth* an account of her own work as a woman writer.[10]

The first moment of self-reflectivity encompassed by the act of sewing in *Ruth* exists on the level of the physical labor of writing where the representation of the writer's labor is embodied in the descriptions of Ruth and the other dressmakers at work. Generally, Gaskell portrays the labor of creation as tedious and taxing. The seamstresses sit up extremely late, their eyes and body aching from their tasks. Ruth wonders how she will "get through five years of these terrible nights! in that close room! and in that oppressive stillness!" (10). Indeed, like the scratching of a pen, the narrator notes that the "sound of the thread can be heard as it goes eternally backwards and forwards" (10).

Accompanying the physical hardships of sweated labor, Ruth also suffers from anxieties about her own skill and dexterity in creative labor, anxieties that are very well-founded. The narrator states that Ruth was "not inclined for, or capable of, much extra exertion; and it would have tasked all her powers to have pleased her superior" (10). When asked about a dress that she is working on, Ruth has to confess that "I was to have done it, but I made a mistake, and had to undo it. I am very sorry" (19). When she is invited to attend the ball to mend gowns, Ruth tries to decline the honor stating that "I was not one of the most diligent . . . I was very tired; and I could not help thinking; and when I think, I can't attend to my work" (11). When Ruth mends a dress at the ball, the owner of the dress declares that "I had no idea any one could have spent so much time over a little tear. No wonder Mrs Mason charges so much for dress-making, if her work-women are so slow" (16).

The apprehensions that Ruth feels about her artistic competence and the anguish she encounters in the act of creation correspond to Gaskell's own misgivings about *Ruth*. Aside from her worries over whether the fallen woman theme was too hazardous a topic for her middle-class readers, Gaskell also fretted that the novel as a whole was not well-written. While writing *Ruth,* Gaskell feared its publication, recording that she had lost her "own power of judging," and that she could not tell whether she had "done it well or ill." Immediately after its publication, Gaskell claimed that her mortification over having the book in print made her feel like "St. Sebastian tied to a tree to be shot at with arrows" (Gaskell 1985, viii). Comments like this made by Gaskell about *Ruth* have led to the recent belief that *Ruth* was considered both morally shocking and poorly written by Gaskell's original audience. In fact, praise for *Ruth* in the 1850s was the rule rather than the exception. According to reviewers of 1853, *Ruth* "rivalled some of the finest passages of Currer Bell" and was "one of the most charming novels since Mrs. Inchbald, Miss Austen, or Miss Edgeworth and is unsurpassed in loftiness, truth, beauty, and courage"(quoted in Easson 78). One reviewer declared that "if Wordsworth had written in prose he might have written this," while another found it "vastly superior to *Mary Barton* in emotional profundity," and a third deemed *Ruth's* deathbed scene "worthy of Shakespeare" (quoted in Easson 81). Well into the early twentieth century, many commentators thought *Ruth* to be Gaskell's most important novel and the inspiration for both George Eliot's *Adam Bede* and Thomas Hardy's *Tess of the D'Urbervilles*.

Ruth was Gaskell's second novel, yet her struggle with writing persisted throughout her career. Like George Eliot, finishing a novel left Gaskell exhausted, and she had to take many vacations in order to recover from the draining experience of creative labor. While working on *The Life of Charlotte Brontë*, for example, Gaskell writes of her "sick wearied feeling of being over-worked" (Gaskell 1967, 451). Likewise, as much as Ruth struggled to please Mrs. Mason, so did Gaskell battle with her editors, especially Dickens, who was often "puzzled by [Gaskell's] inability to work steadily at her task." Gaskell's difficulties with her writing point in part both to the pervasive self-doubt displayed by Victorian women writers (discussed at length by critics such as Elaine Showalter, Sandra Gilbert, and Susan Gubar) as well as the constant domestic interruptions she faced while trying to create.[11] Yet her creative travails also indicate Gaskell's uneasiness with her chosen medium, an uneasiness she expresses in part through the negative images of textile labor in *Ruth*. In her disapproving associations of fabrication with images of artifice, fashion, show, seductiveness, and prevarication, we can read Gaskell's profound ambivalence towards her role as a writer of fiction.

Perhaps above all, the velvet, silks, feathers, and "fly-away" veils stand in for the unreliability of language itself. For everywhere in *Ruth*, as in many of Gaskell works, words misfire. When accounting for Ruth's mother's failure to warn Ruth of the dangers of seduction, the narrator expresses doubt that "wise parents ever directly speak of what, in its depth and power, cannot be put into words" (43). When Ruth's old servant Thomas tries to warn Ruth of sexual danger, "the words fell on her ear but gave her no definite idea" (50). When the minister Benson first meets Ruth his "words do not touch her." When she tries to tell her son about her past she "could not find words fine enough, pure enough to convey the truth" (339). In another conversation with Ruth, Benson feels that "words seemed hard and inflexible, and refused to fit themselves to his ideas" (451). When Bradshaw learns of Ruth's death he "could not speak . . . for the sympathy which choked up his voice and filled his eyes with tears" (454).

This failure of words, accompanied by Bradshaw's repentant tears, points to the competing analogy for imaginative labor offered by sick-nursing in *Ruth*. The analogy between nursing and writing has not been articulated as clearly as that between sewing and writing, yet for the Victorians, as we have seen, nursing gained as much use as did textiles as an analogy for creative labor. Nursing represents a number of different aspects of creativity, but in *Ruth* nursing predominantly symbolizes morally pure labor and thus the spiritual and ethical aspects of fiction-writing. As such, the model of creativity embedded in nursing represents art as a spiritual service rather than a material craft, art as a serious social activity rather than a frivolous adornment or a pleasurable pastime. Unlike male uses of the nurse/seamstress coupling that allow the two elements of writing to coexist, as in *The Scarlet Letter* and the character of Jenny Wren in Dickens's *Our Mutual Friend*, Gaskell, like other Victorian women writers, seems compelled to have nursing obliterate sewing—to battle with sewing and conquer it.[12] Thus because Gaskell has nursing clearly triumph over sewing in the competition between the two models of creative labor in *Ruth*, she seems not surprisingly to be endorsing the notion that the ultimate goal of a novel is to serve humanity for spiritual reasons rather than to function as a pleasurable object of art: service wins out over craft.

Yet in *Ruth*, the moral purity of nursing gets undermined. To see the negative imagery surrounding nursing, we must return to the analogy between the labor of the Victorian nurse and Mary Magdalen's treatment of Christ that the novel sets up. This analogy is not immediately apparent since nursing is more an imitation of Christ's actions, that is, ministering to the outcast sick, than comparable to Magdalen's bathing of Christ's feet with her tears and hair.[13] What links Mary Magdalen's ministering to Christ with nursing for the Victorians are the images that both evoke work that is at once worship and punishment. The fundamental imagery of new-style nursing connects up with nursing as both an imitation of Mary Magdalen's service to Christ and the idea of the work itself as a form of prayer. The early-twentieth-century nursing historian Sarah Tooley, for example, aligns Victorian nursing with the legend of St. Paula, a fourth-century Roman widow who was "oft by them that were sick." St. Paula's nursing is very akin to Mary Magdalen's deeds. With the sick, she "rubbed their feet and boiled water to wash them," and her nursing is also a form of prayer: "it seemed to her that the less she did to the sick in service, so much the less service did she to God" (Tooley 3-4). When the anonymous author of the 1843 *Fraser's* article "Hospital Nurses As They Are And As They Ought To Be" argues for England's need to develop a nurses' training program, it is to "fit them for their work" by awakening them "to a sense of the dignity of their calling" (540). This training "must be done under the guidance of the religion which is to supply the motive" for their work. Like the "hospital chaplains," nurses must realize that they "have a religious work to do" (540). As the narrator-nurse in Tennyson's "In the Children's Hospital" declares: "O, how could I serve in the wards if the hope of the world were a lie? / How could I bear with the sights and the loathsome smells of disease / But that [Jesus] said, 'Ye do it to me, when ye do it to these'?" (Tennyson 1971, 448).

However, a fine line runs between nursing as prayer and nursing as punishment. Mary Magdalen's tending to Christ evokes an image of labor as worship that is also a form of chastisement. At the Pharisee's Mary is humbled, indeed, it can be argued that she grovels at Christ's feet. Likewise, Victorian nursing was seen as humbling, humiliating labor. Tooley writes of the transition between nursing as a strictly religious vocation and a vocation inspired by humanitarian sympathy. Here she claims that the nursing sister of old "nursed as a penance, in the same spirit that she mortified the flesh by doing other menial offices, or by self-inflicted torture" (15). Yet despite Tooley's assertion that St. Vincent de Paul "taught his sisters that nursing and the care of the poor . . . were a duty they owed to humanity" rather than a "self-inflicted torture," remnants of nursing as punishment remained.

In *Ruth*, two Eccleston citizens discuss Ruth's work at the fever hospital. One claims that "they say she has been a great sinner, and that this is her penance." The other villager disagrees, stating that "such a one as her has never been a great sinner; nor does she do her work as a penance, but for the love of God, and of the blessed Jesus" (429). In reading *Ruth*, however, her death from nursing Bellingham does seem like a harsh punishment, thereby undermining two of Gaskell's major premises in the novel: that a sexual misdeed in youth should not ruin one's entire life and that women should not bear the social stigma of sexual transgression while men are left unscathed. Many of *Ruth's* first readers, while basically sympathetic to the novel, felt that Gaskell indulged in an illogical and overly harsh castigation of Ruth in having her atone for her sins through her nursing martyrdom. Charlotte Brontë, for example, writes of *Ruth's* conclusion: "why should she die? why are we to shut up the book weeping?" (quoted in Gaskell 1985, xix). In 1853, an anonymous critic writes that *Ruth* is "the most gloomy picture of the great 'inquisition' of the moral and intellectual world that we have ever seen depicted by artist's hand," since unlike "our Saviour," the author does not allow her fallen woman to be absolved in life but, in a "ghastly conclusion," forces her to die (Easson 18).

Although Gaskell attempts to claim nursing as pure prayer with no hint of penance, the chastisement associated with nursing undermines her assertions of the nonpunitive role of nursing in *Ruth*. In "Hospital Nurses," for example, the author acknowledges "the natural shrinking" from nursing work (539). Of all early Christians, the Roman deaconesses, whom the writer characterizes as "the very ideal of nurses" were "foremost in endurance and in action" as they were not hindered by "the danger or the loathsomeness of [their] work." Drawing on Cardinal Newman's *Essay on Development,* the anonymous author claims that the labor of nursing is so "evil" that only "the fear of purgatorial punishment" could motivate nurses "to sustain the cares and toils of an occupation like this" (541). For the Victorians, the labor of nursing invoked powerful fears for a variety of reasons, most predominately including the forbidden nature of physical illness, the stigma attached to working with the human body, and the taboo status of the nineteenth-century hospital. These three elements worked to bring about the belief in the "evil," "loathsome," and "dangerous" nature of nursing.

In "Hospital Nurses," the author notes that before Christian enlightenment elevated the "dignity" of the sick, society's impulse had been to "keep [the sick] out of sight" (539). Yet despite the nineteenth century's aestheticizing of debility and death—in 1852, for example, Thoreau writes that: "death and disease are often beautiful, like . . . the hectic glow of consumption" (quoted in Sontag 20)—there was a continued belief in the odiousness of the sick. Susan Sontag, for example, claims that even today illness "is felt to be obscene—in the original meaning of that word: ill-omened, abominable, repugnant to the senses" and that "disease widely considered a synonym for death is experienced as something to hide" (8-9). Theologically, illness is often seen as both a sign of divine retribution and a mark of the devil. Practically, it is perilously contagious and sensually repugnant. Further, sickness results in idleness, a transgression against the Protestant work ethic itself. Sontag notes that in the nineteenth century, "the notion that the disease fits the patient's character, as the punishment fits the sinner, was replaced by the notion that it expresses character. It is a product of will" (23). Falling ill represents a failing of personal ambition and transforms the sufferer into both a social and familial burden, the invalid thereby entering a realm of what Foucault has termed "social uselessness" (1975, 74).

The punitive image of nursing is further evoked through the taint associated with working in the hospitals themselves. In *Ruth*, Ruth's most noble act is to volunteer to work as the matron at the fever hospital during a typhus epidemic. It is the hospital that becomes the sight of terror during the epidemic, even though Ruth's matronship in the fever ward leaves her unscathed and she catches her fever during the domiciliary nursing of Bellingham. The narrator specifies that the fever did not have one exact locale: "the plague" had "burst forth in many places at once—not merely among the loose-living and vicious, but among the decently poor—nay, even among the well-to-do and respectable" (424). Nonetheless, in *Ruth* the hospital becomes the site of the epidemic, a "lazar-house," a place of horror replete with "malignant cases," and "pestilent air" (425). The Victorian hospital derived its taint from the stigma associated with it not just as a place of contagion and death, but from the general dishonor connected with all places of confinement: hospitals, jails, and asylums. Foucault has argued that this taint most specifically originated in the taboo of idleness surrounding institutes of confinement (1965, 52-61). Thus what better locale for a moral apotheosis to occur? For Ruth's transgressive dalliance with Bellingham represents precisely a crisis of work and a falling into pleasurable idleness. Consequently, nursing helps her to achieve atonement for her fall from labor into lethargy.

In *Madness and Civilization*, Foucault delineates the "great confinement" that swept Catholic and Protestant Europe during the seventeenth century. From the creation of the Parisian *Hopîtal Général* in 1657, from the opening of the first houses of correction in Germany (1620) and in England, the age of reason confined "spendthrift fathers, prodigal sons, blasphemers . . . [and] libertines," assigning the same space to "the poor, to the unemployed, to prisoners, and to the insane" (1965, 42 and 62). What united this seemingly heterogeneous group of prisoners was an inability or an unwillingness to work, the great confinement finding its impetus in a new reaction to the economic problems created by unemployment and idleness. During this phase of incipient industrialization, labor was not yet perceived of as contributing to economic instabilities. On the contrary, labor was viewed as a "general solution, an infallible panacea, a remedy to all forms of poverty" (Foucault 1965, 54).

During the classical age, labor and poverty were located in simple opposition. Idleness replaced "the exclusion of leprosy" and the idle poor became the new moral lepers of the age of reason (Foucault 1965, 57). Hospitals, prisons and the workhouse became "fortresses of moral order" in which was taught "whatever was necessary to the peace of the State" (1965, 60). Thus the great institutions of confinement were figured as "haunted place[s]" in the "landscape of the moral universe": "these [were] places of doomed and despised idleness . . . space[s] invented by a society which had derived an ethical transcendence from the law of work. . . . The community of labor acquired an ethical power of segregation, which permitted it to eject, as into another world, all forms of social uselessness. [Houses of confinement became an] *other world,* encircled by the sacred power of labor" (1965, 56-57, Foucault's emphasis). During the seventeenth century, Foucault argues, institutes of confinement were not solely sanctuaries for those whom "age, infirmity, or sickness" kept from working. Rather, they were both "forced labor camps" as well as "moral institutions" responsible for punishing and correcting the sin of sloth (1965, 58).

Within 150 years an important shift occurred: the shared characteristic of idleness uniting criminals, debtors, the unemployed, and the insane would come to be lost. By the eve of the French Revolution, the great houses of confinement were seen to contain an "abusive amalgam of heterogeneous elements," and the monumental "crisis of confinement" would begin (Foucault, 1965, 57). Foucault explains this crisis in terms of a profound reorganization of both social temperament and economic relations during the eighteenth century. Poverty, which had been seen as a sign of depravity and a peril to the social body, was now seen as a concealed but indispensable national benefit—the nation's wealth depended on a low-consuming, under-paid, underemployed workforce. From this view, population evolved into a benefit rather than a threat to the strength of the nation, and confinement became a "gross error, and an economic mistake" (1965, 188). Yet the great houses of confinement were not merely definitive failures, on the contrary, their articulation reinforced a momentous ethical conception:

> Measured by their functional value alone, the creation of the houses of confinement can be regarded as a failure. Their disappearance throughout Europe, at the beginning of the nineteenth century, as receiving centers for the indigent and prisons of poverty, was to sanction their ultimate failure: a transitory and ineffectual remedy, a social precaution clumsily formulated by a nascent industrialization. And yet, in this very failure, the classical period conducted an irreducible experiment. What appears to us today as a clumsy dialectic of production and prices then possessed its real meaning as a certain ethical consciousness of labor. (1965, 188)

The institution of the hospital, then, has at its very core a concern with the sin of idleness and the ethics of work: "before having the medical meaning we . . . like to suppose it has, confinement was required by something quite different from any concern with curing the sick. What made it necessary was an imperative of labor" (1965, 48).

Yet the anonymous author of "Hospital Nurses" presents a reading quite different from Foucault's of the origins of the nine-teenth-century hospital. Here the hospitals were not built to punish and confine the nonworker, rather, hospitals "owe their origin to Christian[ity]" since that "pure faith" gave to "sickness and suffering a dignity which they had never possessed before" (539). Hospitals are not taboo spaces of confinement for the idle poor, instead, due to Christian charity, the sick poor are now "viewed with a kind of reverence." Nonetheless, this author cannot mask his or her revulsion towards the sick. As much as the "sufferers" are "revered," the writer also recognizes the "natural shrinking" that accompanies the work of hospital nursing (539). Far from successfully arguing that the "sick and suffering" possess "dignity," the anonymous author rather rein-scribes a general abhorrence for the sick poor.

Not only is the innate morality of nursing that Gaskell tries to assert in *Ruth* called into question through nursing's punitive associations, the role of creative labor it stands for—the realm of invisible work and service-versus-craft—also gets undermined by the opposition of nursing and sewing. Nursing is labor that leaves no mark, no artifact, thus it represents the sphere of "invisible work." Towards the end of *Ruth*, the narrator describes Ruth's nursing of an impoverished widow. Here Ruth sits "deep in study of the Bible, in which she had read aloud to the poor old woman, until the latter had fallen asleep" (388). Similarly, when Mary Garth nurses Peter Featherstone in *Middlemarch*, the narrator describes Mary's choosing to watch Peter's sickroom at night because she could "sit perfectly still . . . revolving . . . the scenes of the day, her lips often curling with amusement at the oddities to which her fancy added fresh drollery" (Eliot 1977, 217). These images of nursing as a representation of intellectual and creative meditation seem specifically to exist in opposition to creativity's association with handicraft. In *Middlemarch* the narrator states that "Mary was fond of her own thoughts and could amuse herself well sitting in twilight with her hands in her lap," while Ruth's nursing work is characterized by "her left hand truly" not knowing "what her right hand did" (429).

In contrast, sewing is very much presented as a craft in *Ruth*. Like painting and writing, sewing leaves a imprint on the world—there is a created object left that can well outlast the life of its creator. In the "Custom House" preface to *The Scarlet Letter,* Hester Prynne has been both village sick-nurse and seamstress, yet what is left of her is the scarlet "A" that "had been wrought, as was easy to perceive, with wonderful skill of needlework; and the stitch gives evidence of a now forgotten art" (Hawthorne 61). Indeed, it is this crafted artifact that triggers the narrative of Hester's story. In Rochester's attic, Jane Eyre finds antiquated chairs upon whose "cushioned tops were yet apparent traces of half-effaced embroideries, wrought by fingers that for two generations had been coffin-dust" (92). When Ruth sews in Mrs Mason's sweatshop, she chooses to sit near flowered panels, the remnants of the former grandeur of the house. These panels were painted "with the careless, triumphant hand of a master" and the narrator states that "surely Monnoyer, or whoever the dead and gone artist might be, would have been gratified to know the pleasure his handiwork, even in its wane, had power to give to the heavy heart of a young girl" (7). Towards the end of the novel, when Ruth reencounters her former lover, she runs to a local church for solace and finds comfort in the "intense expression of suffering" carved into the face of an ancient gargoyle. Here the narrator speculates "what a soul the unknown carver must have had! for creator and handicraftsman must have been one; Whatever it was—however it came there—imaginer, carver, sufferer, all were long passed away. Human art was ended— human life done—human suffering over; but [the gargoyle] remained; it stilled Ruth's beating heart to look on it" (283).

Gaskell's assertion in this quotation is that art should transcend historical specificity and that what ultimately matters is the skill of the craftsman and the survival of the artifact. The invisible work of creation embodied by the nurse, that is, the gathering of thoughts and the preparation for creation, are all well and good, but in an aesthetic creed akin to that expressed in Keats's famous "Ode on a Grecian Urn," Gaskell privileges the surviving object itself, asserting that the crafted object provides crucial historical and spiritual inspiration for succeeding generations. Thus along with the negative images of crafting in *Ruth* is the pleasure in writing and the pride in craft. For example, when Mrs. Mason's apprentices rest during their labors, the narrator recounts how "some held up admiringly the beautiful ball-dress in progress, while others examined the effect, backing from the object to be criticized in the true artistic manner" (4).

Finally, in terms of the ethics of *Ruth* itself, Gaskell seems to posit that it is your mark in the world that ultimately counts. Like Hardy and Hawthorne, Gaskell was very concerned with the issue of disavowal—you leave your mark on the world, the world leaves its mark on you and you cannot disavow your actions. The "scar" that Ruth bears for her sin of sexual transgression, her illegitimate child, becomes the means through which she achieves moral redemption (Hawthorne makes a similar point in his depiction of Hester and Pearl). This "scar" is precisely why society judges women more harshly than men when it comes to sexual misdeeds, and the inequity of uneven blame is an important part of Gaskell's argument in *Ruth*. However, because women bear the indelible "mark" of childbearing, this "scarring" can paradoxically lead to their redemption because they cannot easily disavow their actions. As Ruth says to Bellingham:

"'the time that has pressed down my life like brands of hot iron, and scarred me forever, has been nothing to you'" (302-3).

For Gaskell, as for George Eliot and Hardy, disowning one's past deeds considerably hampers the potential for personal and social redemption. Thus despite Gaskell's ostensible critique of materiality via her condemnation of sewing and her apparent valuing of invisible deeds via her depiction of nursing, *Ruth* actually affirms the material over the invisible. Gaskell builds an argument of redemptive versus damning labor, yet paradoxically, the damning occupation of seam-stress conveys life in the form of Ruth's illegitimate son, an emblem for Gaskell's own novel, while the saving occupation of nursing symbol-izes the annihilation of the material world. Similarly, within the formation of sewing-as-corrupting rests a tradition of positive images connected with sewing, especially as a metaphor for female art. Hence the simple opposition of sewing as a cliché for fallen, dangerous labor and nursing as a means of soul-making and salvation collapses. Gaskell's evocation of nursing as atonement cannot erase the images of nursing as social punishment and self-flagellation.

An important part of Ruth's atonement through nursing rests in the notion of nursing as a manifestation of female heroics. In the following two chapters, I explore in more depth this particular aspect of nursing, showing that the heroic nurse was created through a series of complex ideological formations within the discourse of the Victo-rian nurse, and that this heroism was ultimately always contentious and problematic.

"A Female Ulysses": Mary Seacole, Homeric Epic, and the Trope of Heroic Nursing (1854-1857)

MARY SEACOLE'S WONDERFUL ADVENTURES OF MRS. SEACOLE in Many Lands (1857) is a crucial and problematic text in the canon of both Caribbean autobiography and nineteenth-century black women writers. Unlike Mary Prince's seminal Afro-Caribbean autobiography The History of Mary Prince, A West Indian Slave (1831), Seacole's narrative refuses to critique the ravages of British colonialism. Sandra Pouchet Paquet has argued that Seacole's narrative "reflects an enthusiastic acceptance of colonialism in the aftermath of slavery. In her narrative, Seacole celebrates her subject status in an empire that had systematically exploited and abused her native land and the majority of its inhabitants since the British captured Jamaica in 1655" (651). However, Paquet argues, despite Seacole's explicit quest for English recognition and English approval, Seacole's "surrender" to the dominate culture is "not absolute": "Seacole's revolt against the marginalization imposed by race and gender qualifies her embrace of the civilizing values she professes to honor" (652). In this chapter I explore the ways Seacole creates oblique resistance to her otherwise evident acceptance of "English values at the margins of Empire" (Paquet 662). Through her rewriting of both Homeric epic and the popular hagiography of Florence Nightingale—icons of both British domesticity and imperialism—I argue that Seacole creates a heroic self that cannot be contained by the exigencies of her English audience.

SEACOLE AND THE CRIMEAN WAR

On July 5, 1856, a brief notice appeared in the London *Times*. Situated between two advertisements—one for the Unity Joint-Stock Mutual Banking Association and another for a new military adventure novel, *The Green Hand or, Adventures of a Naval Lieutenant*—the announcement read: "Mrs. Seacole, the celebrated proprietress of the provision store in the Crimea, intends setting up a similar establishment at Aldershott [sic]. Her fame in this particular department of business is as well known among all military men that success in her new speculation is almost certain" (*Times* (London), 5 July 1856, p. 10).[1] However, contrary to the *Times* optimistic predictions, Mary Seacole's provision store in Aldershot did not flourish. Rather, Seacole and her business partner Thomas Day appeared before the London Bankruptcy Court on November 6th of that year.[2] Although the *Times* had overestimated Seacole's financial serendipity, they were not exaggerating her renown. If anything, the *Times* depreciated Seacole's fame by limiting it to "all military men"—for by 1855 Seacole emerged, along with William Howard Russell, Alexis Soyer, and Florence Nightingale, as one of the most celebrated heroes of England's disastrous Crimean War.

Each one of these public figures makes an unexpected war hero, but then the Crimean War was an unusual war. A failure for the government despite Britain and her allies's ultimate victory over Russia, Britain entered the Crimean War with expectations of a swift conquest that would reassert to the world her incontrovertible supremacy.[3] Instead, due to the ineptitude of her aged aristocratic military leaders, astounding bureaucratic mismanagement in London, and the subsequent starvation, mistreatment, and deprivations suffered by the largely working-class soldiers, the war reflected the immense social problems brought about by the Industrial Revolution and Britain's colonial enterprises. Out of 20,000 dead British soldiers, only 3,000 died as a direct result of battle wounds: the remaining 17,000 perished from starvation, exposure, and disease, particularly cholera and yellow fever.[4] The scandalous abuse of the British troops served to trigger a serious crisis in government and a loss of the general public's faith in Britain's military and political leadership.[5] As prominent heroes of the Crimean War, and in contrast to the martial exploits upon which the fame of more traditional military heroes rests,

Russell, Soyer, Nightingale, and Seacole were seen to share attributes of self-sacrifice, compassion, and philanthropy, and as a group they projected a sense of their working towards the exposure and correction of corruption and incompetence in England's government. They were, in other words, heroes of reform.

Russell, the war correspondent for the London *Times*, decried the calamities of the front. Serious errors such as furnishing the soldiers with green coffee beans and other inedible supplies and failing to provide basic health care or warm clothing so that many soldiers froze to death during the first harsh Crimean winter were duly chronicled by Russell and dispatched back to an indignant English readership.[6] Soyer, the world-renowned French chef who had already achieved fame with the soup kitchens that he opened and supervised in Dublin during the Irish Famine (1845-49), traveled to the Crimean Peninsula in order to establish similar kitchens for the British troops stationed at the front.[7] Florence Nightingale, by far the most prominent of the Crimean heroes, gained global fame for what was seen as her Christ-like ministrations to the working-class soldiers at Britain's military hospital in Scutari. Nightingale's role of national and international secular saint generated a hagiographical rhetoric that often obscured her real aims and accomplishments, aims that were firmly aligned with pragmatic, Benthamic programs of public health and institutional reforms, and the administration of the general health of the British army. Like Nightingale, Seacole's fame derived from her compassionate treatment of infirm British soldiers. The ongoing comparison between Seacole and Nightingale was immediate and long-lasting. For example, a letter to the *Times* signed by "Da Meritis" queries whether the "humbler actions of Mrs Seacole [are] to be entirely forgotten" while the "benevolent deeds of Florence Nightingale are being handed down to posterity with blessings and imperishable renown" (*Times* (London), 24 November 1856, p. 24).[8]

Mary Jane Grant Seacole was born in 1805 in Kingston, Jamaica. Her mother was a free black Jamaican and her father was a Scotsman and an officer in the British Army. From her mother, Seacole learned the art of both medicine and hotel management and, widowed at a young age, she used these skills to ensure her economic survival. At the time of the outbreak of the Crimean War, Seacole had recently finished nursing British soldiers and Jamaican citizens through a yellow fever epidemic in Kingston. In September of 1854, she sailed to England in order to volunteer to work with Nightingale nursing the wounded in Scutari. However, due to her race, Seacole's application was rejected despite her considerable qualifications. Seacole recounts going to Sydney Herbert's house in London to apply for a position as one of Nightingale's nurses: "many a long hour did I wait in his great hall, while scores passed in and out. . . . The flunkeys, noble creatures! marvelled exceedingly at the yellow woman whom no excuses could get rid of, nor impertinence dismay."[9] Upon finally securing an interview with "one of Miss Nightingale's companions," Seacole was informed that "the full complement of nurses had been secured . . . . and I read in her face the fact, that had there been a vacancy, I should not have been chosen to fill it." Upon meeting these rebuffs, Seacole wonders "was it possible that American prejudices against colour had some root here? Did these ladies shrink from accepting my aid because my blood flowed beneath a somewhat duskier skin than theirs?" (79).

Although she avoids a direct critique of English racism at this point, earlier, Seacole described the racism encountered during her first trip to London undertaken when she was a young woman: "some of the most vivid of my recollections are the efforts of the London street-boys to poke fun at my and my companion's complexion. I am only a little brown—a few shades duskier than the brunettes whom you all admire so much; but my companion was very dark, and a fair (if I can apply the term to her) subject for their rude wit . . . [thus] our progress through the London streets was sometimes a rather chequered one" (4).[10] Notwithstanding Seacole's disingenuous speculations about English color prejudice, she could not have been unaware, for example, of Britain's much debated "black wars," that is, its genocidal policies then in progress in Australia and especially Van Diemen's Land or Tasmania as it came to be known. Further, the publication of Seacole's *Wonderful Adventures* coincided with the events of the Indian Mutiny, an event that inflamed British racism. The historian Thomas Macaulay writes in his diary in June of 1857 that "the cruelties of the Sepoy natives have inflamed the Nation to a degree unprecedented within my memory. Peace Societies [and] Aborigines Protection Societies . . . are silent" (quoted in Semmel 1963, 21). Indeed, Bernard Semmel characterizes the progress of British racism as one that began with "a kindly view of the native races" that had "taken hold upon the British public early in the century." By 1857, the British inclined towards a distrust of different races, as any compassion was "whittled away by the apparently ceaseless wars which Britain was waging against coloured peoples, as part of their operations to safeguard what England already possessed and to extend commerce and the area of colonization" (Semmel 1963, 20).[11]

It was in this climate that Seacole sailed to the Crimean Peninsula and set up the British Hotel, a canteen, club, and grocery store (or "sutler shop") for soldiers and officers stationed at the front. At the time, sutlers had a deservedly poor reputation for overcharging their customers and thereby profiting from the agonies of war. Yet through her hospitality, and especially through her treatment of sick and wounded British soldiers, Seacole was seen to have "redeemed the name of sutler" as the journalist William Howard Russell characterized it in his preface to Seacole's memoirs (Seacole viii). Earlier, in his bulletins from the front, Russell had reported on the "hoards of sutlers" selling provisions in Gallipoli who did not bear "the highest character in the world" (W. H. Russell 45).[12] Both before and after her bankruptcy, many eyewitnesses attested to Seacole's skill and generosity on the battlefield, and her actions during the war prompted another newspaper correspondent to deem Seacole "both a Miss Nightingale and a Soyer" (*Morning Advertiser,* 19 July 1855).

When the war ended in March of 1856, Seacole was left with a large quantity of stock that was now useless and could be neither salvaged nor sold. Seacole records that at the end of the war: "we had lately made extensive additions to our store and out-houses—our shelves were filled with articles laid in at a great cost, and which were now unsalable, and which it would be equally impossible to carry home" (189). This overstock, along with her disastrous undertaking at Aldershot, led to her bankruptcy in November of 1856. Yet her plight did not go unnoticed by the English public. After a series of letters to the London *Times* and articles about her past deeds and her current dilemma in *Punch* magazine, a musical fund-raiser was planned in order to enrich the recently established "Seacole Fund."[13]

THE SEACOLE FUND

The Seacole Festival took place over four evenings at the Royal Surrey Gardens in late July of 1857.[14] On July 30, the *Times* reported that "on no previous occasion have the Royal Surrey Gardens been thronged by a greater multitude. The music-hall was literally crammed, many hundreds of persons being compelled to remain in the grounds, unable to penetrate into the interior of the building" (*Times* [London], 30 July 1857, p. 5). However, due to the September 1857 bankruptcy of the Surrey Gardens, Seacole received only a few hundred pounds from the proceeds of the concert and so continued to face financial difficulties.[15]

It was in the climate of these ongoing pecuniary mishaps that Seacole wrote and published her memoirs, *Wonderful Adventures of Mrs. Seacole in Many Lands*. While the originating momentum behind Seacole's narrative no doubt derived from her need to rescue herself from her monetary troubles, her autobiography is, of course, far more complex a work than simply a means of fund-raising. Despite her celebrity after the war, Seacole seems not to have sought fame, for aside from her memoirs and a few letters to the London *Times* and one to *Punch* during the height of the "Seacole Fund" affair, no extant writing appears to exist before or after 1856-57. Thus we can infer that Seacole did not place herself or her deeds before the public eye except during this year of financial upheaval: she seems to have been a seeker of fortune, but not necessarily of fame. Rather, her medical skills, her talent as a hostess, and her generosity during the war made her famous, perhaps despite her wishes. Yet, having once been propelled into public view, Seacole was not content to let others speak of her and for her without having her own say in the creation of her public persona. Indeed, she writes in her memoirs that "unless I am allowed to tell the story of my life in my own way, I cannot tell it at all" (147).

The media-created image of Seacole that appeared during her bankruptcy depicted her as someone who should receive equal measures of charity and esteem from the English public. When the London *Times* first announced Seacole's store in Aldershot, it described Seacole simply as the "celebrated proprietress of the provision store in the Crimean." Once the store failed, however, Seacole became an object of both pity and veneration in the London popular press. The letters in the *Times* from "Da Meritis," "A Friend to Merit," and William Howard Russell, extol Seacole's past deeds while characterizing her as currently decrepit and pathetic. These letters repeatedly describe Seacole as a "good old soul," an "old mother," an "old lady," a "good old lady," "poor Mrs Seacole," and "poor woman" (*Times* [London], 24 November 1856, p. 8 and 24 November 1856, p. 8). Russell's letter, for example, states his hope that the *Times* readership will "give enough to Mrs Seacole to set her up—late in life, poor soul, though it be" (*Times* [London], 11 April 1857, p. 8).

Punch was soon to follow the Time's lead, and in their poetry, articles, and comic dialogue published during 1857 and likewise aimed at eliciting donations for the Seacole Fund, Punch mixes great praise for Seacole's generosity, bravery, and skill with images of her as quite on her last legs. This is especially true in the long poem, a "Stir for Seacole," which was written in imitation of "Old King Cole," and hence repeated phrases such as "kindly old soul," "good old soul," and "jolly old soul" (Punch, 6 December 1856, p. 221). The article "The Mother of the Regiment" (Punch, 2 May 1857, p. 180) opens with the statement that "poor old Mrs Seacole is hard up," and in the comic dialogue between Mr. Punch and Lord Palmerston, "Poking Up the Sea-Cole Fire," Lord Palmerston states that he is very glad to hear of the success of the Surrey Gardens musical benefit because Seacole is a "most deserving old soul, and it will help to keep her deserving old body in comfort" (Punch, 5 September 1857, p. 102)[16]

This picture of a dottering and infirm Seacole contradicts not only her self-presentation in her autobiography but also Seacole's physical condition as far as it can be inferred. At the time of her bankruptcy, Seacole was only fifty-two years old and apparently in vigorous health. Indeed, she was to live for another twenty-four years, dying in London from a stroke in 1881. During this time, she not only recouped her losses from the Crimean and the failure at Aldershot, but left at her death an estate valued at £2,615, a sum equivalent to thousands of pounds in today's money. Seacole's subsequent accumulation of this respectable fortune underscores the fact that, above all, she was a businesswoman and an entrepreneur. Thus the public broadcasting of her bankruptcy in 1856-57 must have been a humiliating experience at some level. Seacole writes that "although I was not ashamed of poverty; beginning life again in the autumn—I mean the late summer of life—is hard up-hill work" (193).[17] Furthermore, although she considered herself to be a British citizen, Seacole did not forget the fact of her race and her colonial status.[18] As a black woman and a Jamaican, her self-presentation to a largely white British audience for the sake of raising money placed her in an obviously problematic position. Finally, the writing of her memoirs coincided with the Indian Uprising of 1857 (known to Victorian England as the "Indian Mutiny"), a momentous event that, among other things, revealed the depths of racial hatred in England, a hatred that Seacole alludes to encountering on several occasions.[19] In seizing the terms of her own story, Seacole's literary self-representation displays several strategies of transformation that serve not only to defend her from her necessarily complex relationship with her white British audience, but also to place her in an unusual position of authority. Through the adaptation of male military memoirs, the popular hagiography of Florence Nightingale, and perhaps above all, Homeric epic, Seacole forges a self-image of personal strength, while further making claims for the unique powers of Jamaican women of African descent.

"QUITE A FEMALE ULYSSES"

In describing her "inclination to rove" and her "will powerful enough to carry out my wishes" at the beginning of her narrative, Mary Seacole recounts that "some people, indeed, have called me quite a female Ulysses." In the jocular style that typifies her autobiography, Seacole dismisses this comparison: "I believe that they intended it as a compliment; but from my experience of the Greeks, I do not consider it a very flattering one" (2). Despite this disclaimer, however, Seacole's text does indeed evoke and retell Homeric epic. As we shall see, Seacole's affiliation with both Odysseus and Florence Nightingale helps to elucidate some of the most salient (and often problematic) aspects of her self-representation, especially with regards to her position as an independent Anglo-African woman, and her economic self-interest that is at odds with her claims of partaking in the self-sacrifice implicit in her role of army nurse.

Oblique or overt comparisons to Homeric epic are standard tropes in the adventure narrative genre, yet Seacole's *Wonderful Adventures* moves beyond generic convention to manifest correlations between Homeric epic and the Crimean War specifically. For the British, the Crimean War evoked both *The Iliad* and *The Odyssey* despite the fact that the English public ultimately viewed the war as an embarrassing and antiheroic conflict. That the *Iliad* and the *Odyssey* stood as fundamental texts of nineteenth-century British cultural identity set the stage for the easy association of the Trojan and Crimean wars.[20] For example, well before the Crimean War broke out, many ships in the British fleet had been christened with names from Greek mythology including the *Aeolus,* the *Agamemnon,* the *Cyclops,* the *Euryalus,* the *Gorgon,* the *Penelope,* and the *Polyphemus.*[21]

Furthermore, the British focus on Homeric epic was strongly exacerbated by the geographic situation of the Crimean Peninsula. Due to the peninsula's relative proximity to the Aegean Sea, many of the English who sailed through the Aegean on their way to the front were reminded of stories from Greek mythology. As his ship sailed past the Castles of the Dardanelles, for example, Russell meditated on the fact that "the mountains of the Morea, for the first time since they rose from the sea to watch the birth of Venus, echoed the strains of 'God Save the Queen,'" and that this was "the first time that the blast of English light infantry trumpets broke the silence of those antique shores" (W. H. Russell 27-28).[22] Additionally, the fact that the war's main objective was to capture and demolish Russia's great naval base at Sebastopol echoed the siege of Troy that had occurred at the west entrance of the Dardanelles. Hence references to Homeric epic and Greco-Roman literature were common in the memoirs of, and letters from, the Crimean War.[23] From this perspective, it is not surprising that Seacole should invite a comparison of her situation with Odysseus at the opening of her narrative, even if she quickly disavows this correlation.

One might wonder to what extent Seacole was familiar with Homeric epic and how deliberately she used the model of Odysseus to structure her story. At one point in her narrative, while describing the ease with which she found takers who wanted to purchase shares in her pigs' legs in Spring Hill, Seacole writes that "if the poor thing had possessed as many legs as my editor tells me somebody called the Hydra (with whom my readers are perhaps more familiar than I am) has heads, I should have found candidates for them" (119). Yet this is the only instance of Seacole claiming cultural naïvety. More typically, she alludes familiarly and unapologetically to literary works.[24] Further, she seems deliberately to enter into a mock-Odyssean mode when she recounts an "amicable arrangement" made with a ship's cook to "lash me on to a large hen-coop" when a fire breaks out in the hold on one of her voyages home from England to Jamaica (5).

While Seacole's comic tone and her emphasis on the legendary and the anecdotal places her war narrative firmly within a Homeric or Herodotean tradition, her specific situation invites further parallels between herself and Odysseus.[25] Like Odysseus when he washes ashore on Scheria, Seacole is alone and "naked" (that is, bankrupt) before her British readers, and like Odysseus, she possesses only the news she brings of foreign countries, offering exotic tales to her readers in exchange for provisions.[26] We learn that Seacole has a gift for wandering, and that she has mastered the secrets of travel. Paul Zweig characterizes Odysseus as one who like the shaman "crosses over into the mythic realm and returns with stories of his journeys— he is shipwrecked in a world of strangeness and magic. . . . The adventurer brings back news of the gods. The lands of myth, Hades, even death and Elysium have been within his reach. His story recreates this distant world, enlarging the boundary of what men know" (23). Like Odysseus, Seacole brings back news from what her British audience would have seen as the margins of the world, margins that seem to be either disintegrating (Jamaica or the Crimea) or inchoate (Panama), and whose chaos has been generated especially through the exigencies of British imperialism.

For Odysseus and for Seacole, their stories will become the source of their fortune. Aiolos keeps Odysseus "one full month to hear the tale of Troy," and "when in return" Odysseus "asked his leave to sail and asked provisioning," Aiolos "stinted nothing" (Homer 164). Yet the seeking of patronage does not address the question of *why* Seacole and Odysseus are wanderers. George Dimock notes that the name "Odysseus" derives from a verb that translates to mean a "general sort of hostility." Dimock interprets the name of Odysseus as "trouble": simultaneously making it for others and suffering it at the hands of others (quoted in Zweig 25). As a persecuted figure both blessed and cursed by the gods, we can see how Odysseus would offer a powerful analogy for the situation of nineteenth-century African-Americans. Indeed, in her novel *Beloved*, set in the mid-nineteenth century, Toni Morrison bespeaks this parallel in her reworking of Odysseus through the character of Paul D.[27] By comparing herself to Odysseus, Seacole's narrative becomes in a sense a rewriting of the *Odyssey*, thereby putting into play what Henry Louis Gates describes as the trope of the "talking book," that is, the way that nineteenth-century African-American writers make the "white (written) text 'speak' with a (black) voice" (55).[28]

Yet unlike many nineteenth-century African-American autobiographers, Seacole does not seem directly to address the pain and chaos of black colonial experience. In his introduction to the Schomburg Library edition of *Wonderful Adventures*, William Andrews argues that Seacole appeared to be "well protected from the tentacles of slavery," and that to obtain an "intimate view" of West Indian slavery, one would do better to read Mary Prince's *History* (1831). Seacole shares with many nineteenth-century African-American writers a propensity to leave painful scenes unwritten. Bernard Bell has attributed the silences in the slave narratives to the writer's relationship with both the "white audiences and . . . self-masking from a painful past" (8). In *Beloved*, the narrator describes Ella, a worker on the underground railroad, as one who "listen[s] for the holes—the things the fugitives did not say," and Seacole's narrative exhibits a similar penchant for narrative gaps (Morrison 187). For example, as readers, we know only that her mother was a free black and her father a Scotsman, her family history remaining otherwise undelineated. Tellingly, at the end of her description of a cholera epidemic in Cruces, Panama (then New Grenada), Seacole writes that: "life went on as briskly and selfishly as ever with the Cruces survivors, and *the terrible past was conveniently forgotten*. Perhaps it is so everywhere; but the haste with which the Cruces people buried their memory seemed indecent" (35, my emphasis). If Seacole censors her past in her narrative, it does not necessarily indicate that she has forgotten that past. In describing the Kingston cholera epidemic, Seacole writes that "I do not willingly care to dwell upon scenes of suffering and death, but it is with such scenes that my life's experience had made me most familiar" (60).[29]

That Seacole is "most familiar" with "scenes of suffering and death" is not surprising considering the continued discrimination against people of African descent in post-manumission Jamaica. This, coupled with the moribund state of Jamaican economy in the nineteenth century, an economy characterized as being plagued by "debt, disease and death," amplified the agonies of black colonial experience. Although England abolished slavery in Jamaica in 1834-38, the structures of a slave society remained—especially in the continued exploitation of Jamaicans of African heritage by a white racist minority. Notwithstanding the probability of Seacole being removed at least one generation from slavery, the racism she would have encountered in Jamaica would nonetheless have been extreme. For example, ten years before slavery ended in Jamaica, the Lewis Lescene and John Escoffery case, which was debated in England's Parliament on June 16, 1825, became a cause célèbre that exposed the mistreatment by whites of the free blacks of Jamaica. During this trial, Stephen Lushington argued before Parliament that the whites of Jamaica could not be "speedily brought to view the importance of the people of mixed blood" in Jamaican society because "the prejudices which had for so many generations led them to consider the blacks as an inferior race, naturally extended to all who had a mixture of African blood in their veins" (quoted in Hurwitz 108).[30]

Like other nineteenth-century African-American writers, Seacole displays what Bell characterizes as the "complex double vision of Americans of African descent whose humanity and culture had been historically devalued and marginalized by people of European descent" (7). A part of this struggle involves creating a subjectivity in a dominant culture that seems to say, as Franz Fanon describes it, "turn white or disappear" (100). From this perspective, we can see how the figure of Odysseus would offer one of the most salient examples of the heroic struggle for recognition and selfhood in the face of a threatened obliteration or denial of subjectivity. Zweig, for example, notes that Odysseus spends his life avoiding engulfment, whether by the sea, by the narcotic lotus flower, by Charybdis, by the Cyclops, or by Calypso's grotto. Odysseus must "struggle from trouble to trouble, adventure to adventure, for that is the only defense he knows against the oblivion of No Name" (31).

For Seacole, this "engulfment" or oblivion bespeaks her experience both in the face of the alienating diaspora of post-manumission Jamaica and in her encounters with American and European racism that cast doubt upon the humanity of anyone with African blood. Gates has argued for the crucial role the production of literature had for African-Americans during the eighteenth and nineteenth centuries:

> what seems clear on reading eighteenth-century texts created by
> black writers in English or the critical texts that responded to these
> black writings is that the production of "literature" was taken to be

the central arena in which persons of African descent could, or could not, establish and redefine their status within the human community. Black people . . . had to represent themselves as "speaking subjects" before they could even begin to destroy their status as "objects," as commodities, within Western culture. In addition to all the myriad reasons for which human beings write books, this particular reason seems to have been paramount for the black slave. At least since 1600, Europeans had wondered aloud whether or not the African "species of men," as they most commonly put it, *could* ever create formal literature, could ever master "the arts and sciences." If they could, then, the argument ran, the African variety of humanity and the European variety were fundamentally related. If not, then it seemed clear that the African was destined by nature to be a slave.(53)

In his *Autobiography of a Fugitive Negro* (1856) published a year earlier than Seacole's *Adventures,* Samuel Ringgold Ward addresses the issue of the continued doubts expressed by many American and European whites over the status of black humanity: "it is perhaps admissible to step aside to profane history for a few passages of testimony concerning the ancient Negro . . . Carthage was not the meanest of countries, though Hannibal, like his subjects, was black."[31] Ward refers to a white America that is "exceedingly unwilling to believe that anything good or great ever emanated from one wearing a black skin," and he urges his readers to "trace this very civilization, of which we are so proud, to its origin, and where do you find it? We received it from our European ancestry; they from the Greeks and the Romans; those from the Jews; but whence did the Jews receive it? From Egypt and Ethiopia—in one word from Africa!"(274-75). Ward points out that due to the "superior learning of ancient Africans . . . those stirring spirits, Homer, Pythagoras, and others, travelled among those Africans, as did the sons of the wealthy Greeks and Romans, to acquire the completion of their education, and to give the finishing touch to their verses, just as our sons and poets now travel in Germany and Italy for a like purpose . . ." (275). Thus Seacole's allusion to Ulysses, however brief, is potentially weighted with the sense that Ward conveys of needing to establish the historical links between ancient and modern civilizations in order to establish Anglo-African identity, and the possible centrality of Homeric epic within the establishment of those links.

We could interpret Seacole's self-presentation as Ulysses as partaking of the classic paradigm of bourgeois individualism, especially in her embodiment of the opposition, as Max Horkheimer and Theodor Adorno characterize it, of the "surviving individual" pitted against a "multifarious fate" that threatens to swallow her.[32] Indeed, in describing her recently widowed condition at the beginning of her memoirs, Seacole asserts that "I was left alone to battle with the world as best I might. The struggles which it cost me to succeed in life were sometimes very trying . . . but I have always turned a bold front to fortune" (6). Seacole further posits herself as a universal example of *homo economis* when she declares that "my fortunes underwent the variations which befall all. Sometimes I was rich one day, and poor the next" (7). Yet Seacole's paradigm of individual survival in the face of shifting fortune takes on a historical specificity that bespeaks not simply a universally shared experience of bourgeois individualism, but further the distinctive disintegration, fragmentation, and confusion of colonial experience itself.

At times, Seacole's representation of colonialism suggests a celebration of its modernity, an intimation that colonial expansion symbolizes the progress of civilization itself. For example, in describing the newly developed trade routes through the isthmus of Panama, Seacole avows that "it was reserved for the men of our age to accomplish what so many had died in attempting, and iron and steam, twin giants, subdued to man's will, have put a girdle over rocks and rivers, so that travellers can glide as smoothly . . . over the once terrible Isthmus of Darien, as they can from London to Brighton" (10).[33] Yet Seacole does not unequivocally celebrate the modernity and "progress" that the newly plotted trade routes embody. Rather, the images of chaos and disorder contained within Seacole's text invoke a specific critique of expanding world markets at the same time that Seacole seems to commemorate them.

This critique is often aimed xenophobically at the residents and refugees of the newly created marketplaces: "not yet, however, does civilization rule at Panama. The weak sway of the New Grenada Republic, despised by lawless men, and respected by none, is powerless to control the refuse of every nation which meet together upon its soil" (10).[34] However, Seacole simultaneously recognizes the human cost of colonial expansion. Seacole's narrative is filled with displaced wanderers, refugees from the exigencies of war, famine, slavery, and plague. For example, in describing the construction of the Panamanian railroad, Seacole recounts that "beneath leaky tents, damp huts, and even under broken railway waggons, I saw men dying from sheer exhaustion. . . . Every mile of that fatal railway cost the world thousands of lives. I was assured that its site was marked thickly by graves, and that so great was the mortality among the labourers that three times the survivors struck in a body, and their places had to be supplied by fresh victims from America . . ." (11-12).

Seacole survives this colonial chaos thanks to what she characterizes as fortune or fate. But her dependence on fate raises the issue of the double valence of the word "fortune" not only in its meaning of luck, chance, or *fortuna,* but also in its economic register: fortune as a species of mercenary exploitation or plunder. In his reading of the *Odyssey,* Zweig notes that Odysseus is "no less a brutal pirate at the end of the poem than at the beginning," and he claims that for Nietzsche, the "essential accomplishment" of the Homeric poems was to express "energies of hatred and cruelty, while creating an integral human form which transmutes their nihilistic power" (208). Odysseus's often overlooked manifestation as a brutal pirate echoes the themes of domination and exploitation that permeate Seacole's narrative and remain its most disturbing elements: her bellicosity and jingoism, her racism (expressed especially against the "lazy" indigenous Panamanians and the Turkish and Greek troops and civilians in the Crimean Peninsula), her unabashed entrepreneurial spirit, her pillaging after the fall of Sebastapol, and her violence towards her own servants.[35] Like Odysseus, an integral part of Seacole's survival leads her into realms of doubtful ethics, and it is this ethical instability that creates Seacole's need to reconcile her economic with her heroic self: that is, her need to "redeem the name of sutler" as Russell characterizes it in his preface to her memoirs.

This redemption occurs above all through Seacole's role as a sick-nurse, and it is nursing alone that bolsters Seacole's declaration of purification from the economic taint inherent in her role as entrepreneur and "brutal pirate": "my one and only claim to interest the public, viz., my services [as nurse and doctor] to the brave British army in the Crimea" (124). Yet Seacole's are not the ordinary avowals of cleansing based on domestic ideology—avowals used to fix Nightingale's position as the ultimate figure of purification for the Crimean War. Because Seacole is a product of colonialism, because she has lived through slavery, plague, and the exploitations of colonial life in Jamaica, Panama, Haiti, and Cuba as well as the Crimea, she can lay claim to being uniquely positioned to understand the horrors of colonialism, and therefore uniquely gifted at healing these very horrors. For example, in a letter that Seacole quotes in her narrative, John Hall, Inspector-General of the Hospitals during the war, writes that Seacole was "enabled to administer appropriate remedies" for the Railway Labourers' Army Works Corps and Land Transport Corps "during the winters of 1854 and 1855" due to the "knowledge she had acquired in the West Indies" (129).

In quoting John Hall in her narrative, one wonders to what extent Seacole was familiar with the intense conflict and rivalry between Hall and Nightingale that was a shaping force in the nursing policies creating during the Crimean War. Sue M. Goldie recounts the "bitter personal confrontation[s]" between Hall and Nightingale. When Nightingale fell ill during the war, Hall "hoped that she might be forced by ill health to retire. When it was apparent that she was not to be so easily got rid of, he set about making her position in the Crimea untenable" (6).[36] Although Seacole pays due reverence to Nightingale in her narrative, she nonetheless positions herself as an alternative nursing heroine: "I shall make no excuse to my readers for giving them a pretty full history of my struggles to become a Crimean *heroine!*" (Seacole's emphasis, 76).[37] Seacole bases her medical authority not only on the British domestic ideology that informed the avowal of woman's "sacred office of healer" as Charles Kingsley writes, but also upon her unique training in "masculine" European medical techniques such as surgery, pharmacology, and autopsy—training she received during her years working with the British Army surgeons stationed at the Up-Park and Newcastle army camps in Jamaica.[38]

Above all, however, Seacole indirectly affirms her superior potency to both the female healing powers exemplified by Nightingale and the male medical skills of the military doctors due to her knowledge of Afro-Caribbean medicine learned from her mother and grandmother, for Seacole implies that Afro-Caribbean medicinal arts were especially suited to treating the "tropical" diseases that were at once the foe of the British army and the scourge of all of Europe, which felt the threat of a second "great plague" (especially vis-à-vis cholera) as trade routes with Asia, Africa, and India continued to expand. Thus the recurrent motif of Seacole restoring order in the midst of chaos is informed in part by the unique amalgamation of her European and Afro-Caribbean medical talents. Seacole devotes much of her narrative to recounting these singular medical abilities. In just one example, during the cholera epidemic in Cruces, Seacole puts her "medical skill and knowledge . . . to the test." While everyone around her panics, Seacole diagnoses "the terrible truth" of the cholera epidemic with "a single glance" (24). All come to her "eager for advice," and there is no other medical authority except a "little timid dentist who was there by accident and refused to prescribe for the sufferer[s]" (25) and a Spanish doctor who "was not familiar with the terrible disease he was called upon to do battle with, and preferred trusting to one who was [that is, to Seacole]" (27). While Seacole hopes that the "kind reader" will not think that "in narrating these incidents, I am exalting my poor part in them unduly" (25), or that "the account of what Providence has given me strength to do on larger fields of action be considered vain or egotistical" (26), she nonetheless presents herself as the sole hero of the Cruces cholera epidemic.

Seacole's frequent claim at the end of these stories of general crisis is that "at last I restored some order" (29) both in Panama and in the Crimean war zone: "mismanagement and privation there might have been, but my business was to make things right in my sphere, and whatever confusion and disorder existed elsewhere, comfort and order were always to be found at Spring Hill" (113). In her eagerness to manage and control the disorder and suffering incurred by colonialism, Seacole seems, like Nightingale, to be an apologist for the status quo. She does not appear to want to halt British imperial expansion and exploitation, but rather improve conditions and keep the colonial project on course. Indeed, in her narrative Seacole writes that she is ready to "take any journey to any place where a stout heart and two experienced hands may be of use," a journey earlier reported by *Punch* to have the British army camps in China or India as its destination (198).[39]

Yet there is a way in which the recurrent apocalyptic images contained in Seacole's narrative undermine her pro-imperialist stance: her fascination with fire and flood indicates an underlying impulse not to redeem Britain's colonialist project, but rather to destroy it. In discussing the aftermath of the yellow fever epidemic in Jamaica, Seacole asserts that "indeed, the mother country pays a dear price for the possession of her colonies" (60). Seacole has delineated this "price" in numerous places in her text: her discussion of U.S. slavery, her continuous expression of fears of privation, and the images of disease, mortality, and human misery work to bring home the magnitude of global suffering that accompanies imperialism—whether British, Russian, or American. In one telling example, Seacole is walking on the "wretched streets of Navy Bay [Panama]" when she notices "3 long boxes, loosely covered with the *debris* of a fallen house." She asks her companion to explain these boxes and he replies "oh, they're only 3 Irish men killed in a row a week ago, whom its nobody's business to bury" (63-64). The "fallen house" evokes Ireland, devastated only a few years earlier by the Great Famine, and the unburied Irishmen, no doubt refugees from that very famine, are its "debris." Yet the "house" of Ireland is ultimately the responsibility of the "mother country"— the famine being yet another "great price the mother country pays for its colonies." Due to its rigid adherence to laissez-faire economics, England, as the world knew, refused for several crucial years to offer any relief during the famine, and what relief it did proffer came late and was inadequate. Thus England's irresponsibility is underscored by the laconic summation that "its nobody's business to bury" the dead Irishmen. Seacole inhabits a world where no one takes responsibility for the violence and the death colonialism brings about, neither in the Irish Famine, the Crimean War, nor the death of the navvies building the trade-routes of Empire.

Throughout her narrative, Seacole characteristically glosses over, represses, or denies the horrors of her world:

> if I were to speak of all the nameless horrors of that spring as plainly as I could, I should really disgust you (135); my memory prefers to dwell upon what was pleasing and amusing, although the time will never come when it will cease to retain most vividly the pathos and woe of those dreadful months (136); we seldom talk about its horrors; but remem[ber] its transient gleams of sunshine (136); I could give many other similar instances [of war horrors], but why should I sadden myself or my readers? [The real history of the

Crimean trenches] has never been written, and perhaps it is as well
that so harrowing a tale should be left in oblivion (153); I have
refrained from describing so many scenes of woe, that I am loath to
dwell much on these (176).

Despite Seacole's vigilant repression of the atrocities underlying
her text, an increasing tension builds within her narrative. Seacole
symbolizes this explosiveness when she describes her stay on the
British ammunition ship the *Medora*. Here she sleeps "over barrels of
gunpowder and tons of cartridges" with the "by no means impossible
contingency of their prematurely igniting, and giving us no time to
say our prayers before launching us into eternity" (102). Although
the ship's English captain orders all passengers to extinguish their
lights every evening at eight o'clock, Seacole "evade[s] the regula-
tion" by hiding her "lantern into a deep basin, behind some boxes"
(102). In this anecdote, Seacole not only exemplifies her own bravery
in the face of a profoundly unstable, potentially explosive world, she
also illustrates that while being forced to "hide her light in a barrel,"
she will defy British authority, a defiance that engenders possibly
spectacular, incendiary consequences.

Similarly, after Britain has made peace with Russia, Seacole is
forced to sell her stores to the Russians who will soon reclaim the
Crimean Peninsula. Seacole states that "it makes my heart sick to talk
of the really alarming sacrifices we made," feeling that the Russians
had come not to engage in fair trade but to plunder her supplies.
Seacole responds to this exploitation by passionately destroying her
valuable wine collection: "I could not stand this, and in a fit of
desperation, I snatched up a hammer and broke up case after case [of
wine], while the bystanders held out their hands and caught the ruby
stream. It may have been wrong, but I was too excited to think" (196).
Seacole's smashing of the wine caskets bespeaks both a re-creation of
the bloodletting that she has witnessed and a release of the violent
energies engendered during her horrific life experiences. Seacole
justifies this symbolic bloodletting with the claim that "there was no
more of my own people to give [the wine] to, and I would rather not
present it to our old foes" (196). As readers, we are meant to interpret
Seacole's reference to "my own people" as alluding to the British
soldiers and "our old foes" as referring to the Russians. Yet Seacole's

narrative raises the possibility that she regards her "own people" to be black Jamaicans, and the English as her "old foes," and that the sort of economic exploitation engaged in by the Russians at the end of the war mirrors the centuries of exploitation experienced by black Jamaicans at the hands of English colonists.

As simultaneous relief, reenactment, and purification, Seacole's apocalyptic imagery echoes Odysseus's "cleansing" of his home hall with fire and brimstone upon his return home: "So I went out, and found Odysseus erect, with dead men littering the floor. . . . Now the cold corpses are all gathered at the gate, and he has cleansed his hall with fire and brimstone, a great blaze" (Homer 430). Seacole, too, views fire as "the great purifier": "right glad was I one day when the great purifier, Fire, burnt down the worst of these places and ruined its owner" (162). Seacole's persona of "a female Ulysses," conveys the implication that there is disarray back in her homeland, and like Odysseus, she must return home to restore order and purify her homeland by purging it of its parasitic and exploitative suitors.

For Seacole there can be no easy return to Jamaica. For economic reasons, her longing for home cannot be fulfilled. At the end of the Crimean War, Seacole recounts her identification with an enlisted (very likely Irish) soldier: "with him I acknowledged to have more fellow-feeling than with the others, for he, as well as I, clearly had no home to go to. He was a soldier by choice and necessity, as well as by profession. He had no home, no loved friends; the peace would bring no particular pleasure to him. . . . Was it not so with me?" (192). This theme of exile is a common trope in Caribbean literature. Sandra Paquet notes it in *The History of Mary Prince* and twentieth-century texts such as Aimé Césaire's *Return to My Native Land,* George Lamming's *In the Castle of My Skin,* and V. S. Naipaul's *Finding the Center.* Exile is, of course, one of the fundamental issues at stake in *The Odyssey* as well, Horkheimer and Adorno registering the "unequivocal purposiveness of [Odysseus's] own self-preservation, and his return to his homeland and fixed estate" (47):

> The sweet days of his life time were running out in anguish over his exile. . . . When day came he sat on the rocky shore and broke his own heart groaning, with eyes wet scanning the bare horizon of the sea . . . each day I long for home, long for the sight of home. If any

god has marked me out again for shipwreck, my tough heart can undergo it. What hardship have I not long since endured at sea, in battle! Let the trial come. (Homer 85 and 87)

Yet as Zweig notes, *The Odyssey* differs from other quest stories because Odysseus will never reach his goal, his tribulation is perpetual in that he must leave Ithaka after a brief reunion with his wife and son and journey inland to appease the anger of the gods. Seacole, too, will continue to wander after the close of her narrative. She appears to have divided her time between Jamaica and London, and now lies buried in the Catholic section of London's Kensall Cemetery, in a state of permanent exile.

In the following chapter, I continue to explore the complications of nursing and female heroics. This chapter takes as its starting point the Victorian debate over defining a sphere of female heroics. While focusing on Florence Nightingale and George Eliot's implicit struggle for heroic eminence, I argue that the figure of the nurse played a crucial role within this struggle. In seemingly distinct ways, both Eliot and Nightingale appropriate the image of the nurse in order to structure a heroic self, and thereby a voice of social leadership: what I wish to explore in this chapter is the way these prominent social spokeswomen distinguished their partisanship at the contested site of the nurse. While Nightingale's employment of the nurse draws its power from an amalgamation of domestic and martial tropes, Eliot's use of the nurse seems born solely out of domestic melancholy— thereby suggesting a resignation to disillusionment encouraged by the realist ethic itself. However, by looking at those moments in her novels where the nurse embodies not sympathy and connection, but solipsism and aggression, I argue for a subtle convergence between the militancy of the Nightingale nurse and the humanitarian sympathy embodied in Eliot's nursing persona.

CHAPTER SIX

Nursing and Female Heroics: George Eliot and Florence Nightingale (1835-1873)

WHEN *MIDDLEMARCH* WAS PUBLISHED in 1873, praise for the novel was widespread.[1] One of the few dissenting voices belonged to Florence Nightingale, who criticized Middlemarch in an article on modern spirituality that she had written for Fraser's Magazine. Here she writes that George Eliot

> once put before the world (in a work of fiction too), certainly the most living, probably the most historically truthful, presentment of the great Idealist, Savonarola of Florence. This author now can find no better outlet for [Dorothea Brooke]—also an Idealist—*because* she cannot be a 'St. Teresa' or an 'Antigone,' than to marry an elderly sort of literary impostor, and, quick after him, his relation, a baby sort of itinerant Cluricaune (see *Irish Fairies*) or inferior Faun (see Hawthorne's matchless *Transformation*) (1873, 567).

Middlemarch marked an abrupt change in Nightingale's opinion of Eliot's work, since she had fervently admired all of Eliot's previous novels—most especially *Romola*.[2] *Middlemarch*, however, so disturbed her that Benjamin Jowett (the Oxford classicist and a friend to both women) finally requested that she cease complaining to him about Eliot: "will you not let poor Middlemarch alone. [Eliot] has gone wrong, not only in the literary way, but I have a respect & regard for her. And, moreover, she has more of the spirit which you want to introduce into literature than any one else in the present day. Let her be at peace: this is my request . . ." (Jowett 256).

In her *Fraser's* essay, Nightingale's objections to the novel stem primarily from Eliot's portrayal of Dorothea Brooke. In Nightingale's view, Eliot had an obligation to inspire her readers—especially impressionable, idealistic young women. Nightingale's opposition to Dorothea derives in part from the ongoing Victorian debate between aesthetic idealists who believed that art should show an ideal, inspiring world, and realists who felt that art must show the world as it is.[3] As a heroic woman manqué, Dorothea Brooke offered a strongly dispiriting image of female heroic potential: "it is past telling the mischief that is done in thus putting down youthful ideals. There are few indeed to end with— even without such a gratuitous impulse as this [that is, Eliot's portrait of Dorothea] to end them" (Nightingale 1873, 567).

Nightingale modestly suggests that Eliot had at least one good model for modern heroic womanhood in Octavia Hill, the nurse and social reformer: "Yet close at hand, in actual life, was a woman—an Idealist too—and if we mistake not, a connection of the author's, who has managed to make her ideal very real indeed. By taking charge of blocks of buildings in poorest London . . . she found work for those who could not find work for themselves. . . . Could not [Dorothea], the 'sweet sad enthusiast,' have been set to some such work as this?" (1873, 567).[4] In offering the example of Hill, Nightingale no doubt realized the forceful promise her own life presented to idealistic women who possessed "ardently willing souls."

At the time that Eliot was writing *Middlemarch*, many Victorians believed that a heroic female "sphere of action" had best been exemplified by Nightingale's nursing during the Crimean War and in her continued projects on public health and hospital and nursing reforms. Just as Eliot implies Dorothea's "saintly" potential, so was Nightingale seen as a living British saint. Indeed, nursing seems a conspicuous solution to the heroic crisis that faces Dorothea. Eliot obviously foregrounds health care and the medical profession in her tale of the reform years, and she could have turned from J. Rutherfurd Russell's *History and Heroes of the Art of Medicine* (one of the first books she read while beginning to write *Middlemarch*) to create an image of "Heroines in Medicine" via nursing.

In the course of their vocational frustrations, both Dorothea Brooke and Mary Garth end up occupying themselves with nursing. Yet despite the considerable amount of time they spend in the sickroom, neither they nor anyone else in the novel considers that they are engaged in potentially professional work, let alone work that could be seen as heroic. Far from presenting nursing as a profession or a calling, Eliot naturalizes nursing as something that all wives, mothers, and daughters do, thereby apparently reinforcing Borthrop Trumbull's belief that "a man whose life is of any value should think of his wife as a nurse" (1977, 217).[5] Nightingale's larger argument with Eliot possibly resides in the representation in *Middlemarch* of nursing as purely domestic and therefore nonprofessional labor, for Nightingale and many other mid-Victorian women regarded nursing as a means of breaking with the domestic realm and as a path to social power. F. B. Smith, for example, notes that "outside [of] conducting a London salon or presiding over charities, controlling a sisterhood was the one avenue to power open to ambitious single women of the upper classes" (1982, 19).[6]

Nightingale seemed personally offended by Eliot's portrayal of Dorothea, an offense that caused her to repudiate a writer whom she had previously championed.[7] Yet Eliot's point, the purport that Nightingale misses or misreads, is that her tale is set in the past.[8] In *Middlemarch*, Eliot explores the historical conditions of the past that make the present possible. Unlike Eliot's earlier heroines such as Dinah Morris, Agatha, or Romola, who are Methodist or Catholic, Dorothea is "helped by no coherent social faith and order which could perform the function of knowledge for the ardently willing soul" (3). The "coherent faith" inchoate in the 1830s but blossoming during the '40s, '50s, and '60s included the growth of positivism, and the burgeoning public-health and women's movements.

In *Middlemarch*, Eliot implies a Whiggish view of history with her assertion of the gradual amelioration of social ills, and the correspondent implication that idealistic women of the 1870s were emancipated from the handicaps of Dorothea's fate due paradoxically to the vocational martyrdom of women like Dorothea:

> Certainly those determining acts of [Dorothea's] life were not ideally beautiful. They were the mixed result of young and noble impulse *struggling amidst the imperfect social state.* . . . For there is no creature

whose inward being is so strong that it is not greatly determined by
what lies outside it. . . . [The] growing good of the world is partly
dependant on unhistoric acts, *and that things are not so ill with you
and me as they might have been* is half owing to the number who lived
faithful a hidden life and rest in unvisited tombs. (838, my emphasis)

Of course there is always the possibility that *Middlemarch's*
narrator is sarcastic when s(he) recounts the "dark ages" of the
1830s—especially in terms of women's art and fashion. For example,
when the narrator states that Dorothea should be excused from having
no interest in the "feminine fine arts" because they consisted merely of
"small tinkling and smearing at that dark period" an irony no doubt
exists in that Eliot would maintain that feminine fine arts of the 1870s
were not in a much advanced position (see, for example, her essay
"Silly Novels by Lady Novelists"). On the other hand, the narrative
clearly emphasizes the great upheavals of the early Industrial Revolution including the real advances in medicine and science, the building
of the railroads, and the ongoing political reformations.

While far from ideal, the position of women in 1870 was undoubt-
edly more open than that of the provincial gentlewoman in the 1820s
and 1830s. George Levine writes that "it would be a mistake to dismiss
as an irrelevant sentimentalism, the narrator's talk . . . of 'the growing
good of the world.' The wise (and almost cynical) narrator knows that
political reform . . . is deceptive; history does not follow the purposive
intellectual grooves of its most alert people, but changes develop
organically and biologically, through the incremental inheritance of
the qualities developed in the characters of such 'diffusively' good
people as Dorothea. . . . " (1980, 166). No doubt Eliot believed that
pioneering rebels like Nightingale paved the way for modern idealists
to act. Yet anticipating even Nightingale would be those "unhistoric"
women whose selfless dedication to others allowed world historical
figures such as Nightingale, Octavia Hill, and Eliot herself to appear.

Eliot's restriction of Dorothea's possibilities involves two significant
assumptions. First, Eliot asserts that modern heroism grows not out of
public but out of private acts. For Eliot, the domestic realm is where true
heroism, and concomitantly social change, derives. Secondly, Eliot
predicates her positive teleology of modern life on the growth of a
"coherent social faith and order" that existed by the 1870s and was in

infancy during the 1830s. Yet Eliot's representation of Dorothea's frustrated heroism offers a misleading view of the heroic possibilities available to women in the 1830s. Along with late- eighteenth- and early-nineteenth-century renowned women of other countries—George Sand, Germaine de Stael, and Marie de Sévigné were three greatly admired by George Eliot herself—there were many celebrated women in England during the 1830s and well before who could have served as inspirational models for Dorothea in her intellectual and spiritual quests.[9] Nonetheless, Eliot could not have told Nightingale's heroic story through the character of Dorothea Brooke, for Eliot's chosen genre, the realist novel, necessarily excludes the celebration of heroic idealism—even if this heroism is based on historical fact.

George Levine, for example, sees the prohibition of heroic idealism as one of the determining characteristics of the mid-Victorian realist novel, claiming that "disenchantment is the restraint of the ideal, the idea seen from the perspective of complicating experience" (1981 205).[10] Ironically, this "disenchantment" or failure of idealism was an aspect of heroism with which Nightingale was familiar, and her vendetta against Eliot over Dorothea surprises the reader when one realizes that Nightingale previously held a theory of heroism analogous to Eliot's. In a letter to her father written in 1846, Nightingale posits that "trials must be made, efforts ventured—some bodies must fall in the breach for others to step upon, failure is one of the most important elements of success—the failure of one [will] form a guide-post to others—till, at last, a dog comes who, having smelt all the other roads, & finding them scentless & unfeasible, follows the one which his Master has gone before" (1990, 30). This canine analogy's remarkable parallel to the role that Eliot gives Dorothea as a "fallen body" used to fill the "breaches" on the road towards female heroism points to the overdetermined nature of Nightingale's protests over *Middlemarch*: Why should Nightingale become vexed over Dorothea when she herself had imagined a similar mechanism governing the structure of female heroic possibility?

THE ARTIST VS. THE NURSE

Jowett writes to Nightingale in February of 1873: "I think that you are very intolerant & persecuting to George [Eliot]. She has painted—

what often takes place in real life—the failure of an ideal. Why should not this be described as well as any other chapter in the life of a family?" (237). Nightingale's dismay over Dorothea's fate points in part to a clash in defining the possibilities of female heroic capacity, a conflict that was further heightened by an implicit struggle over who would become the spokeswoman for that heroism. Along with Jowett's statement that Eliot "has more of the spirit which you want to introduce into literature than any one else in the present day" (256), he further declares to Nightingale that Eliot "is the only woman in this generation who can do much, besides yourself" (250).

Just as Nightingale may have viewed Eliot as a challenge to her authority, so Eliot would have been aware of Nightingale's bid for heroic preeminence, if only because of her immense popularity following the Crimean War. In a letter written in 1855 to the essayist and art historian Anna Jameson, Elizabeth Barrett Browning praises Nightingale, but expresses her frustration at the "general . . . approbation," of Nightingale's actions in Scutari, especially on the part of men:

> Every man is on his knees before ladies carrying lint, calling them "angelic she's," whereas, if they stir an inch as thinkers or artists from the beaten line (involving more good to general humanity than is involved in lint), the very same men would curse the impudence of the very same women. . . . I can't see on what ground you think you see [in nursing] the least gain to the "woman's question," so called. It's rather *the contrary*, to my mind. . . . I acknowledge to you that I do not consider the best use to which we can put a gifted and accomplished woman is to *make her a hospital nurse*. If it is, why then woe to us all who are artists! . . . For the future I hope you will know your place and keep clear of Raffaelle and criticism; and I shall expect to hear of you as an organiser of the gruel department in the hospital at Greenwich, that is, if you have the luck to *percer* and distinguish yourself. (Barrett Browning 2:189, original emphasis)[11]

In setting up a dichotomy between the nurse and the artist as alternative models of heroic womanhood, Barrett Browning overlooks the fact that the image of nursing was being appropriated by both social activists like Nightingale and artists such as Eliot in their contention for the position of Victorian female sage. Unlike Barrett

Browning, however, Eliot does not repudiate the figure of the heroic nurse. Rather, as we shall see, the nurse is as important an image for Eliot's consolidation of prophetic power as she was for Nightingale. Ultimately, the image of the nurse becomes a disputed site in the construction of Victorian female heroics. Nightingale, a social activist, literally became a nurse in order to escape from "the oppressive liberty of the gentlewoman's world." Eliot, while sharing Nightingale's goals of gaining a position of moral leadership, felt the inherent danger in direct action, and thus conversely used the figure of the nurse to create an image of a prophet whose wisdom lay in a realm removed from direct political action.

Competition for the role of social prophet was particularly fierce during the mid-nineteenth century, and, as Carol Christ points out, many male writers worked to circumscribe, or even exclude, female leadership from their utopic (or dystopic) social visions. Thus it is not surprising to find Victorian women writers establishing their own positions as sages. Not unexpectedly, fissures and antagonisms complicated the creation of a locus for female leadership, and as two of the strongest contenders for this role, both Eliot and Nightingale seemed tacitly aware of their potential rivalry. However, unlike Barrett Browning, Eliot never directly criticized Nightingale. Indeed, in 1852 she writes to Sara Hennell that "I had a note from Miss Florence Nightingale yesterday. I was much pleased with her. There is a loftiness of mind about her which is well expressed by her form and manners" (1954, 2:45).

Nonetheless, in 1859, at the commencement of her own eminence as a novelist, Eliot responds to a letter about Nightingale sent to her by Hennell:

Thank you for sending me that authentic word about Miss Nightingale. *I wonder if she would rather rest from her blessed labours, or live to go on working?* Sometimes, when I read of the death of some great sensitive human being, I have a triumph in the sense that they are at rest; and yet, along with that, such deep sadness at the thought that the rare nature is gone for ever into darkness, and we can never know that our love and reverence can reach him, that I seem to have gone through a personal sorrow when I shut the book and go to bed. (1954, 3:15, my emphasis)

Eliot, troubled by the consequences of direct action, urges Nightingale not only to rest but to death. Here Eliot moves quickly from the contemplation of Nightingale's "blessed labours" to a general statement about the death of "great sensitive human beings." By obliquely including Nightingale in this group of the inspirationally dead, Eliot seems to be stating a preference for being enkindled by Nightingale's death rather than by her living deeds. Yet included in this awe for the "rare natures" who have "gone for ever into darkness," is a feeling of "triumph" over the dead. Eliot imagines Nightingale as a dead hero who can at once remain forever unreachable ("we can never know that our love and reverence can reach him") and also safely shut up in a book ("I shut the book and go to bed").

Fourteen years earlier, Nightingale anticipates Eliot's urging her to give up her labors for "rest" when she writes to the Howe family that:

> one does not like the poets and the doctrines and remedies for uneasiness of the day. The spirit they breathe is sweet, but it is the spirit of the evening, of the long shadows on the grass, and of the repose which has been earned, and may be given way to. It is not the spirit of the morning . . . All that weight of bitterness, which must have accumulated in our Saviour's heart during those thirty private years, did not teach him resignation—he stood upon it, and it lifted him up, till he rose upon that last highest Cross, and so ascended, not into his rest, but into his victory . . . [W]hat is peace? according to all the definitions of all the poets—the essence, the ne plus ultra of peace, would be lying in bed. (1934, 334-35)

Eliot's "sweet-breathed" letter of 1859 does indeed seem to evoke the "spirit of the evening," and the tenets of "earned repose," and "lying in bed."

The distinction between Eliot's quietism and Nightingale's activism can further be seen in their respective rhetorical styles, for despite Barrett Browning's exclusion of Nightingale from the category of "artist and thinker," Nightingale was primarily a writer, her literal manifestation as a nurse spanning only a few years of her sixty-odd-year career. As George P. Landow has argued, Nightingale's chosen genre was "sage writing," a style best exemplified by Thomas Carlyle, a writer whose own interest in defining heroics is well recognized. Sage writing of the sort seen in Nightingale's essay *Cassandra* (1852) is characterized by an aggressiveness grounded in the writings of Jeremiah and Daniel. Landow claims that *"Cassandra* positions the sage's voice outside society and in opposition to the audience." Unlike the wisdom speaker or Augustan satirist, both of whom speak and write as if they "confidently embody their culture's accepted wisdom," the sage writer "stands apart from others" presenting a "far more aggressive attitude towards the audience and its beliefs" (32-3). In contrast to the sage writer, the "wisdom speaker" abstains from the truculence contained in the rhetoric of sage writers such as Nightingale, Carlyle, and Ruskin. In George Eliot's novels, we can detect the moderate voices of both the wisdom speaker and the Augustan satirist.[12] Nonetheless, as we shall see, there is an bellicose element in Eliot's writing, a contentiousness that works to link the moderation of her realism with the aggressive and utopic positivism exemplified by Nightingale.[13]

In the following pages, I explore the ways in which both Nightingale's and Eliot's youthful evangelical passions, passions that encouraged a sense of social responsibility and compelled both women to attempt to mitigate the distresses accompanying England's expanding industrialism, shifted by mid-century to a blend of secular humanism, domestic ideology, and the science of positivism, and that this blend of ideas, crucially emblematized by the figure of the nurse, played an important role in shaping both Eliot's and Nightingale's claims for positions of heroic leadership.[14]

MORNING AND EVENING SPIRITS

Born only six months apart, Nightingale and Eliot were swayed by similar imperatives in their teens and early twenties to act as social reformers. Both women underwent familial and spiritual crises during the turbulent and evangelically tinged 1840s, both hungered for intellectual, vocational, and spiritual recognition and evinced a keen interest in serving God, especially through the melioration of social ills. In 1841, for example, Eliot proclaimed to Maria Lewis that the "prevalence of misery and want in this boasted nation of prosperity and glory is appalling, and really seems to call us away from mental luxury. O to be doing some little toward the regeneration of this groaning travailing creation! I am supine and stupid, overfed with favours, while the haggard looks and piercing glance of want and conscious hopelessness are to be seen in the streets" (1954, 1:116).

Similarly, Nightingale displayed her awareness of the social imperative to alleviate human suffering, especially the sufferings of the poor. In a 1845 letter to the Samuel Gridley Howe family, she wrote:

> I saw a poor woman die before my eyes this summer, whom her well-intentioned nurses had poisoned, as certainly as if they had given her Prussic Acid. She died of ignorant nursing—and such things happen constantly—as well as all sorts (some, from pure ignorance) of misery and profligacy, which good healthful intimacies among the poor people, made by the better educated, under the shelter of a rhubarb powder or a dressed leg, might go far to avert. . . . It is so much easier and more *prevenant* to approach the poor people with medicine for their bodies, than in any other way . . . (1934, 334-35).

Nightingale's desire to "approach the poor" through medicine led to her frequent visits to the needy who lived near her family homes in Derbyshire and Hampshire and her customary caretaking of sick relatives and servants. By the late 1840s, she had begun her quest to receive medical training and in 1851 she stayed for three months at Pastor Fliedner's Institution of Deaconesses at Kaiserwerth. She supplemented this training in 1853 with several weeks in the Parisian Maison de la Providence run by the Sœurs de la Charité and in August of 1853, Nightingale gained her first professional position as "Superintendent of the Hospital for Invalid Gentlewomen" at Harley Street in London. Within eighteen months of her tenure at Harley Street, Sidney Herbert was to appoint Nightingale "Superintendent of the Female Nursing Establishment of the English General Hospitals in Turkey" during the Crimean War.

Nightingale's decision to dedicate her life to good works came early. In 1837, she had the first of four mystical experiences where she heard God call her to his service (see Nightingale 1990, 19). By 1844, she was contemplating a career in nursing and by 1847 she would write after spending over a month nursing sick villagers at Lea Hurst that "I found my business in this world. My heart was filled. My soul was at home. I wanted no other heaven" (quoted in Huxley 34). Nightingale believed that there were only three paths open to her in life—those being "a married woman, a literary woman, or a Hospital Sister." The third course was her "greatest wish" that, due to the objections of her family and her own depression ("I did not think it worth while to get up in the morning"), seemed "not to be the calling for *me*" (1990, 42, Nightingale's emphasis). The potential failure of her nursing ambitions led Nightingale into a severe depression that was lifted only by her mother's and sister's reluctant permission, after a six-year-long battle, to allow her to pursue her nursing career.[15]

In her youthful search to serve God, Eliot, too, visited the poor. In 1841, she writes of her expedition to the House of Industry, an almshouse at Bedworth, to tend to "poor Mrs. Kelley" whom she found "as comfortable as in her afflicted state she can be made" (1954, 1:77). During her first journey to London, in the summer of 1838, Eliot writes to Lewis that "I think Greenwich Hospital [the home for aged and disabled soldiers] interested me more than anything else" (1954, 1:6). Yet unlike Nightingale, who quite soon decided that her spiritual service rested in medical work, Eliot, although interested in the caretaking of the sick poor, felt that her altruistic path lay in hermeneutic inquiry and intellectual labor: "I do think that a sober and prayerful consideration of the mighty revolutions ere long to take place in our world would by God's blessing serve to make us less grovelling, more devoted and energetic in the service of God. Of course I mean only such study as pigmies like myself in intellect and acquirement are able to prosecute; the perusal and comparison of Scripture and the works of pious and judicious men on the subject" (1954, 1:12).

Although Nightingale shared Eliot's intellectualism, she ultimately emphasized deeds over words. In her early twenties, she wrote to Mary Clarke Mohl: "You ask me why I do not write something. I had so much rather live than write—writing is only a substitute for living . . . I think one's feelings waste themselves in words, they ought to be distilled into actions and into actions which bring results" (quoted in Huxley 26-27). Similarly, in 1846, Nightingale posited that "In this too highly educated, too little active age, the balance between Theory & Practice seems destroyed—the just connexion between Knowledge & Action lost sight of—the inspiration unacknowledged, which is to be sought in effort, even more than in thought, the actual addition to our store of *Knowledge*, which is supplied by every *deed*, & the positive subtraction from Thought, which a life of thinking suffers—not considered" (1990, 30). In *Cassandra*, Nightingale confirms her mistrust of writing when she maintains that being read aloud to is "the most miserable exercise of the human intellect. It is like lying on one's back, with one's hands tied, and having liquid poured down one's throat" (1979, 24).

Nonetheless, aside from her term as Superintendent at the Harley Street hospital and her labors in Scutari, Nightingale's life work was essentially discursive in nature. In their introduction to her selected letters, Martha Vicinus and Bea Nergaard note that Nightingale "left her papers, including around 10,000 letters, manuscripts of many of her major works, and drafts of others, to the discretion of her executor. The collection forms one of the largest manuscript collections at the British Library. An additional 3,000 to 4,000 letters are held in private hands and other libraries" (1). Further, in a private note written in 1851, Nightingale outlined her New Year's resolutions: "to offer a religion to the working Tailors," and "to translate the Prophets" (1990, 56). She accomplished the first goal with her *Suggestions for Thought to the Searchers after Truth Among the Artizans of England* (1859), an 829-page-treatise that proposed to intellectual artisans a rationale for religious belief.[16] Although she saw these literary projects as secondary activities undertaken to keep her "healthy" while she was waiting for her life's work to begin, after the Crimean War Nightingale spent the remainder of her days almost exclusively confined to her bed working on manuscripts and reports and maintaining her vast correspondences.

As with many positivist reformers, Nightingale's utopic social vision entailed a spirit of invasiveness that balanced on the point of the apocalyptic. In 1843, her sister Parthenope wrote that: "I believe [Florence] has little or none of what is called charity or philanthropy, she is ambitious—very, and would like well enough to regenerate the world with a grand *coup de main* . . . " (quoted in Nightingale 1990, 56). Indeed, Nightingale's public persona of heroic nurse is replete with martial and active qualities. She is a figure of the public realm, of the military, and of institutions. Yet Nightingale's martial interests were obscured in the creation of her hagiography, which is one of Lytton

Strachey's salient points in his reading of Nightingale in *Eminent Victorians*: "She was heroic. . . . Yet her heroism was not of the simple sort so dear to the readers of novels and the compilers of hagiographies—the romantic sentimental heroism with which mankind loves to invest its chosen darlings: it was made of sterner stuff. . . . It was not by gentle sweetness and womanly self-abnegation that she had brought order out of chaos in the Scutari Hospitals . . . it was by stern discipline, by rigid attention to detail, by ceaseless labour, by the fixed determination of an indomitable will" (155-6).

Nightingale would have been the first to agree with Strachey's assessment of her heroism, although she accepted the sentimental portrait of her work in Scutari because it granted her more leverage with the British public. While it is true that martial imagery played a significant part in the creation of the heroic Nightingale (as, for example, in the comparisons drawn in various popular narratives between Nightingale and Iphigenia, Joan of Arc, and Athena on the battlefield), it was the image of Nightingale as a "housewifely woman" (in the words of Harriet Martineau), which had the most lasting public impression. The comparisons of Nightingale to Christ, for example, emphasized the same sympathetic and feminized Christ extolled by proponents of domestic ideology.[17]

Throughout the nineteenth century, Nightingale's mythic persona continued to be seen primarily in terms of saintly maternalism. Although Nightingale never contradicted the romantic image of her work at Scutari, she did not personally embrace the sentimental model of domestic ideology prevalent among writers such as Sarah Stickney Ellis, Elizabeth Gaskell, George Eliot, Charles Dickens, and Charles Kingsley. Far from being an advocate of domestic reformation—that is, the belief that social reform should be based on the diffusion of maternal sympathy and that the model of middle-class domesticity should penetrate all realms of society—Nightingale consistently displayed a cynicism about domestic life. For example, in *Cassandra* Nightingale writes that:

> Mrs. A. has the imagination, the poetry of a Murillo, and has sufficient power of execution to show that she might have had a great deal more. Why is she not a Murillo? From a material difficulty, not a mental one. If she has a knife and fork in her hands for three hours

of the day, she cannot have a pencil or brush. . . . Women are never
supposed to have any occupation of sufficient importance *not* to be
interrupted, except "suckling their fools"; and women themselves
have accepted this, have written books to support it, and have trained
themselves so as to consider whatever they do as *not* of such value to
the world or to others. . . . *The family? It is too narrow a field for the
development of an immortal spirit, be that spirit male or female.* (1979,
43, my emphasis)

Indeed, Nightingale felt that the family was the site of moral and
physical suffocation, especially for women, and went so far as to
believe that all children should be removed from their families and
raised in "a well-managed crèche" (quoted in Gaskell 1967, 320).
Although Nightingale shared with adherents of domestic ideology
the belief in an innate superiority possessed by women, this
supremacy was not predicated on maternal and nurturing
"instincts." Rather, Nightingale's sense of female preeminence
stemmed from her tenet that women held a unique aptitude for
management and that the female eye was distinctively skilled at
noting the particularities of everyday life.[18]

Eliot, too, shared Nightingale's belief in the superiority of the
female gaze. Yet in contrast to Nightingale's aggressive message of
social reform, what comes through powerfully in Eliot's novels is the
need to retain social equilibrium, evoking change only through the
slow hand of time: "Eliot saw her own literary practice as a primary
mechanism for social reform. As such, it becomes an *alternative*, at
least for the foreseeable future, to political representation. The working class, faulty and degenerate as it is, should be represented, not in
Parliament, but in novels. Such novels would increase the classes'
understanding of each other, but concentrating as they must (in Eliot's
view) on the disabilities of the lower classes, they would also prevent
premature moves toward the direct political representation of those
classes" (Gallagher 1984, 224).

Although Eliot conceived of her literary practice as an important
method of social activism, this activism was rooted ironically in
quietism, and in this way seemed markedly distinct from Nightingale's
positivist agenda, grounded as it was in vigorous and immediate
reform.[19] Nevertheless, both Eliot and Nightingale appropriated the

figure of the nurse to serve as a crucial metaphor for their apparently disparate political positions. While it is clear that the image of the heroic nurse was decisive in shaping and consolidating Nightingale's social power, the place of the nurse was less manifest but nonetheless integral in the creation of Eliot's prophetic persona.

Sandra Gilbert and Susan Gubar notice the pattern of female aggression played out through female resignation that I am interested in here. While they locate a subtext of "authorial vengeance in the service of female submission" in certain of Eliot's nursing scenes, most particularly those of Janet Dempster's nursing of her husband and the Reverend Tryan, they ultimately conflate nursing with other images of female resignation or martyrdom in Eliot's novels (Gilbert and Gubar 484-93). Nor are they interested in the function of the trope of nursing as a metaphor for Eliot's work as a novelist. Conversely, in a recent study, Miriam Bailin pays sustained attention to the motif of nursing, illness, and the sickroom in Eliot's works, particularly "Janet's Repentance," *Romola*, and *Daniel Deronda* (Bailin does not discuss *Middlemarch*). However, Bailin's purpose and conclusions differ from my readings in a number of ways. First, Bailin's primary focus is on the issue of the crisis of subjectivity that she reads as being resolved for Eliot's characters within the "idyll" of the sickroom (120). Second, Bailin attributes Eliot's interest in the sickroom, and her belief in its restorative powers, to her nursing of her father on his deathbed (110-11). In my deliberation on the parallels between Nightingale's and Eliot's adolescent interests in helping the sick poor, I have suggested that the ideological power of the sickroom scene for Eliot derives from a wider range of social and political pressures than the strictly personal considerations of her relationship with her father. Third, Bailin accepts at face value the claims that Eliot's narrators make for the "quarantine" and "sequestration" of the sickroom, asserting that both the "'stir and glare of the world'" and the "self as conscious agent with all its capacities for miscarriage, are eliminated" in Eliot's sickroom scenes.[20] In antithesis, I will argue in the following pages that in fact Eliot's declarations of the simplicity and purity of human relations within the sickroom do not hold up under scrutiny, and that by extension her claims for the purity of the cultural realm as the realm of reconciliation and understanding likewise are troubled.

THE WORSHIP OF SORROW

During the year of 1848, Eliot nursed her father, Robert Evans, on his deathbed. She "made him as comfortable as possible, gave him the required medicines, read to him, played the piano for him, and did whatever gave him comfort or pleasure during the long, weary year. . . . She never left him." (Sprague 70). At this time, Eliot wrote that "my chair beside my father's bedside is a very blessed seat to me" and further avowed that "these will ever be the happiest days of my life. . . . The one deep strong love I have ever known has now its highest exercise and fullest reward [in nursing my father]—the worship of sorrow is *the* worship for mortals" (1954, 1:70). In her novels and poems, Eliot continued to express the notion that nursing was a "high exercise" and a "full reward."[21] In tracing the way that the scene of suffering in Eliot's writing "exemplifies her art," Daniel Cottom recognizes the figure of the nurse as a metaphor for Eliot's conception of her relationship to her readers: like the attendant "angel of duty" who supervises the sickbed scene, Eliot's novels advocate a passivity on the part of the reader, while simultaneously offering consolation and sympathy for suffering through the narrative itself.[22] The suffering of the sickbed is "shared by the attending angel of duty, by the sympathetic reader, and by the writer who supervises the whole scene, suffering in the writing of it and yet feeling this suffering necessary to the therapeutics of literary art" (142). Human pain, and the sympathy that accompanies it, becomes for Eliot the one means of binding society together because it appears as a universal, as opposed to a local, truth.[23]

In "Janet's Repentance," written at the inception of Eliot's career as a novelist, the narrator asserts that:

> the sick-room and the lazaretto have so often been a refuge from the tossings of intellectual doubt—a place of repose for the worn and wounded spirit. Here is a duty about which all creeds and all philosophies are at one: here, at least, the conscience will not be dogged by doubt, the benign impulse will not be checked by adverse theory; here you may begin to act without settling one preliminary question. To moisten the sufferer's parched lips through the long nightwatches, to bear up the drooping head, to lift the helpless limbs, to divine the want that can find no utterance beyond the feeble

motion of the hand . . . these are offices that demand no self-questionings, no casuistry, no assent to propositions, no weighing of consequences (323-24).

Eliot posits the sickroom as a site freed from the "stir and glare of the world" where a "human being lies prostrate, thrown on the tender mercies of his fellow" (323-24). It is this physical helplessness and the benevolent response to it that bring about an extreme clarification of human relationships: "the moral relation of man to man is reduced to its utmost clearness and simplicity [during nursing]; bigotry cannot confuse it, theory cannot pervert it, passion, awed into quiescence, can neither pollute nor perturb it" (Eliot 1975, 324). This longing for a space of relational lucidity corresponds with a crucial theme in Eliot's novels: that is, the quest for freedom from self-consciousness, and the utopic consequence of social empathy and reconciliation such a loss of subjectivity allows.

It is in the activity of nursing, perhaps exclusively, that Eliot believes she has found a locus for the dissolution of ego. In a letter written to Eliot in 1879, Benjamin Jowett articulates the parallels between the selflessness of nursing and the selflessness of imaginary labor when he writes to Eliot about her concept of self-dispersement:

> your notion of 'diffusing ourselves,' making the most of one life for the good of many:—that is a phrase of yours which often comes into my mind: and, especially in the case of a great sorrow the first thing is to bear it and to feel it; and the next thing is to convert the particular sorrow into a wider and deeper sympathy for men and women everywhere, and having suffered ourselves, to lighten the hearts and minds of others: I hardly think you are aware how great a good and comfort your writings have been to numberless persons (quoted in Eliot 1954, 9:284).[24]

Thus just as nursing expresses the ability of the sickroom watcher to convert personal sorrow into compassion, thereby echoing Christ's experience of suffering and forgiveness, so too does Eliot's own imaginative labor reflect her empathetic position as a writer. Her novels, then, like the lazaretto, are imagined to be locales free from creed, ideology, and doubt where the reading public can, in their imagination, meet and effect reconciliation, pointing to what Raymond Williams has characterized as the English custom of seeking consolation for the disruption engendered by industrialism in the realm of culture (1958, 132).

In *The Ethics of George Eliot*, John Crombie Brown conflates George Eliot's authorial persona with that of Romola, the character he feels most embodies Eliot's ethical project: "imagination has seldom placed before us a fairer, nobler, and completer female presence. . . . [C]ombining such deep womanly tenderness with such spotless purity; so transparent in her truthfulness; so clear in her perceptions of the true and good, so firm in her aspirations after these; so broad, gentle, and forbearing in her charity, yet so resolute against all that is mean and base" (33-34).

Brown asserts that Romola's nobility of spirit gets expressed most clearly through her nursing, a "path of voluntary self-consecration" that makes the "mystery of sorrow intelligible to us" (37):

> In the streets of the faction-torn, plague-stricken, famine-wasted city . . . she moves and stands more and more before us as the "visible Madonna." . . . How sharply the sword has pierced her heart, how sorely the crown of thorns is pressing her fair young brow. . . . Meek, steadfast, she devotes herself to every duty and right that life has left to her. . . . [She] takes up the full burden of her cross . . . [She is carried into] the midst of terror, suffering, and death [during the plague]; and there, in self-devotedness to others, in patient ministrations of love amid poverty, ignorance, and superstition, the noble spirit rights itself once more . . . (J. Brown 37-40).

Romola's role of nurse mirrors Eliot's work as healer-writer, and both become heroic figures through their labors. Not only are they "visible Madonnas," they are also Christ-figures wearing their "crown of thorns" through the self-sacrifice and suffering their work entails. But this suffering is not purposeless, rather, their "voluntary self-consecration" effects a healing in the "faction-torn, plague-stricken, famine-wasted" states of fifteenth-century Florence and, by analogy, nineteenth-century England.

JAEL AND SISERA

Yet the heroism of the nurse, and by extension, the writer, becomes problematic when we recognize that Eliot's acknowledged ethical mission within her writing was ambiguous. In June of 1857, Eliot wrote to her editor John Blackwood that she "should like *not* to be offensive—I should like to touch every heart among my readers with nothing but loving humour, with tenderness, with belief in goodness" (Eliot's emphasis, 1954, 2:348). Here we can discern the wisdom writer's reasonable voice, characterized especially by Eliot's avowedly benevolent relationship with her audience. Yet, as we have seen, Eliot's more clearly stated purpose in her writing is not only, or not primarily, to bring "loving humour, tenderness and a belief in goodness," but also to arouse sorrow: "the vision of something that life might be and that one's own ignorance and incompleteness have hindered it from being, presses more and more as time advances. The only problem for us, the only hope, is to try and unite the utmost activity with the utmost resignation. Does this seem melancholy? I think it is less melancholy than any sort of self-flattery" (1954, 8:383). Here Eliot voices the realist writer's sense of earthly melancholia, a pessimism derived in part from the transformation of an evangelical vision of the world as a "vale of tears" meant only to be endured into the concept that the "reality" of life is located in human suffering.

Like Nightingale, Eliot bore a personal sense of the world's anguish, and this burden caused Eliot's definition of realism to be distinctly involved with a deflation of ideals: grimness envelops reality. In her essay "The Natural History of German Life" (1856), Eliot contends that the limits of Dickens's realism stem precisely from his idealizing, and thereby distorting, his working-class characters:

> he scarcely ever passes from the humorous and external to the emotional and tragic, without becoming as transcendent in his un-reality as he was a moment before in his artistic truthfulness. But for the precious salt of his humour, which compels him to reproduce external traits that serve, in some degree, as a corrective to his frequently false psychology, his preternaturally virtuous poor children and artisans, his melodramatic boatmen and courtezans, would be as noxious as Eugene Sue's idealized proletaires in encouraging

the miserable fallacy that high morality and refined sentiment can grow out of harsh social relations, ignorance, and want; or that the working-classes are in a condition to enter at once into a millennial state of *altruism*, wherein everyone is caring for everyone else, and no one for himself (Eliot's emphasis, 1990, 111).

As a corrective to Dickens's and Sue's "noxious" idealizing, Eliot felt compelled to write about the painful "truth" of life, a truth that for Eliot lay expressly in reality's ugliness—an ugliness that she paradoxically reads as "beauty." In a renowned passage from *Adam Bede*, the narrator exhorts the reader to

love that other beauty too, which lies in no secret of proportion, but in the secret of deep human sympathy. . . . do not impose on us any aesthetic rules which shall banish from the region of Art those old women scraping carrots with their work-worn hands, those heavy clowns taking holiday in a dingy pot-house, those rounded backs and stupid weather-beaten faces that have bent over the spade and done the rough work of the world. . . . In this world there are so many of these common coarse people, who have no picturesque sentimental wretchedness! It is so needful we should remember their existence, else we may happen to leave them quite out of our religion and philosophy, and frame lofty theories which only fit a world of extremes (1968, 153).[25]

In reasserting the Wordsworthian imperative to represent England's poor in art, the narrator of *Adam Bede* implies both an admiration for those who have done "the rough work of the world," and a contempt for those same "heavy clowns" with their "dingy pot-house[s]," and "stupid weather-beaten faces."

Eliot's critique of Dickens and Sue derives from the debate Nightingale raises over the ethical purpose of art—whether it was meant to instigate inspiration or resignation. That Eliot felt the pull of this contention is seen in the frequent generic splitting in her novels between her wish to provide consolation and inspiration on the one hand, and her vision of social satire and tragic melodrama on the other. Indeed, Levine has argued that "Eliot's voice is often the voice of disenchantment. It impresses on us the failures of history, the littleness of the self, the pervasiveness of death. Yet she struggles against the wisdom of her own insight" (1980, 169-70).

Eliot's hesitation over whether her writing was a vehicle for anguish or "loving humour" and the implicit aggression in her notion of the "worship of sorrow" is vividly anticipated by the infamous wooden doll anecdote of her childhood: "the attic [in Griff House] was also [Eliot's] refuge where she hid her storms of tears after being punished. She had a wooden doll, on which she used to take out her rages by driving nails into its head—a picture of Jael and Sisera was the inspiration for this action—and then, when her temper was spent, she would hold the doll and sing to it, in recompense for having hurt it" (Sprague 8-9). This image of Mary Ann Evans inducing and then assuaging pain bodies forth the possibility that the "worship of sorrow," rather than imparting empathy and expanding the humanity of her readers is, in part, a means of aggressivity and control. Accompanying Eliot's belief that the writer's moral duty towards the reader includes reminding them of human suffering, is the prospect that these images would serve not to inspire but rather to deaden and dishearten.

Further, the claim Eliot makes for the sickroom, and by analogy, the realist novel, as a space of social reconciliation, breaks down when we realize that Eliot characteristically restricted the scene of suffering to the position of the nurse or "watcher." In "Janet's Repentance," Eliot writes: "As we bend over the sick-bed, all the forces of our nature rush towards the channels of pity, of patience, and of love, and sweep down the miserable choking drift of our quarrels, our debates, our would-be wisdom, and our clamourous selfish desires. This blessing of serene freedom from the importunities of opinion lies in all simple direct acts of mercy, and is one source of that sweet calm which is often felt by the watcher in the sick-room, even when the duties there are of a hard and terrible kind" (1975, 324). Here the narrator idealizes the relationship between nurse and patient, but even in this idealization, the coupling is not one of equality, but objectification. Nursing in Eliot's novels does not trigger the communal understanding that Eliot claims for it: rather, it heightens the nurse's solipsism and the alienation of nurse from patient. Thus Janet Dempster seals her redemption through her forgiving nursing of her husband—but Robert Dempster is offered no such opportunity for conversion. Similarly, it is Romola whose heroism is assured through her nursing, her patients remaining as unshriven as before.

"I WILL NOT TOUCH YOUR KEYS"

The solipsistic nature of nursing in Eliot's novels is expressed vividly in Mary Garth's nursing of Peter Featherstone in *Middlemarch*. As Featherstone's nurse, Mary Garth faces duties that are, like those of Janet Dempster, of a "hard and terrible kind." However, in contrast to Janet's response to her husband's illness, there is no rush of "pity, patience and love" as Mary bends over Featherstone's sickbed (1975, 323). Rather, Mary Garth's "thought was not veined by any solemnity or pathos about the old man on the bed: such sentiments are easier to affect than to feel about an aged creature whose life is not visibly anything but a remnant of vices" (1977, 218). Unlike Janet, Romola, and Dorothea, Mary Garth does not display "saintly" nursing skills: "To be anxious about a soul that is always snapping at you must be left to the saints of the earth; and Mary was not one of them" (218). Still, Mary finds solace in the sickroom, solace that derives not from caretaking, but, like the Nurse in Alma-Tadema's painting, from the silent meditation offered to her during the nightwatch: "That night after twelve o'clock Mary Garth relieved the watch in Mr. Featherstone's room, and sat there alone through the small hours. She often chose this task, in which she found some pleasure, notwithstanding the old man's testiness whenever he demanded her attentions. There were intervals in which she could sit perfectly still, enjoying the outer stillness and the subdued light" (217). Any "sweet calm" Mary feels in the sickroom arises not from performing "simple, direct acts of mercy" for Mr. Featherstone, but from those moments when he leaves her alone.

Mary uses the lulls in Featherstone's demands to conduct a private review of her remarkably narrow daily life: "Mary was fond of her own thoughts, and could amuse herself well sitting in twilight. . . . She sat to-night revolving, as she was wont, the scenes of the day, her lips often curling with amusement at the oddities to which her fancy added fresh drollery . . ." (217). In depicting Mary's ability to transform the meager scraps of her existence into an amusing and pleasurable narrative, Eliot reasserts the transformative powers of the imagination itself. Mary, in her review of the "scenes of the day" to which "her fancy added fresh drollery" becomes as much a symbol for the imaginative labor of the novelist as does Lydgate with his desire to "pierce the obscurity of those minute processes which prepare human misery and joy, those invisible thoroughfares which are the first lurking-places of anguish, mania, and crime, that delicate poise and transition which determine the growth of happy or unhappy consciousness" (113).[26] From this perspective, the sickroom functions not as a space of social reconciliation, but rather a realm of solipsism, solipsism associated specifically with the isolation imaginative labor can require. The private pleasures of nursing for Mary derive from the "twilight," the peace of the "small hours" and the "intervals in which she could sit perfectly still, enjoying the outer stillness and the subdued light." Indeed, the chapter's epigraph from Shakespeare's *Henry the IV Part II* reads: "Close up his eyes and draw the curtain close; / And let us all to meditation," thereby underscoring nursing's association with meditative, creative, and isolated states (217).

As with Lydgate, Mary's imaginative space is a fragile locale, easily violated or disrupted by the harsh exigencies of everyday life—in Mary's case this violation is personified by the "testy" demands of her dying patient. Rather than a space of peaceful meditation, the sickroom exists for Mary as a site of intense conflict, conflict that echoes the obstacles Lydgate encounters in his quest for medical knowledge. Indeed, of the five nursing scenes that occur in *Middlemarch*, three (those between Mary and Peter; Dorothea and Causaubon; and Bulstrode, Mrs. Able, and Raffles) are not only central to the workings of the plot, but also become the locus of acute power struggles over money, sexuality, vengeance, and gender and intergenerational contestations. Through the conflicts contained within the "private" space of the sickroom, Eliot offers domestic parallels to the factionalism of Middlemarch's "public" realms, that is, the political, religious, and medical battles that Eliot delineates in her novel. In this way, Eliot invites the reader to see that the "private" domestic realm is not a quarantined, politically neutral locale.

If, as I am arguing here, Mary Garth's function as a meditative nurse offers us an analogy for the creative labor of the novelist, then what sort of allegory is being played out? Perhaps above all, Mary's meditative state embodies the "purity" of what Eliot might have termed "invisible" work: that is, the conception and planning of a story before having to commit it to paper. In 1856, at the inception of her career as a fiction writer, Eliot writes: "besides these trifles and the introduction to an article already written, I have done no *visible* work. But I have absorbed many ideas and much bodily strength; indeed, I do not remember ever feeling so strong in mind and body as I feel at this moment . . . I am anxious to begin my fiction writing" (Eliot's emphasis, quoted in Sprague 34). This "invisible" work, the gestation of a creative scheme, exists in counterdistinction to the commitment of that idea to paper, a slippage that George Levine has described as "the terrible paradox that leaves writing as the only possible action [for the novelist who realizes] . . . that writing can affirm ideas only in the recognition that they have no connection with the reality they purport to describe" (1981, 315). With both Lydgate and Mary Garth, Eliot implies a purity in the creative gathering of ideas, a purity that can become corrupted in its translation into concrete work: be it a novel or the testing of a scientific hypothesis.

As we have seen, the actual labor of nursing interrupts the peaceful meditation of the sickroom. On the night of Featherstone's death, Mary's work takes on a terrible aspect due to Featherstone's request that she take his key, go into his closet, open his iron chest, and burn one of the two wills that he has had drawn up. The two "wills" in conflict here, however, are Mary's and Featherstone's, their struggle becoming a duet with Featherstone's refrain of "I shall do as I like" being countered by Mary's "I can not touch your iron chest or your will" (219). Logically there is no reason for Mary to be as trapped as she is by Featherstone and his request. Stone Court is full of visitors, including Fred Vincy and his mother, and Mary would certainly not be faulted for leaving the sickroom to seek help. Yet Eliot depicts the pair as being locked into a private, perverse, and ineluctable battle of the wills.

In denying Featherstone's request to burn the second will, Mary states that she "will not let the close of your life soil the beginning of mine" (219), and indeed, Eliot imbues this sickroom fracas with strongly sexualized imagery, thereby underscoring Featherstone's "*testiness* whenever he demanded Mary's attentions" (my emphasis 217). Featherstone, a mere "remnant of vices," has the power on his deathbed to pollute Mary with his "iron chest," his corrupt wills, and his "erect" key: "the old man paused with a blank stare for a little while, holding the one key erect on the ring; then with an agitated jerk he began to work with his bony left hand" (219). The "agitated jerk[ing] work" of Featherstone's "bony left hand" refers to his removal of money from a tin box that he keeps by his bed, money that the old man offers to Mary if she will obey him: "Missy . . . take the money—the notes and gold—look here—take it—you shall have it all—do as I tell you" (219).

Featherstone's urging that Mary take his gold places her in a potential situation of prostitution, a role that Mary resoundingly rejects: "I will do anything else I can to comfort you; but I will not touch your keys or your money" (220). Featherstone asserts that he "want[s] nothing else" and orders Mary to come to his bed where he drops his "erect key" and clutches instead "his stick" with which he hopes to strike her: "Mary approached him cautiously, knowing him too well. She saw him dropping his keys and trying to grasp his stick, while he looked at her like an aged hyena, the muscles of his face getting distorted with the effort of his hand. She paused at a safe distance" (220). The battle finally ends when Featherstone "impotently" throws his stick at Mary: "he lifted the stick, in spite of her being beyond his reach, and threw it with a hard effort which was but impotence. It fell, slipping over the foot of the bed" (220).

The sexual imagery of this deathbed scene and Featherstone's attempts to transform Mary into a species of prostitute can be read as allegories for Eliot's own fears of her art being corrupted by the marketplace. Here Eliot implies that the move from the private, meditative realm of creativity embodied in Mary Garth's peaceful reflections at the chapter's opening to the "work" of professionalizing that creativity can be a corrupting and polluting journey. Like many Victorian writers, Eliot struggled throughout her career with her ambivalence about becoming commodified and marketable as a professional writer, of writing, as Eliot declared "drivel for dishonest money" (1885, 2:262). The conflict that Victorian writers felt over the commercial aspects of publishing was profound during the mid nineteenth century. George Meredith conveys a sense of this uneasiness in his novel *Rhoda Fleming* when one of the characters proclaims that "you can buy any amount for a penny, now-a-days—poetry up in a corner, stories, tales o' temptation" (73). In *Lucretia*, Francis Edward Paget expresses this fear even more bluntly: "most of the worst sensational novels are republished, vile type and vile paper combining to secure for the dissemination of still viler sentiments a very low price" (302). Mary Poovey writes of the confusion felt by male writers during the mid nineteenth century over their place in society, the status of their profession, and their double ancestry of both medieval court scribes and Renaissance intellectuals and "early and mid-eighteenth-century hacks who sold ideas by the word and fought off competitors for every scrap of work," an uneasiness women writers shared in the nineteenth-century literary marketplace (1988, 103). In this sense we can read Featherstone with his "notes and gold" as an allegory for the venality of the marketplace itself.

Accompanying the motif of professional anxieties, the sickroom conflict between Mary and Featherstone further points to the crucial issue of the "ownership" of culture. Part of the horror involved in Featherstone's attempt to bribe Mary with his gold is the potential for the subsequent suspicion that Mary in fact robbed Featherstone of this money while he was dying or even after his death. Although Eliot's portrayal of Featherstone as a desperate miser longing to "take it with him" deliberately points to the futility of holding on to material possessions, any exchange of money at the deathbed from the dying or dead to the living is regarded with an even greater dread. The Victorian motif of the living plundering the dead (as in Old Sally's pilfering of Oliver's mother's necklace in *Oliver Twist*, Hexam's corpse-robbing in the opening scene of *Our Mutual Friend*, or the widespread representations of grave-robbing and body-snatching) indicates a general ambivalence about the transmission of culture itself: this transmission must occur in a lawful, forthright manner. Were Mary to accept Featherstone's money, she would be furtively interfering with the just transmission of his legacy.

Bernard Semmel discusses the "theme of inheritance" in Eliot's novels and concludes that it registers two important issues: the first is the "passing on of goods and property to heirs, which [Eliot] saw as emblematic of family affections and obligations."[27] The second issue of the theme of inheritance, one that Semmel sees Eliot stressing in her later writings, is the notion of the inheritance of the nation's "culture and historical traditions" (6). Semmel argues that while "a parent was obliged to will his goods to his children, a child, as an independent, self-directed being, was free to reject such a bequest and the duties accompanying it" (6). Thus a parent has a moral obligation to pass on a legacy to a child, but a child has the free will to disinherit him or herself. From this viewpoint, Featherstone's bequest of his name and land to his illegitimate son Joshua Riggs (a bequest present in both wills) is in fact quite ethical under Eliot's schema of inheritance. Conversely, the deliberate disinheritance of Aunt Julia by Causaubon's maternal grandparents and Ladislaw's mother Sarah Dunkirk by her stepfather Bulstrode are morally reprehensible acts. On the one hand, the parent is obligated to the child. On the other, the child retains the option of rejecting a corrupt or tainted legacy. Indeed, this renunciation can be a noble or heroic act, as when both Will Ladislaw and Sarah Dunkirk abjure the ill-gotten Dunkirk fortune.[28]

This personal code of inheritance translates readily into a metaphor for the relationship between the individual and his or her cultural or political inheritance. While the state has incurred an obligation to its citizens not to disinherit or disenfranchise them, the "children" do not have to accept the legacy of the past but are free to renounce it and to create their own inheritance, as do Dorothea and Will Ladislaw. Indeed, the nursing scene between Mary and Featherstone finds its echo in the struggle between Dorothea and Causaubon over her submission to his will—she too must "touch" his "key"—in this case Causaubon's life's work, his "Key to all Mythology." Here Eliot draws a parallel between Dorothea's and Mary Garth's quests to free themselves from their vampiric, incestuous captors: captors whose "Dead Hands" hold the power to blight the young lives of their nurses. On many levels, these "dead hands" represent both the ownership and the inheritance of British and Western culture itself.[29] Causaubon, whose privileges of gender, class, and education grant him an undeserved status, embodies a patriarchal hoarding of cultural knowledge that is at once exclusionary and condescending. If we read the nurse in this instance as a figure for the female novelistic imagination, then we can see, especially in the nursing relationship between Dorothea and Causaubon, both a desire for access to forbidden masculine realms of knowledge, and the stultifying deadening that quest can entail. Finally, Eliot implies that the female novelistic imagination must be free to resist, renounce, or re-create the masculine models of knowledge inherited from the past.

"OUR DEEDS STILL TRAVEL WITH US FROM AFAR"

In comparing Mary Garth's and Dorothea's nursing to Janet Dempster's, we can discern a shift from *Scenes of Clerical Life* to *Middlemarch*,
a loss of the pathos that distinguished the narrator's voice in the
sickroom scenes in "Janet's Repentance," a quality that George Levine
describes as Eliot's "to ugh-minded disenchantment" (1981, 256).
Likewise, if we correlate Romola and Dorothea, we can trace a course,
as Nightingale did, towards increasing realism in *Middlemarch*, an
increase that meant a diminishment of representations of heroic
nursing such as that exemplified by Romola: indeed, Romola's nursing
of the plague village has been considered to be one of the most
unrealistic moments in all of Eliot's novels.[30]

This shift from "Janet's Repentance" and *Romola* to *Middlemarch* can
be perceived despite Eliot's disclaimer in 1876 that she saw no divergence between her initial and later works.[31] Within the nursing scenes
in *Middlemarch*, Eliot displays a cynicism quite distinct from the
sincerity apparent in her initial representations of nursing. Despite these
differences, however, there remains a sense of isolation and miscommu-
nication evident not only in Mary Garth's caretaking of Featherstone,
but also in Eliot's earliest nursing scenes. For example, Janet's nursing of
Robert Dempster is characterized not by the mutual reconciliation of
husband and wife, but by continued misunderstanding and separation:
"It seemed as if her husband was already imprisoned in misery, and she
could not reach him—his ear deaf for ever to the sounds of love and
forgiveness. His sins had made a hard crust round his soul; her pitying
voice could not pierce it" (319). Janet's nursing of Robert typifies Eliot's
sickbed scenes: they are moments in the narrative where communica-
tion breaks down utterly, the patients becoming "doomed carcasses"
that serve to nourish the souls of their attendants.

Further, despite the narrator's claim in "Janet's Repentance" that
the sickroom exists as a space unfettered by "creeds and all philosophies," the sickroom houses, and even precipitates, complex ideological conflict—there are no "simple, direct acts of mercy" (Eliot 1975,
324). Indeed, *Middlemarch* foregrounds the political battles being
waged for control of the medical community during the 1830s, a
struggle that was only to intensify during the 1870s. The "blessings of
serenity from opinion" that Eliot claims for the sickroom in "Janet's

Repentance" no more exist in the face of Dempster's corruption and brutality than they do in Mary Garth's deathbed struggle with Featherstone or Bulstrode's capitulation to Mrs. Abel's request to supply Raffles with alcohol. Thus Eliot's utopic envisioning of the sickroom as a space of social reconciliation and individual peace disintegrates, underscoring the problematic task of locating political solutions within the ostensibly universalizing cultural realm.

NURSES

The nurse stands as an important figure for both Eliot and Nightingale in demarcating their positions as social leaders. For both writers, the image of the nurse was one that was especially able to convey heroism and the martyrdom that often accompanies heroism. Yet Eliot and Nightingale apparently employed the nurse in very different ways: for Nightingale she was a symbol of the active "morning" spirit, a manifestation of a martial Christ, and a symbol of Nightingale's own social activism. Nightingale applauded Eliot for the activism that she saw in Eliot's representation of Romola, but she chided Eliot for her turning away from this activism with her creation of Dorothea. For Eliot, immediate political action and sweeping social change threatened to disrupt, or even destroy, English culture. Eliot believed that social change must take place gradually and only after mutual comprehension between classes and individuals had been achieved: a comprehension brought about in part through the realist novel itself. Thus for Eliot, the figure of the nurse embodied the patience and self-sacrifice necessary for ideal social change.

However, distinctions between Eliot's and Nightingale's uses of the nurse ultimately founder, for the aggressiveness inherent in Nightingale's manifestation as a nurse is echoed in Eliot's scenes of nursing: scenes that she claims are the sites of social reconciliation. Further, the dissolution of the distinction between the social activist and the writer troubles the accepted notion of a fixed dichotomy between political and literary labor; both can be seen, rather, as pieces of a larger puzzle. Thus the politics of the novel and the politics of medical reform conjoin, displaying the confluence, rather than the distinction, contained in strategies of middle-class reform.

Notes

Preface

1. Traditionally there have been many terms for nursing in Great Britain. In this instance, the phrase "dry-nurse" is being used to indicate nursing of the mother after she experiences childbirth. "Dry-nurse" was employed beginning in the sixteenth century to denote either a child's nurse who did not suckle her charges (as opposed to a "wet-nurse"), or in the sense of general sickbed nursing. To be "at dry-nurse" was a common expression, especially during the seventeenth and eighteenth centuries. By the nineteenth century, "dry-nursing" was an old-fashioned expression. Thus when Charlotte Brontë uses the phrase "Mrs. Horsfall had him at dry-nurse" in her novel *Shirley*, the term probably seemed quaint to her readers. To be "dry-nursed" was also synonymous with being "brought up by hand" as Pip is said to be in Dickens's *Great Expectations*—that is, to be raised from birth without breast-feeding. Another very popular term in the nineteenth century was "sick-nursing," an expression meant to indicate all forms of nursing apart from child-care nursing (infant and child care was also termed "health-nursing" in order to distinguish it from "sick-nursing"). A term for nursing that was used particularly in Ireland, was "nurse-tending." For the sake of focus, I have limited this study to the complex debates and representations of what the Victorians would have called sick-nursing, and what we call nursing, to the general exclusion of wet-nursing, midwifery, or child-care nursing.
2. As I explain in chapter one, the miasmatic theory of contagion held that disease was spread by rotting matter such as standing cesspools or heaps of garbage that turned into a lethal gas or "miasma." Epidemics were believed to occur when people inhaled this "poisoned" air (hence, for example, the term "malaria" or "bad air").

Introduction

1. In 1854, England joined Turkey and France in their war against Russia. The focus of the war was to contain Russia within the Black Sea as well

as to destroy Russia's important naval base of Sebastapol located on the Crimean peninsula. Although the battles took place on the Crimean peninsula, England established its military hospital in Scutari, a suburb situated across the Strait of Bosphorus from what was then known as Constantinople. In other words, the sick and wounded British soldiers had to be transported from the Crimean peninsula across the Black Sea to Scutari—just one of the many enormous problems the English encountered during this war. For a detailed discussion of the Crimean War, see chapter 5.

2. "Benthamic" refers to influence of the political philosopher of utilitarianism Jeremy Bentham (1748-1832). His theory of the "greatest good for the greatest number" became the underpinning of nineteenth-century British liberalism. F. B. Smith (1982) and Mary Poovey (1988) pp. 169-98, discuss Nightingale's Benthamic projects at length.

3. See, for example, Martha Vicinus, pp. 46-61, and Anne Summers (1989). Recent revisionist works on nursing history in Britain and the United States include Celia Davies; Robert Dingwell and Jean McIntosh; Charles Rosenberg (1987); Elizabeth Brown Prior; Susan Reverby; Anne Hudson Jones; Monica Baly (1980); Ellen Condliffe Lagemann; and Eva Gamarnikow. For writings focusing especially on Victorian nursing, see Martha Vicinus pp. 1-120, Baly (1985), Ruth Gilpin Wells, and Judith Moore. For works that address the class conflicts involved in Victorian nursing, see especially Summers (1988 and 1989), Baly (1984), Christopher Maggs, Charles Rosenberg (1979), Sandra Holton, and Poovey (1988), pp. 164-98. See Darlene Clark Hine for class and racial conflict in U.S. nursing from 1880-1950. See, also, the recent collections of Nightingale's letters edited by Sue M. Goldie and Martha Vicinus and Bea Nergaard, as well as the collection of Benjamin Jowett's letters to Nightingale edited by Vincent Quinn and John Prest.

4. In her fine reading of Florence Nightingale's heroic image, Poovey declines to trace the historical foundation of that persona. For example, although she recognizes that Nightingale was "responding to rather than creating th[e] idealized image" of the Crimean nurse, Poovey credits Nightingale's immediate inspiration to a series of letters published in the London *Times* detailing the management atrocities at the British military hospital in Scutari (1988, 166-68). These letters queried "why have we no Sisters of Charity?"—thereby indicating the competition between England and their old enemy (now their ally) France. However, as we can see from Robert Southey's nearly identical question raised in 1829 (discussed in chapter 1), interest in the heroic nurse was heightened, but did not originate, during the Crimean War. Further, as I argue in chapter 2, Nightingale's desire to become a sick-nurse developed during the late 1830s and early 1840s.

5. I am using the term "positivism" not in the strict sense of the doctrinaire system of Comte's "philosophie-positive," but rather in its broadest

meaning to designate the seminal philosophical movement that swept Europe during the nineteenth century, a movement whose important adherents and theorists included not only Auguste Comte, but also Jeremy Bentham, John Stuart Mill, and Herbert Spencer. Positivism is associated most literally with the philosophy of Auguste Comte who articulates a full social, political, philosophical and religious program in his *Cours de philosophie* (1830-42) and his later work, the *Système de politique positive*. In its wider definition, however, positivism indicates a social philosophy based on a creed of scientific inevitability coupled with a secular "religion" of humanity. Positivism signifies a belief in a secular, rational, and scientific society—a "mature" society that has developed progressively from "immature" theological and metaphysical creeds. Jerome Buckley points out that "it was the business of the Positivists to ascertain by the empirical method the basic facts relevant to social action and from such facts to determine the 'laws' by which all data might be related and interpreted" (192). Defining the term in a broader sense than doctrinaire Comtism, the tenants of positivism crucially informed much of England's, and Western Europe's, reforming and humanitarian policies. In his discussion of the innovative reaction among Western European intellectuals in the 1890s against "what was felt to be a positivist stranglehold on European thought" Martin Jay, for example, notes that "variants of positivism . . . flourished in Western Europe during much of the nineteenth century" (68). For discussions of the impact of positivism on nineteenth-century European thought, see, for example, Herbert Marcuse 323-88; Peter Alan Dale; Walter Michael Simon; and Michel Foucault (1965; 1975; 1979; 1980).

6.   For a discussion of the notion of the ideologeme, see Fredric Jameson 115-19.

7.   Alma-Tadema, considered by some to epitomize high Victorian and Edwardian art, was not a Pre-Raphaelite. Rather, he is credited with the founding of England's "marble school" of painting (a "marbellous painter" sallied *Punch* magazine). Profoundly influenced by the Elgin marbles, which he studied in 1862, and a trip to Pompeii and Hercu-laneum made in 1863, Alma-Tadema frequently painted scenes from everyday life in Greco-Roman times: "Victorians in togas" as some have described them. He is best known for his paintings from the 1870s to the 1900s, including *In the Tepidarium* (1881), *Expectations* (1885), *Silver Favorites* (1903), *Vain Courtship* (1900), and *A Coign of Vantage* (1895). *The Nurse*, with its medieval setting and lush color scheme, is a departure from Alma-Tadema's usual subject matter and pastel palette. See Bram Dijkstra (125) and *Alma-Tadema* (1-3).

8.   In an effort to control prostitution and curtail the spread of venereal disease, Parliament passed a series of Contagious Disease Acts in 1864, 1866, and 1869. These acts mandated that the British police could arrest and force into "lock" hospitals for up to nine months any woman

suspected of being a prostitute, especially if she manifested symptoms of venereal disease. Lock hospitals were hospitals that contained a venereal ward. In 1869, Josephine Butler organized the "Ladies' National Association" (LNA), which worked to repeal the acts—they were finally fully repealed in 1886.

9. Quoted in James Morris (380).

10. A fungal blight destroyed Irish potato crops for several years, creating a devastating famine in which perhaps as many as 2 million Irish people died from starvation or famine-related diseases. British relief was woefully inadequate due to a stubborn adherence to a free market economy. For the Crimean War, see note 1. The Indian "Mutiny" was the rebellion of north Indian people against the rule of Great Britain's East India Company. It took British troops two years to quell the uprising and the reprisals, executions, and torture endured by the Indians were severe. The Governor Eyre Controversy centered on the reaction of Edward Eyre, an Englishman and governor of Jamaica, to a rebellion of independent ex-slave farmers who resisted pressure to return to the sugar plantations of Jamaica. Thirty-nine white Jamaicans were killed and in reprisal Governor Eyre gave free rein to martial law during which time military forces shot or hanged nearly 400 farmers and burnt more than 1,000 farms. The main source of controversy centered on the hanging of one of Eyre's political opponents after a kangaroo-court trial. Radical factions in England believed that Eyre should be brought to trial for political murder. Efforts to indict Eyre failed, but the controversy divided the British intellectual community. See Semmel 1963. Beginning in 1831, Britain experienced severe cholera epidemics that ultimately killed at least 140,000 people. The major epidemics occurred in 1831-32, 1848-49, 1853-54, and 1866. These epidemics brought an intensity to Britain's public- health reform plans.

11. Alma-Tadema was justly celebrated for his dedication to historical specificity in his paintings. The style of clothing, furniture, and book-binding in *The Nurse* all point to a late-medieval, low-country setting.

12. After first meeting Florence Nightingale in 1854, for example, Elizabeth Gaskell writes that Nightingale is "so like a saint" and "is [she] not like St. Elizabeth of Hungary?" (1967, 307). See, also, Charles Kingsley's play based on the life of St. Elizabeth of Hungary, *The Saint's Tragedy* (1848).

13. For more detailed discussion of the distinction between old- and new-style nursing, see chapter 2.

14. Among the profusion of recent discussions of the fallen woman and the prostitute, see especially Walkowitz, who can be credited with pioneer-ing recent interest in the image of the prostitute. Helena Michie contends that middle-class representations of the prostitute reflect the ambivalence Victorian women writers felt towards the sexual power and sexual display associated with professional writing (59-78). Catherine

Gallagher explores the primacy of the metaphor of the writer-as-prostitute, regardless of the writer's gender, in her essays on Aphra Behn and George Eliot (1986 and 1988). Dijkstra illustrates the role of the prostitute as an icon of decadence and disease in the male imagination (352-75). Amanda Anderson's and Elsie Michie's books exemplify two fine recent studies of the centrality of prostitution and "fallenness" in Victorian literature.

15. See, for example, Jerome Hamilton Buckley (66-86).

16. See note 2.

17. Welsh's seminal attention to the sickbed attendants in the Victorian novel differs from my project in that he does not register their medical function and their association with the complex Victorian discourse of nursing that I am interested in delineating here. As I discuss in chapter 1, Welsh focuses exclusively on the nurse as an "angel" and on her quasireligious role. Oddly, neither Langland, in her study of Victorian "angelology," nor Bailin, with her interest in the motif of the sickroom, engage with Welsh's pioneering attention to the motif of the "angelic" nurse in the Victorian novel. For a discussion of Welsh's "angels of death" that emphasizes the general role of servants as the harbingers of death, see Bruce Robbins 117-18.

18. Tracey Alison Baker and Nancy Lee Sobal are also interested in literary representations of the nurse. Sobal's work analyzes the interplay between the ongoing debates about women's work and the role of women in the nineteenth century's developing medical fields. Her investigation centers on the depictions of female doctors and nurses in American literature (with comparative references to English fiction), and her examination of the figure of the nurse commences with works written in the early twentieth century by authors such as Sinclair Lewis and Ernest Hemingway.

19. For example, Marian Bailin's *The Sickroom in Victorian Fiction* takes as its starting point the "pervasive presence of the sickroom scene in Victorian fiction," claiming that such scenes provided a "crucial therapeutic function within Victorian realist narrative" (1994, 3). Although Bailin is interested to some extent in the cultural, particularly the biographical, histories that inform the sickroom scene, she maintains in her preface that the steady rise in the medical profession's status and advances made in medical research in the nineteenth century had "relatively little impact upon the representation of illness and recovery in early and mid-Victorian fiction" (2-3). While this is a controversial and intriguing thesis—an argument for the cordoning off of Victorian narrative from the myriad of political and social pressures that surrounded it—I do not believe that Victorian representations of illness, recovery, and death reside in a strictly "personal" space. See, for example, my discussion of Bailin's reading of the sickroom in George Eliot's fiction, in chapter 6.

20. Interestingly, nineteenth-century nursing reformation stems not directly from hospital improvement, as might be expected, but rather descends from penal reorganization, particularly the work of John Howard and Elizabeth Fry (Baly, 46-50). Foucault would claim that this distinction is not crucial due to his concept of the "carceral continuum"—that is, the way in which nineteenth-century institutions such as hospitals, schools, and prisons echo one another in spirit and function. See my discussion of the carceral continuum in chapter 3.

21. Edwin Chadwick was a leading mid-Victorian sanitarian and the author of the enormously important 1842 bluebook report on the health of towns. He worked very closely with Nightingale on public-health issues until his death in 1890. Chadwick began his career as Jeremy Bentham's secretary, and he was the chief architect of the controversial New Poor Law of 1834. See Finer.

22. For an extensive reading of the crucial role public-health reform played in the formation of Victorian British culture, see Poovey (1995), especially chapters 1-6.

23. See, for example, Frank Mort and Bruce Haley.

24. See, for example, A. Susan Williams.

25. For an interesting discussion of domesticity and sanitary reform, see Poovey's chapter on domesticity and Chadwick's 1842 *Sanitary Report,* 1995, pp. 115-31.

26. Poovey contends that the power of Nightingale's popular image rests within this confusion of military and domestic tropes because these images were the basic paradigms of gender for mid-Victorians. See Poovey, 1988, 169-72. See, also, *Punch's* 1855 poem "Florence Nightingale." Here Nightingale is portrayed by turns as a "blessing, bred of gentleness" who falls "like balm on passion wrung from festering wound or fever-pain," and as a general who leads "her great army" and "face to face with pain and death, bore bravely a worse battle's brunt / Than any soldier."

27. Jordanova contends that a fully historical view of science is hard to attain, because virtually everything in our culture "conspires to reinforce a separation between the study of science and the pursuit of the humanities, both of which are needed to understand the social and cultural history of science" (15), and that in earlier centuries, including the nineteenth, "few of the institutions maintaining present-day discipline boundaries existed. . . . [Indeed] the entire notion of a discipline is a recent one" (16). In 1825, for example, Hazily wrote that the "two greatest names in English literature [are] Sir Isaac Newton and Mr. Locke" (quoted in R. Williams, 1986 10).

28. Other possibilities include the "analysis of metaphors and of grammatical forms [and] the analysis of areas of interaction between different forms of writing" (R. Williams 1986 12).

29. See, for example, Richard Selzer, Enid Rhodes Peschel, Edmund D. Pellegrino, and Marie Borroff.

30. Some seminal studies of literature and medicine include the works of Gillian Beer; Michel Foucault 1975; Catherine Gallagher 1986a; Thomas Laqueur; George Levine 1981; Frank Mort; Mary Poovey 1988 and 1995; Elaine Scarry 1987; Elaine Showalter 1985; Elise Michie and Athena Vrettos 1990 and 1995.

31. For a detailed discussion of thematic criticism, see Werner Sollors.

32. For this reading of the Victorian novel, see George Levine 1981 and Lawrence Rothfield.

33. In *The Political Unconscious*, Fredric Jameson argues that the revolt of the "weak and the slaves against the strong, and the 'production' of the secretly castrating ideals of charity, resignation, and abnegation, are, according to the Nietzschean theory of *ressentiment*, no less locked into the initial power relationship than the aristocratic system of which they are the inversion" (117). My reading of *Jane Eyre* precisely is interested in the way in which the act of nursing allows Brontë's charitable, resigned and self-abnegating heroine to participate in, and win, her power struggle with the masculine and aristocratic "rulers" of her world. In Brontë's depiction of the nurse's gaze, I argue, we see a depiction of "carceral" or disciplinary power played out in a decidedly feminine realm. For a detailed definition of "carceral power" and "the carceral," see Foucault, 1979.

Chapter 1

1. See Welsh 194-228 and Humphrey House 132. For more recent overviews of the prominence of death and disease in the Victorian novel, see Vrettos 1990 and 1995, Rothfield, and Bailin 1987 and 1994.

2. Ruskin also speculates on the possibility that the "infliction of violent or disgusting death" in the Victorian novel stems from syphilitic lesions on the author's brain that cause him or her to produce distasteful images: "the reader who cares to seek it may easily find medical evidence of the physical effects of certain states of brain disease in producing . . . images of truncated and Hermes-like deformity, complicated with grossness" (164).

3. Although there are important differences between French and British medicine, the growth of the medicalization of modern culture was an international phenomenon with much theory and policy being shared among European countries as well as with the United States. For example, in *The Birth of the Clinic* Foucault discusses the way that the practice of setting up chairs in clinical medicine spread from Leyden to the University of Edinburgh by 1720, and from there expanded to London, Oxford, Cambridge, and Dublin. At the same time, the Leyden influence also moved into Vienna, Gottingen, and Padua (57). In the

eighteenth and nineteenth centuries, an active exchange of ideas within the international medical community was the rule rather than the exception. For the increasing influence of French medical theories and policies on British public-health issues, see, for example, Walkowitz, pp. 36-38, 44-46, and 50.

4. In her essay on Henry Mayhew and Thomas Malthus, Catherine Gallagher recognizes the pervasive Victorian "social discourse obsessed with sanitation," where "society was imagined to be a chronically, incurably ill organism that could only be kept alive by the constant flushing, draining, and excising of various deleterious elements" (1986a, 90).

5. For sanitary reform in the United States being particularly the province of women, refer to the work done during the Civil War by the Woman's Sanitary Association and by health reformers such as Clara Barton and Dorothea Dix. For female activism in Great Britain, see Vicinus.

6. The emphasis on nursing as an innate female skill conceals the actuality that not all nurses in the nineteenth century were men. F.B. Smith notes that: "the notion that 40 nurses could cope with 3,000 patients, . . . and that ten—in another letter at this time Miss Nightingale put the number at eighteen and five in successive sentences—would really suffice . . . highlights the fact, which Miss Nightingale—followed by her biographers—managed to obscure, that the greater part of the nursing [in Scutari] was done, as it always had been done, by male medical orderlies" (1982, 43). Inasmuch as there were male nurses, there were also female doctors in England—Queen Victoria herself had been delivered by Mademoiselle Siebold, a "female obstetrician . . . who had qualified as a physician and surgeon at the University of Gottingen, 'like a man,'" and who later delivered Prince Albert (Woodham-Smith 1972, 44-45). Yet, as with the male nurses at Scutari, England was very anxious to screen the existence of a female doctor—for ideological reasons the categories of doctor and nurse needed to remain firmly gendered. Thus Nightingale will state in *Notes on Nursing* that "every woman is a nurse" (3) while Cecil Woodham-Smith notes the powerful mid-nineteenth-century myth that Victoria's birth was too difficult for Siebold to handle by herself, and that a Welsh male doctor, David Daniel Davis, "intervened, safely delivered the Princess Victoria and saved the lives of both [mother and child]" (1972, 50).

7. See, for example, John Norris, F. R. and Q. D. Leavis (183, 240, 267-68, and 179-83), Myron Brightfield, and especially Rothfield.

8. Many influential Victorian writers aligned their writing with medical methodology and authority. In *Characteristics,* for example, Thomas Carlyle claims to examine society with a "practical, medical view," while in *London Labour and the London Poor,* Henry Mayhew declares that "the science of anatomy is not confined to hospitals and dissecting-rooms, nor restricted in its application to the human frame" (Mayhew 4:xii).

9. A striking example of the amalgamation of Christ and the sick-nurse can be seen in a letter Nightingale wrote from Cairo in 1849 where she lists three examples of "divine greatness"—Moses, Christ, and the St. Vincent de Paul nursing sisters who where then working in Egypt (1987a, 34). Correspondingly, in her essay *Cassandra* Nightingale suggests that "the next Christ will perhaps be a female Christ." These examples point to the Victorian feminization of Christ, a process that emphasized Christ's human qualities and his earthly deeds while subordinating his martial and supernatural manifestations. The result was an image of Christ as a philanthropist and a healer characterized by "feminine" attributes of compassion, pity and sympathy. Thus when Holman Hunt came to paint his portrait of Christ in his *Light of the World,* he used Elizabeth Siddall's hair and Christina Rossetti's face as models for Christ. Interestingly, Christina Rossetti was herself an avid nurse who begged to accompany Nightingale to the Crimean while Elizabeth Siddall was one of the "distressed gentlewomen" nursed for a time by Nightingale at the Harley Street Hospital.

10. In the "Prelude" to *Middlemarch,* Eliot writes "Theresa's passionate, ideal nature demanded an epic life . . . Many Theresas have been born who found for themselves no epic life wherein there was a constant unfolding of far-resonant action . . . for these later-born Theresas were helped by no coherent social faith and order which could perform the function of knowledge for the ardently willing soul" (xiii).

11. "Beguines" are members of a Flemish lay sisterhood established in the twelfth century and devoted, like Catholic nursing orders, to nursing and religious life. However, they are not bound by irrevocable vows.

12. My use here of the terms "medical" and "sanitary" is based upon the divisions engendered by the British debates on the best route the "medicalization" of society should take. In his book on the Parisian cholera epidemic of 1832, François Delaporte makes the distinction between a theory of sanitary (contagious) practices and health (infectious or miasmic) practices, subsuming both categories under the "medical" realm (cf. Delaporte, 13-14). For the British, the terms "medical" or "medicine" delineated a contagionist philosophy of disease while a "sanitary" approach stood for the belief in infectious (miasmic) transmission of disease.

13. Chadwick, for example, had a "deep-rooted distrust" of doctors, and found curative medicine to be "nothing but *consulate maim* . . . [the doctors] pretending to alleviate disease which if they had the will they had not the skill to *prevent*" (Edwin Chadwick to J. Kay-Shuttleworth, 15 May 1843. Quoted in Finer, 157-58).

14. For example, the anticontagionist Chervin was unanimously elected to the Royal Academy of Medicine in 1832 at the same time "that the Society for the Propagation of the Idea that Cholera Morbus Is a

Contagious Disease, proposed by Pariset, was dissolved before it could hold a single meeting" (Delaporte 14).

15. Ruskin calls this pervasive focus on the medical realm and public-health reform in Victorian discourse the "Divinity of Decomposition," and characterizes it as "partly satiric, partly consolatory, concerned only with the regenerative vigour of manure, and the necessary obscurities of fimetic Providence; showing how everybody's fault is somebody else's, how infection has no law, digestion no will, and profitable dirt no dishonour" (1900, 157).

16. For this interpretation of the Vatic poet, see Abrams, especially p. 128. For a discussion of the relationship between medicine and poetry in Keats's writing, see de Almeida, Goellnicht, and Holstein.

17. Shelley wrote the "Song of Apollo" for the opening scene of Mary Shelley's verse drama *Midas*.

18. See, for example, the doctors in the jestbook *Tales and Quick Answers,* Beaumont and Fletcher's *Thierry and Theodoret,* Ben Jonson's *Sejanus* and *Volpone,* John Lyly's *Midas,* Christopher Marlowe's *The Tragical History of Doctor Faustus,* Thomas Middleton's *A Fair Quarrel,* Thomas Nashe's *The Unfortunate Traveller,* Thomas Dekker's *That Wonderful Year,* and Robert Burton's *The Anatomy of Melancholy.*

19. See John Donne's *Devotions* or John Milton's "In Obitum Procanceliarii Medici," which Joanna Traumann and Carol Pollard characterize as "unusual in its praise of physicians . . . The poem is almost a parody of the Renaissance commonplace that physicians are spared because they provide death with so many victims" (29).

20. See, for example, George Crabbe's poem "Fragment, Written at Midnight" where he writes "Oh, great Apollo! by whose equal aid / The verse is written, and the med'cine made" (Crabbe, 575), or Dryden's preface to *Absalom and Achitophel:* "he who writes Honestly, is no more an Enemy to the Offendour, than the Physician to the Patient, when he prescribes harsh Remedies to an inveterate Disease" (2:5).

21. "Oorali" is a paralytic drug that was important in vivisection experiments during the nineteenth century. Tennyson based this poem on an incident related to him by Mary Gladstone. Robert W. Hill comments that "Tennyson was susceptible to most, if not all, of the weaknesses apparent in Victorian sentimental literature, and this poem, with its particularly unbelievable nurse, shows enough of them. There is a good deal of truth in the saying that if one wants fully to understand the Victorian period, one must read the third-rate literature" (in Tennyson 1971, 448-49, fn. 5).

22. Late-eighteenth- and nineteenth-century literature contains abundant portraits of diabolic, callous, or incompetent doctors. There is the sinister quack doctor in Maria Edgeworth's *Belinda,* Dr. Quackelben in Walter Scott's *St Ronan's Well,* and Dr. Slop in Lawrence Sterne's *Tristram Shandy.* Chapter 71 (cxxi) in Robert Southey's treatise *The Doctor* is

wholly devoted to a discussion of evil doctors, as is the discussion of the Roman doctor in Thomas De Quincey's "Murder as One of the Fine Arts." Incompetent, competitive, self-interested doctors include Drs. Lewsome and Jobling in Charles Dickens's *Martin Chuzzlewit*, Harold Skimpole in *Bleak House*, Charles Kingsley's portrait of Dr. Heale in *Two Years Ago*, and most of the doctors in George Eliot's "Janet's Repentance" and *Middlemarch*. Other renowned literary doctors include Dr. Fillgrave in Anthony Trollope's *Doctor Thorne*, the philandering Dr. Edgar Fitzpiers in Thomas Hardy's *The Woodlanders*, the depraved doctors in Sheridan Le Fanu's *The House by the Churchyard*, the doctors in Charles Reade's *The Cloister and the Hearth* and *A Woman-Hater*, Dr. Macfarlane in Robert Louis Stevenson's "The Body-Snatcher," Dr. Jekyll in his *Dr. Jekyll and Mr. Hyde*, and the controlling doctor-husband in Charlotte Perkins Gilman's "The Yellow Wallpaper."

23. Perhaps the most substantial element that contributed to a general fear and mistrust of medical doctors during the nineteenth century was the controversy surrounding the "resurrection men" and the whole issue of dissection and anatomy theaters. Before the Anatomy Act of 1832, medical schools were only allowed to dissect the bodies of hanged criminals. Consequently, a black-market trafficking in stolen paupers' bodies sprang up in England and especially Scotland during the 1810s and 1820s. The Burke and Bishop murder trial was the most infamous scandal connected with what came to be know as "Burking" or "body-snatching". The public outcry against "Burking shops" or anatomy theaters continued even after the passage of the Anatomy Act.

24. See, for example, his discussion of the diabolic anatomists of Alexandria who dissected living men: "The natural result of this brutal proceeding, combined with an entire laxity of morals and excessive voluptuousness, was the utter degradation of the art and practitioners of medicine" (70).

25. Like *Bleak House*, Charles Kingsley's *Two Years Ago* offers another example of the pattern of coupling a well-intentioned but ultimately fallible doctor with an heroic and irreproachable nurse—in this case the well-meaning Dr. Tom Thurnall and the idealized, saintly Grace Harvey. Likewise, the Physician in Charles Dickens's *Little Dorrit*, a figure clearly presented to the reader as an analogy for the realist writer, is fundamentally a worldly and helpless man who attains nothing near the heights of saintliness and healing achieved by Little Dorrit—a character whose main activity in the novel is nursing others.

26. There is a similar celebration of female healing power in John Fletcher's play *The Faithful Shepherdess* where Clorin, the steadfast virgin, solves the troubles in the play with her magical healing powers, powers given to her because she, like Marina in *Pericles*, remained a virgin in the face of threatened violation. Edmund Spenser also exalts the healing virgin through the character of Belphoebe in *The Faerie Queene* who cures a wounded squire with herbs and divine grace. John Milton's *Comus*

revives this image through the spirit of the virgin Sabrina who frees the Lady from the spell put on her by Comus, and Philip Sidney's *Arcadia* features Queen Helen of Corinth who restores Parthenia's beauty. See also, Ariosto's *Orlando Furioso,* especially canto 37, which contains several accounts of female healing powers and opens with the argument that male writers deprive women of their due fame. Tasso's epic poem *Gerusalemme Liberata* depicts Ermina skillfully tending to her battle-wounded lover Tancred by using her long hair to bind his injuries.

27.   Neither Ruskin's nor Garber's arguments take into account the healing teams of Prospero and Ariel or Oberon and Puck, two sets of men (or masculine spirits) who work miracles of social restoration and redemption. Inasmuch as these male magicians rejuvenate shattered lives and societies, they offer long-recognized paradigms for the analogy between the work of the magician-healer and the work of the writer.

Chapter 2

1.   For a useful reading of Victorian domiciliary nursing, see Summers (1989).

2.   For general introductions to the mid-nineteenth-century nursing reform movement, see Abel-Smith (1-49) or Baly 1980.

3.   E. P. Thompson writes that the first half of the nineteenth century "must be seen as a period of chronic under-employment" (243).

4.   Some reformers wanted to introduce orphan girls as young as sixteen into the hospitals as nurses, a plan Nightingale vehemently opposed (see Abel-Smith, 22 and 39).

5.   After Nightingale's experiences with the "lady" nurses in the Crimean War, however, she abandoned the notion of replacing working-class hospital nurses with middle- and upper-class women, and felt that, excepting the managerial positions, hospital nursing should be left as a field for working-class women (see Baly 1984, 56).

6.   In discussing Foucault's theory of *scientia sexualis,* Frank Mort sees the deployment of sexuality happening in a slightly different manner. Mort claims that it was the professional experts (that is, medical doctors and sanitarians), not the bourgeoisie in general, who "staked out the new field of sexuality" (46). Furthermore, these experts continually concentrated on working-class, not bourgeois, sexuality. In terms of their own class, sanitarians focused not on sexuality, but on what Mort calls "bourgeois hygienics"—that is, "health-giving rituals of moderation . . . which led to population increase and promised cultural and economic ascendancy" (46). Thus for Mort, working-class sexuality plays a primary rather than secondary role in the deployment of sexuality.

7.   For a careful reading of the Contagious Disease Act, see Walkowitz.

8. For the centrality of De Quincey's *Confessions* in the nineteenth-century British imagination, see Hayter 1971, 21. For the prominence of Ann within the *Confessions*, see Hayter 1968, 128-29. See also Montandon, who claims that "le visage d'Ann est devenu rapidement une figure mythique" in nineteenth-century British, French, and German literature (149).

9. De Quincey's need to present himself as asexual or impotent in his *Confessions* possibly partly derives from the criticisms he received, especially from the Wordsworths and Coleridge, for both his use of opium for pleasurable sensation and his marriage to Margaret Simpson, which was seen by the Wordsworths to be a carnal alliance (cf. Hayter 1971, 11 and 13). In each case, De Quincey tries to defend himself against charges of sensual self-indulgence by seeking refuge in infirmity. He claims that he became an opium eater due to terrible stomach ailments, not because he took pleasure in opium intoxication, and he justifies his marriage to Simpson partially on the grounds that he needed a dedicated nurse to help him through his illnesses. Throughout the *Confessions* and his other writings, De Quincey emphasizes his "lost powers," his "sense of powerless and infantine feebleness," and his "mere childish helplessness," thereby underscoring his self-representation as an impotent invalid.

10. For an excellent discussion of the eighteenth-century French libertine convent novel, see Christopher Rivers.

11. For more on seventeenth- and eighteenth-century anticlerical pornography, see Rivers, Roger Thompson 133-55, and Claude Reichler.

12. "There is no part of the body . . . where a wound occasions more intolerable anguish than upon the knee—Except the groin; said my uncle Toby. An' please your honour, replied the corporal, the knee . . . must certainly be the most acute, there being so many tendons . . . the groin is infinitely more sensible [quoth uncle Toby]—there being not only as many tendons . . . but moreover * * *———. . . The dispute was maintained with amicable and equal force betwixt my uncle Toby and Trim for some time . . . So that whether the pain of a wound in the groin . . . is greater than the pain of a wound in the knee . . . are points which to this day remain unsettled" (Sterne 459).

13. Psychic or literal impotence is obviously a significant theme in both De Quincey's *Confessions* and Sterne's *Tristram Shandy*. The image of a nurse/lover curing impotence is also present in Sigmund Freud's *Dora* in the relationship between Dora's father and Frau K. Here many of the elements of the masculine version of the nurse/patient sexual fantasy are present—that is, a powerful male released from adult responsibilities through illness; the cure of chronic impotence; a disinterested nurse/lover; and the nurse/lover as a maternal figure.

14. See, also, my discussion of scavenging during the Crimean War in chapter 5.

15. For discussions of Victorian male sexual fantasies about working-class women see, among numerous examples, Walkowitz, Gallop (144), Davidoff, Stallybrass and White (149-70), Mort, and Marcus.

16. Mark Pattison, the popular Oxford Don, ecclesiastical scholar, and repudiator of the Oxford Movement, was Dorothy Pattison's brother.

17. During the nineteenth century, "spending" was commonplace slang for achieving orgasm. As Richard Miller notes: "the Stuarts called it 'dying,' the Victorians called it 'spending,' and we call it 'coming'" (vi).

18. Descended from gothic and sentimental fiction of the eighteenth and early nineteenth centuries (for example, Ann Radcliffe's *The Mysteries of Udolpho*, Matthew G. Lewis's *The Monk*, Jane Austen's parodic *Northanger Abbey*), the Victorian sensation novel, associated with writers such as Wilkie Collins and Mary Braddon, grew in popularity throughout the 1860s and 1870s. What sets the sensation novel apart from its gothic predecessors is, as Athena Vrettos notes, the transformation of "the haunted mansion of gothic fiction into the Victorian asylum" (1990, 562). Sister Dora's reading of sensation novels during her guarding of the smallpox hospital takes on resonance as the sensation novel particularly emphasizes issues of surveillance, claustrophobia, and imprisonment—especially in medical or medicalized settings (see Collins's *The Woman in White* and D. A. Miller's discussion of this novel 146-91). For an overview of the development of the sensation novel as a genre, see Winifred Hughes.

19. In an engrossing reading of *Wuthering Heights*, Beth Newman also links the "power of the gaze" to domestic surveillance and familial supervision—especially by way of the storyteller Nelly Dean. Yet even though Newman notes that the most authoritative and "Medusa-like" stares belong to Nelly, Cathy, and Catherine Earnshaw, thus allowing them to slip beyond the masculine rule of Wuthering Heights, Newman nonetheless implies that this forceful feminine gaze depicted in Emily Brontë's novel is a usurpation of, or in collusion with, a masculine gaze: "The gaze is not necessarily male (literally), but to own and activate the gaze, given our language and the structure of the unconscious, is to be in the 'masculine' position" (E. Ann Kaplan quoted in Newman 1029).

Chapter 3

1. John Bender goes even further than Gilbert and Gubar or Miller when he connects the carceral with the realist novel at its very core. In a rewriting of Ian Watt's *The Rise of the Novel*, Bender claims that the eighteenth-century novel, especially by way of Daniel Defoe and Henry Fielding, "enabled the penitentiary by formulating, and thereby giving

conscious access to, a real texture of attitudes, a structure of feeling, that I call the 'penitentiary idea'" (2). For Bender, the realist novel and Georgian penology coincide, yet his argument goes beyond mere correlation to posit an intricate causality between the ethical diagrams of the eighteenth-century novel and the growth of a new kind of penal system later in the century.

2. British lunatic asylums dating from the eighteenth century, of which Grimsby's Retreat is possibly an example, were often modeled after, or indeed had been, manor houses like Thornfield. As Bender notes, "the very few specially constructed [eighteenth-century institutions], York [Retreat] for example, resembled grand houses . . . and w[ere] laid out on a domestic plan" (14-15).

3. Although no one has interpreted Ferndean as a site of incarceration in a continuum with Eyre's other domestic/carceral abodes, many readers have been puzzled by its hidden, sylvan locale. Gilbert and Gubar read Ferndean's "quiet autumnal quality" as symbolic of Eyre's and Rochester's removal from a world where "such egalitarian marriages as theirs are rare, if not impossible" (369). Helene Moglen reads the "decaying house buried in the gloomy, tangled forest" as a metaphor for Rochester's "spirit . . . hidden in his broken body" (58). John Maynard sees Ferndean as signifying a retreat into a space of fecund sexuality, the "rich and thick" wood a "massed version of the masculine vitality associated with trees," mingling with the "series of windings and narrow openings" symbolic of female sexuality (141-42).

4. In some ways the differentiation between the masculine "prison" and the feminine "insane asylum" seems spurious both in light of what Foucault calls the "carceral continuum" (1979, 293-308) and also considering that prisons and insane asylums seem to be equally disagreeable places. If a valuative distinction is to be made, the asylum would be a more desirable locale as one is sent there for a cure, while one is sent to prison for punishment and possible execution. Yet Miller points out that this distinction between criminal men and innocently sick women actually reinscribes woman's oppression by reinserting stereotypes of women as unconscious, subjective, or irresponsible.

5. In this story from Acts, chapter 16, Paul receives a vision to preach and convert in Macedonia. He travels to Philippi with Silas and there meets Lydia, a "seller of purple" from Thyatira. Lydia and her household are converted by Paul's preaching and insist on sheltering Paul and Silas in Thyatira. While they are her guests, they expel the "spirit of divination" possessed by a "certain damsel." The female soothsayer's masters are angered by their loss of income from the exorcism, and thus have Paul and Silas beaten and then imprisoned in the city's jail on the basis that "these men, being Jews, do exceedingly trouble our city" (Acts 16:20). Brontë's allusion to this story is interesting due to its twin themes of female madness and imprisonment.

6. These images of the unknown child and the lonely road stem from the song Bessie sings to young Eyre when she's recovering from her red-room fit (see Gilbert and Gubar 363-64). In this ballad, the horrors of the open road and lonesome wandering are illustrated through the "poor orphan child" who "both of shelter and kindred despoiled" walks alone through moors, mountains and marshes. For readings of Eyre's nightmares that differ from mine see, for example, Gilbert and Gubar 357-59; Bodenheimer 108-9; Homas 113-32; or Poovey 1988, 138-42.

7. For other interpretations of Eyre's wandering journey after fleeing Thornfield, see Moglen 47-51; Gilbert and Gubar 363-65 and Maynard 131-33.

8. Bessie Leaven and Maria Temple act as both metaphoric asylum guards and surrogate mothers for Eyre, thus underscoring the novel's confusion of the institutional and the domestic.

9. For a typical dismissal of Eyre's thoughts about Poole see, for example, Maynard 111 and 117. Conversely, Gilbert and Gubar note a correlation between Eyre and Poole (they list Poole along with Adèle Varens and Blanche Ingram as "negative role models" for Eyre) yet they do not develop Eyre's and Poole's affinities beyond their observation that "interestingly" Eyre "cements her bond with Bertha's keeper" when she notes that they are both "uncomely" (351). Numerous essays mention Poole in passing and almost always in connection with either her caretaking of Bertha or her acting as a beard for Bertha. For two recent essays that consider the crucial role of Grace Poole in *Jane Eyre,* see Kate Lawson and Susan Fraiman.

10. Although the quenching of the fire on Rochester's bed overtly appears to symbolize the dousing of sexual desire, the "wet-spot" on the bed actually reinscribes an image of sexual menace since puddles, pools, and standing, brackish water connote degenerate sexuality in *Jane Eyre,* while "floods" or "flowing" water indicate overwhelming passions (cf. note 15). Conversely, sexual repression in *Jane Eyre* typically is signaled through images of "freezing" and "ice," as with St. John Rivers, rather than the dousing of flames with water. Rochester's reluctance to allow Eyre to depart in this scene, even after he verbally grants permission ("Go, then, Jane; go!"), foreshadows his near rape of Eyre on their aborted wedding day.

11. Biographically, Brontë found the model for both Poole's and Eyre's nursing in her own life. As the eldest daughter, Brontë had primary responsibility for her brother's and father's care during their illnesses and simultaneously welcomed and disliked the responsibility. Peters notes that "deeply resenting both Papa's and Branwell's imposition on her freedom, Charlotte could only comfort herself with the belief that duty was a sacred necessity and blame herself when she resented the weight of its yoke" (193). Brontë's nursing of Branwell during his final years of fatal debauchery echoes Poole's relationship with Bertha Mason.

Indeed, Brontë described Branwell as the family phantom, scourge and "skeleton behind the curtain" (Peters 228). Peters claims that Brontë based her portrait of Bertha Mason at least in part on Branwell (212). Eyre's final position of nurse/wife to the partially blinded Rochester possibly stems from Brontë's nursing of her father Patrick before his successful cataract operation in 1846. In 1845, Brontë writes to Constantin Heger that: "My father is well but his sight is almost gone. . . . [He] allows me now to read to him and write for him; he shows me, too, more confidence than he has ever shown before, and that is a great consolation" (quoted in Peters 168).

12. Marian Bailin contends that in Brontë's novels, raw sexual passion: "'a mere fire of dry sticks, blazing up and vanishing' according to Shirley . . . is [often] converted into the more enduring 'passion of solicitude'" (Bailin 1987, 81).

13. This oddly comical colloquy is almost the only dialogue Poole has in the novel, and is possibly inspired by Dickens's nurses Sairey Gamp and Betsy Prig as depicted in his 1843 novel *Martin Chuzzlewit*.

14. The text in the King James translation reads in part: "Now there is at Jerusalem by the sheep *market* a pool, which is called in the Hebrew tongue Bethesda. . . . [Here] lay a great multitude of impotent folk, of blind, halt, withered, waiting for the moving of the water. / For an angel went down at a certain season into the pool, and troubled the water: whosoever then first after the troubling of the water stepped in was made whole of whatsoever disease he had. / And a certain man was there, which had an infirmity thirty and eight years. / When Jesus saw him lie, and knew that he had been now a long time *in that case,* he saith unto him, Wilt thou be made whole? . . . Jesus saith unto him, Rise, take up thy bed, and walk. / And immediately the man was made whole." (John 5:2-9, original emphasis)

15. In naming her old-style nurses "Poole" and "Horsfall," Brontë reiterates the nineteenth-century myth that working-class nurses were often prostitutes who had grown too old to practice their trade. "Horsfall" evokes "whore" and "fallen woman," while Brontë associates puddles, pools, and floods in *Jane Eyre* with transgressive sexuality. During their courtship, Rochester states to Eyre that: "I envy you your peace of mind, your clean conscience, your unpolluted memory. Little girl, a memory without blot or contamination must be an exquisite treasure—an inexhaustible source of pure refreshment. . . . [When I was 18, my memory was] limpid, salubrious; *no gush of bilge water had turned it to a fetid puddle*" (119, my emphasis). Later, when Eyre discovers Rochester's married state, she writes: "That bitter hour cannot be described: in truth,'the waters came into my soul; *I sank in a deep mire:* I felt no standing; I came into deep waters; the floods overflowed me'" (261, my emphasis).

16. Part of the nineteenth century's emphasis on a nurse's ability to watch, guard, and police the patients derives from the persistent conflation of

workhouses, hospitals, insane asylums, and jails, which Foucault calls the "carceral continuum" (1979, 303). Within this conflation or continuum, the nurse becomes an exchangeable worker: at once teacher, prison-guard, surrogate mother, and nurse. For example, Edward B. Pusey writes in 1839 of forming British nursing sisterhoods where the nurses would "be employed in hospitals, lunatic asylums [and] prisons" (quoted in Austin 181).

17. For a detailed discussion of hierarchical surveillance, see Foucault 1979, 195-228.

18. Yet simultaneously, Nightingale wouldn't trust this chain of gazing and was unable to watch only her immediate subordinates. Rather, Nightingale was driven to be everywhere watching everyone at once. As she writes to Elizabeth Herbert in 1855: "alas! I find that under any guardianship less watchful than mine, I can hardly depend on any Nurse" (1990, 113). This compulsive supervision could partially explain Nightingale's years of agoraphobia, as the need to watch everything overwhelmed her and she ended up literally watching or supervising no one except in her head and through her writing.

19. For an excellent discussion of female domestic management, see Langland 45-52.

20. Nightingale continues: "It may be too broad an assertion, and it certainly sounds like a paradox. But I think that in no country are women to be found so deficient in ready and sound observation as in England, while peculiarly capable of being trained to it. The French or Irish woman is too quick of perception to be so sound an observer—the Teuton is too slow to be so ready an observer as the English woman might be . . . " (1860, 69).

21. Embedded in this description of Eyre tending Richard Mason is a delineation of the labor involved in Brontë's own writing of her novel: that is, a cluster of images that captures the "sheer plod" of the act of writing itself. For example, in her account of Brontë's work habits, Elizabeth Gaskell emphasizes Brontë's meticulousness and patience. She also records that Brontë was often "wakeful for hours in the night" while she was in the midst of a writing project (quoted in Brontë 1977, 415). From this point of view, the basin of blood and water might represent ink, wiping the "trickling gore" evoke the wiping of a pen, and Mason's white lips embody the blank page. The image of Eyre offering the stimulating salts "again and again" could point to Brontë's own incorporation of action and sensation into her realist narratives, for her first novel, *The Professor,* had been rejected for publication precisely because it lacked "thrilling excitement" or "stimulating salts": "I offered [*The Professor*] to a publisher. He said . . . such a work would not sell. I tried six publishers in succession; they all told me it was deficient in 'startling incident' and 'thrilling excitement,' that it would never suit the circulating libraries" (quoted in Gaskell 1975, 419).

22. Nancy Armstrong, for example, examines the question of why Charlotte and Emily Brontë "should occupy a place of such prominence in the British cultural consciousness" (186), which she believes derives from their skill at "formulating universal forms of subjectivity" and converting history into desire (186-224). Raymond Williams states that with the Brontës there came an "emphasis on intense feeling, a commitment to what we must directly call passion, that is in itself very new in the English novel" (1984, 60).

23. In 1855, Margaret Oliphant writes that "suddenly, without warning, *Jane Eyre* stole upon the scene, and the most alarming revolution of modern times has followed th[is] invasion" (quoted in Gilbert and Gubar 337). In 1848, Elizabeth Rigg wrote of Brontë's "proud and perpetual assertion of the rights of man . . . [and her] pervading tone of ungodly discontent . . . We do not hesitate to say that the tone of mind and thought which has overthrown authority . . . is the same which has also written *Jane Eyre*" (quoted in Brontë 1977, 452).

24. Dr. John tells Lucy to "'go with the women, Lucy; they seem but dull; you can at least direct their movements, and thus spare her some pain. She must be touched very tenderly'" (345).

Chapter 4

1. Elizabeth Barrett Browning writes to Gaskell: "I am grateful to you as a woman for having treated such a subject—was it quite impossible but that your Ruth should *die?* I had that thought of regret in closing the book" (Barrett Browning's emphasis, quoted in Gerin 140).

2. See, for example, George Watt's "The Fallen Woman in Nineteenth Century Fiction."

3. See Gallagher 1985, 44.

4. Hawthorne's *The Scarlet Letter* was Gaskell's acknowledged inspiration for *Ruth.*

5. For an extended discussion of the relationship between the Victorian fashion industry and prostitution see Valverde.

6. For an excellent reading of the class contradictions generated by the figure of the Victorian governess, see Poovey 1988, 126-63.

7. For a reading of Gaskell's self-consciousness as a writer in *Ruth* that differs from mine, see Hilary Schor 169-72. For an interesting reading of secrecy and sexuality in *Ruth* see Jill L. Matus 113-31.

8. Gaskell is not unique in uniting sewing and nursing as analogies for imaginative labor. In *Jane Eyre*, Grace Poole's identity as Bertha Mason's nurse is masked through her ostensible occupation as household seamstress. In Dickens's *Our Mutual Friend*, Jenny Wren, a character whom Garrett Stewart claims "symbolize(s) the Dickensian

fancy at its most versatile," is both the dolls' dressmaker and a redemptive sick-nurse (199). In *To the Lighthouse* and *Mrs Dalloway*, Virginia Woolf emphasizes and unites both nursing and sewing (or knitting) in the characters of the knitting nurse in Hyde Park, Lucrezia Warren Smith, and Mrs. Ramsey. For Woolf, Brontë, and Dickens, these nursing/sewing characters stand as images for the labor of writing itself.

9.   See, for example, Emily Dickinson's "spider" poems and an excellent reading of those poems and the general theme of sewing and women's art in Dickinson by Gilbert and Gubar, 633-42.

10.   For extended discussions of the weaving trope in literature, see Gilbert and Gubar 581-650 and Gerhard Joseph.

11.   In one letter she records that "I . . . was writing away vigorously at Ruth when the Wedgewoods, Etc. came: and I was sorry, *very* sorry to give it up my heart being so full of it, in a way which I can't bring back. That's *that*" (Gaskell's emphasis, quoted in Stoneman 37). For more on Victorian female authors' self-doubts, see Elaine Showalter 1977 and Gilbert and Gubar, especially chapters 15 and 16.

12.   This pattern can also be seen in Christine Rossetti's *Maude*.

13.   "[A] woman in the city, which was a sinner, when she knew that Jesus sat at meat in the Pharisee's house . . . stood at his feet behind him weeping, and began to wash his feet with tears, and did wipe them with the hairs of her head" (Luke 7:37-38).

Chapter 5

1.   The announcement for her Aldershot store was placed fortuitously as Seacole's memoirs are remarkable in part because they represent female appropriation of a typically male genre—the war memoirs used by the author of the *Green Hand*, while the "Joint Stock" company echoes Seacole's own interest in entrepreneurial endeavors.

2.   In 1856, Aldershot was a newly created army base located in an ancient Hampshire hamlet thirty-five miles southwest of London. As a garrison town, Aldershot was to be the site of one of the enactments of the Contagious Diseases Acts of the 1860s.

3.   See, for example, Gibbs 100. See, also Tennyson's famous propaganda for entering the war at the end of *Maude* and Punch's ironic reply to *Maude* in "The Laureate's View of the War."

4.   In his dispatches from the Crimean War, William Howard Russell comments that Scutari was "a place then about to acquire a *sad notoriety* as the headquarters of death and sickness and an *immortal interest* as the principal scene of the devoted labours of Florence Nightingale" (Russell's emphasis 1966, 34).

5. It was the criminal ineptitude of the Crimean War that inspired Dickens's angry tone in *Little Dorrit* (1857) as well as his creation of the satiric "office of circumlocution" in that novel. For a detailed account of Dickens's response to the Crimean War, see Ackroyd 707, 718-19, and 733-35.

6. The Crimean War is often considered the first "modern" war as not only was it the first photographed war, but the Black Sea Cable enabled journalists like Russell to send frequent bulletins from the front. An English surgeon, George Lawson, wrote to his family on April 30, 1855, that "the Electric Telegraph across the Black Sea has now been completed. It extends from St. George's Monastery on the shore, to some place near Varna. From there it is carried to Bucharest, where it becomes continuous with the line from Vienna. News will therefore be forwarded to England in a very short space of time, and you will be able to hear in the evening what we have been doing in the Crimea in the morning. The space of time to transmit a message will, I think, be 6 or 7 hours" (193, fn 6). See, also Gernsheim and Savulēscu.

7. Soyer was the chef of the Reform Club, the bastion of London's Whig Progressives. In February 1848, he was officially invited to Dublin to establish and supervise the distribution of government soup (see Soyer). James Morris speculates that during the famine "perhaps never before, at least since the Middle Ages, had a corner of Europe been so horribly devastated. The hospitals, the workhouses, the prisons were packed with starving destitutes. . . . Probably a million people died in the Great Famine—most of them from the diseases of malnutrition" (Morris 154-55). Soyer's soup kitchens at the Crimean front no doubt evoked parallels in the English imagination between the mistreatment and mismanagement of the British troops during the war and the English government's insubstantial response to, and responsibility for, the Irish famine just a few years earlier. Ironically, many of the starving soldiers at the Crimean front were in fact Irish economic refugees: "perhaps a majority of the enlisted soldiers of the British Army were Irish Catholics—*St Patrick's Day* was the most familiar of all the Army's marching songs" (Morris, 159). Further, the £70 million spent by the British government on the Crimean War vastly overshadowed the £9 million spent in response to the Irish Famine.

8. Other famous, or notorious, women who participated in the Crimean War along with Seacole and Nightingale include Mrs. Duberly, Mrs. Rogers, Mary Stanley, Frances Margaret Taylor, Lady Alicia Blackwood, and Dr. James Barry. Ziggi Alexander and Audrey Dewjee note that Barry "qualified at Edinburgh in 1812 and joined the army as a Regimental Surgeon in the following year. Dr. Barry masqueraded as a man and kept her secret until her death. . . . At the time [of the Crimean War, Dr. Barry] was stationed on Corfu. . . . she defied her superiors by going to the front on three months' leave to care for the maimed and diseased in

the camps" (17-18). See Summers 1988, Cooper, Blackwood, Wells, Taylor, and Duberly.

9.   Sydney Herbert, characterized by G. M. Young as a "haughty Border lord" (4), was a Peelite, a talented Cabinet Member, and Secretary of War at the start of the Crimean conflict. Both Herbert and his wife Elizabeth were close friends of Nightingale, having known her for seven years before the outbreak of the war. It was at the Herberts' suggestion that Nightingale formulated her plan for nursing in Scutari. Nightingale shared with the Herberts a passionate commitment to civilian and military medical reform, and their partnership continued after the war's end.

10.   See, also, Seacole 89-90. For discussions of English racial prejudice in the mid nineteenth century, see, for example Elsie Michie 46-78, Bolt, Gregory, Barker, and Ferguson. For race politics in the Caribbean, see Heuman and Sio.

11.   Morris contends that "at heart . . . nearly every Briton considered as his organic inferior everyone who was not white—the less white, the more inferior. Even educated people seldom bothered to hide their racial prejudices" (448-49).

12.   On the other hand, "the regular canteens . . . were kept by a better class of people" (41).

13.   The "Seacole Fund," started sometime around April 11, 1857, was administered by William T. Doyne, Esq. It seems never to have garnered a great deal of donations (see, for example, Thomas Day's letter to the *Times* on April 14, 1857, where he expresses fear that the donations will be limited to a few hundred pounds). This is in sharp contrast to the Nightingale Fund into which poured thousands of pounds. For a history of the Nightingale Fund, see Baly 1986.

14.   For the festival, regimental bands combined with a conventional orchestra to play patriotic, military, and camp music, accompanied by a large chorus and several renowned soloists.

15.   As many as 80,000 Londoners may have attended Seacole's musical benefit over its four-day run.

16.   The *Punch* title the "Mother of the Regiment" is a play on Gaetano Donizetti's opera "La Fille du Regiment," then having a record-breaking revival in London with Jenny Lind in the role of Marie the vivandière. Lind's popularity gave *Punch* more occasion for punning on names as they also insinuated comparisons between Florence Nightingale and "the Swedish Nightingale" as Lind was called.

17.   Seacole writes that "we set to work bravely at Aldershott [sic] to retrieve our fallen fortunes, and stem off the ruin originated in the Crimea . . . at last defeated by fortune, but not I think disgraced, we were obliged to capitulate on very honourable conditions. . . . Perhaps it would be right if I were to express more shame and annoyance than I really feel at the pecuniarily disastrous issue of my Crimean adventures, but I cannot. . . .

When I would try and feel ashamed of myself for being poor and helpless, I only experience a glow of pride at the other and more pleasing events of my career . . ." (197-98).

18. Alexander and Dewjee note that "from the 1830s, black Jamaicans were encouraged to consider themselves to be as British as any citizen in Yorkshire or Midlothian" (12).

19. For a discussion of English reaction to the Indian Mutiny, see Paxton.

20. Joseph Kestner asserts that classical mythology "permeated Victorian discourse" (5).

21. The *Agamemnon,* a new steam battleship, was one of the most important ships in the Crimean War. The naval siege of Sebastopol centered around this flagship.

22. The Dardanelles is the strait that connects the Aegean Sea with the Sea of Marmara and divides the Gallipoli Peninsula of European Turkey from Asiatic Turkey. Also known as the Hellespont, it is the site of the legend of Hero and Leander. The strategic importance of both the Dardanelle and Bosporus straits have been crucial since antiquity. Ancient Troy flourished near the west entrance of the Hellespont.

23. Among other allusions, Russell evokes Thucydides to characterize the conduct of the English and French soldiers during the cholera epidemic as "recklessness verging on insanity" (W. H. Russell 1966, 54). Russell further describes the meadow frogs whose "concerts by day and night would delight the classical scholar who remembered his Aristophanes" (45); depicts the Turkish soil as "just as scratched up by ploughs rather inferior to those described by Virgil 1,800 years ago" (37); and states that Lord Raglan "was brave as a hero of antiquity" (80). In describing the construction of the English camp in Balaklava, Russell writes that "the English Hercules at last began to stir about the heels of the oxen of Augæus" (177), and compares the English siege-works to "a kind of Penelope's web" (178). See, also, Florence Nightingale's letters from Scutari where she images that Athena appears to her and where she compares the war to a Greek tragedy: "I saw Athena last night. She came to see me. I was walking home late . . . when Athena came along the cliff quite to my feet, rose upon her tiptoes, bowed several times, made her long melancholy cry, & fled away—like the shade of Ajax—I assure you my tears followed her" (1987b, 102) and "the whole of this gigantic misfortune has been like a Greek tragedy—it has been like the fates pursuing us—every thing that has been done has been a failure & nobody knows the reason why—the Gods have punished with blindness some past sin & visited the innocent with the consequences . . ." (1987b, 103).

24. Along with many verse quotations (cf. pp. 7, 13, 114, 126, 134), Seacole also alludes to Sterne's *Tristram Shandy* (15); the legend of Hero and Leander (85); the *Arabian Nights* (110-11); the Hebrew Bible (165-66); and Burns's *Tam O'Shanter* (123). Further, Seacole recounts her role as

English teacher to the Turkish ruler Omar Pacha, which formed a basis for a "lasting friendship" (cf. pp. 110-11). Seacole also displays a sophisticated understanding of contemporary political issues in her narrative. Her literacy was not an anomaly. The world of free black urban boarding-house owners formed a respectable middle-class caste in early- and mid-nineteenth-century Jamaica and other Caribbean islands such as Trinidad (Alexander and Dewjee, 9-10). See, also, William Makepeace Thackeray's brief, racist portrait of the heiress Miss Swartz ("the rich woolly-haired mulatto from St. Kitts") sent to Miss Pinkerton's academy for young ladies in England (she is charged "double" for her education) in the opening chapter of *Vanity Fair.*

25. The Homeric and Herodotean patterns of war narrative exist in counter-distinction to Thucydides's methodology that, as George Steiner points out, recounts the Pelaponnesian conflict with a threefold narrative purpose: (1) to narrate the events leading up to the conflict, (2) to analyze both overt and covert causes of the war, and (3) to offer "moral insight into the violence, blinding illusions, cumulative inevitability of great wars" (86). Steiner argues that Thucydides's "uniquely intricate" approach to war narrative "has marked all serious philosophies and sociologies of warfare since" (88).

26. My reading of Odysseus owes a debt to both Paul Zweig's *The Adventurer* and Max Horkheimer and Theodor W. Adorno's discussion of Odysseus in their *Dialectic of Enlightenment* (43-80).

27. For a twentieth-century Afro-Caribbean rewriting of the *Iliad* see Derek Walcott's epic poem *Omeros* (New York: Noonday Press, 1990). Furthermore, Walcott has recently adapted the *Odyssey* for the stage, giving his verse play an Afro-Caribbean emphasis. Walcott's birthplace, the island St. Lucia, is known as the "Helen of the West," because it has been fought over by so many European countries.

28. Gates bases his concept of the talking book on Bahktin's notion of "double-voiced" discourse.

29. See, also, Seacole's statements that: "it is not my intention to dwell at any length upon the recollections of my childhood" (2); "it is all very well to smile at these [disasters] now, but at the time they were heartrending enough" (118); and "although I can laugh at my fears now—I was often most horribly frightened at Spring Hill . . ." (121).

30. White Jamaican racism would again cause a sensational uproar in England during the Governor Eyre scandal of 1864, yet another ignominious event that emphasized the continuation of Jamaica's repressive and racist institutions. See Semmel 1963.

31. Ward offers another example of the connection of the siege of Sebastapol with ancient sieges when he comments that "no doubt there was a good deal going on in Carthage, while Hannibal was besieging Rome, which one could not but be reminded of last winter; but that was not (*so the Crimean campaign shows*) peculiar to blacks" (Ward's emphasis,

274). For an extended nineteenth-century re-creation of the siege of Carthage, see Gustave Flaubert's *Salammbô*.

32. See Horkheimer and Adorno 45-46.

33. E. J. Hobsbawn writes that with the California gold rush, the need for a shorter route from Europe, the Caribbean, and the east coast of the United States to California was "overwhelming," and that this need was answered by the redevelopment of trade routes through the Isthmus of Panama: "the Isthmus of Panama once again became what it had been in Spanish colonial times, the major point of trans-shipment, at least until the building of an isthmian canal which was . . . begun—against American opposition—by the maverick French Saint-Simonian de Lesseps, fresh from his triumph at Suez, in the 1870s" (65-66). Hobsbawn recounts that prior to the construction of the Panama Canal, "the United States government fostered a mail service across the Isthmus of Panama, thus making possible the establishment of a regular monthly steamer service from New York to the Caribbean side and from Panama to San Francisco and Oregon. The scheme, essentially started in 1848 for political and imperial purposes, became commercially more than viable with the gold-rush. Panama became what it has remained, a Yankee-owned boom town, where future robber barons like Commodore Vanderbilt and W. Ralston . . . cut their teeth. The saving of time was so enormous that the isthmus soon became the crossroads of international shipping . . ." (66).

34. Similarly, on her journey to the Crimean battlefield, Seacole stops at the marketplace in Gibraltar where she stands "curiously watching its strange and motley population" (83).

35. Alexander and Dewjee write that Seacole "is not an obvious heroine for modern times. While her snobbery and coyness are counterbalanced by many fine qualities, less endearing are her prejudices against Native Americans, Greeks and Turks, and her glorification of war. In addition, although it is clear from the text that she was proud of her origins, sometimes she conveys contradictory feelings about her status as a black woman" (9). See also Paquet's reading of Seacole.

36. For many sarcastic letters written by Nightingale concerning Hall, see Nightingale 1987.

37. For Seacole's praise of Nightingale, see Seacole 87-91. Although Seacole recites the stock praises of Nightingale's "immortal" deeds ("that Englishwoman whose name shall never die, but sound like music on the lips of British men until the hour of doom" 91), she offers oblique criticism in terms of Nightingale's snobbery, fragility, and possible racism (cf. 78-79, 89-91, and 148).

38. Wilma R. Bailey writes that among the English Army bases on Jamaica, "Port Royal and Fort Augusta, both on dry, sandy peninsulas, had low morbidity and mortality rates. So did the camp at Stony Hill, at an elevation of over 1,250 feet. On the other hand, the troops quartered on

the coastal lowlands at Parade, Up Park Camp, Rockfort and Castile Fort suffered greatly. . . . Up Park Camp [was] disease-ridden . . . [and] the mortality among the men of the 82nd Regiment stationed there was very high" (29 and 31).

39.   On May 8, 1857, Seacole writes that she "believes there will yet be work for her to do somewhere. Perhaps China, perhaps on some other distant shore to which Englishmen go to serve their country, there may be woman's work to do" (quoted in *Punch,* May 30, 1857). The London *Times* reported on July 28, 1857, that "in an interview with the Secretary of War which took place yesterday . . . Mrs. Seacole expressed her desire to set out immediately for India. 'Give me,' said the excellent old lady, 'my needle and thread, my medicine chest, my bandages, my probe and scissors, and I'm off.'" For Nightingale's devotion to the British Army, especially the British Army in India, see Nightingale 1990.

Chapter 6

1.   Eliot writes to Charles Ritter that "*Middlemarch* seems to have made a deep impression in our own country, and . . . the critics are as polite and benevolent as possible to me. . . ." (Eliot 1954-1978, 5:374).

2.   *Romola* was never a very popular novel, yet certain readers felt it to be Eliot's most important work. In 1881, John Crombie Brown writes that "few things in the literary history of the age are more puzzling than the reception given to 'Romola' by a novel-devouring public . . . to probably the majority of readers, even of average intelligence and capability, it was, and still is, nothing but a weariness. With the more thoughtful, on the other hand, it took at once its rightful place, not merely as by far the finest and highest of all the author's works, but as perhaps the greatest and most perfect work of fiction of its class ever till then produced" (J. Brown 31). Nightingale was among the party of Victorian intellectuals who found *Romola* to be a remarkably significant novel. In his introduction to *Romola,* Andrew Brown also includes in this group Robert Browning, Tennyson, Gladstone, F. D. Maurice, Millais, Mazzini, the Trollope brothers, and Nightingale's fiancé Richard Monckton Milnes (A. Brown xliv-xlv).

3.   For a discussion of the debate between aesthetic idealism and realism see Gallagher 1985, 219-22. See also Eliot's statement in "Leaves from a Note-book" where she writes that "to lay down in the shape of practical moral rules courses of conduct only to be made real by the rarest states of motive and disposition, tends not to elevate but to degrade the general standard, by turning that rare attainment from an object of admiration into an impossible prescription, against which the average nature first rebels and then flings out ridicule. It is for art to present

images of a lovelier order than the actual, gently winning the affections, and so determining the taste" (n.d., 208).

4. Octavia Hill (1838-1912) was a "connection of the author" because her sister Gertrude married George Lewes's son Charles Lee Lewes in March 1865. Hill was the leader of the British open-space movement and an innovator in housing reform who established, initially with the financial help of John Ruskin, housing for the poor in the slums of London.

5. In *Middlemarch*, Eliot explores the topic of vocational confusion, a theme particularly played out in the stories of Dorothea Brooke, Will Ladislaw, Fred Vincy, and Mary Garth. Eliot presents these characters in opposition to the (mistakenly) smug Celia Brooke, James Chettam, Rosamund Vincy, and Tertius Lydgate—all of whom know exactly what they want and feel self-confident that they have chosen the correct paths in life. Conversely, Will, Dorothea, Fred, and Mary spend much of the novel trying to avoid the "fatal step of choosing the wrong profession." For Fred and Will, their vocational crises stem from a superabundance of choices. For Dorothea and Mary, it is a question of limited expecta-tions. Mary Garth asserts that she must "go to the school at York . . . I am less unfit to teach in a school than in a family. . . . And, you see, I must teach; *there is nothing else to be done*" (400, my emphasis). As a middle-class woman, Mary's vocational options include becoming a governess, a teacher, or a paid companion. As an heiress, "buried alive" in the "oppressive liberty" of the "gentlewoman's world" (274), Eliot characterizes Dorothea as both more and less constrained than Mary—less in that she has the means to do what she likes, more constrained in that as an heiress she should not work at all. *Middlemarch's* narrator states that the one suitable occupation for heiresses—domestic and "feminine fine art"—consisted only of "small tinkling and smearing . . . at that dark period" (65). Although Eliot does not represent nursing as a potential solution to Dorothea's search for heroic vocation, nonethe-less nursing does play a cardinal role in the novel. Many of the female characters in *Middlemarch* spend time nursing: Mrs. Vincy, Dorothea, Mrs. Bulstrode, Mary Garth, and Mrs. Able all tend the sickroom at crucial moments. Furthermore, as in *Vanity Fair,* faulty nursing becomes the vehicle for murder, thereby putting nursing at the center of the novel's plot.

6. See also Martha Vicinus, chapters 2 and 3.

7. Nightingale's dogged antipathy towards *Middlemarch* can also in part be ascribed to a perceived personal insult towards her family, her close friend Charles Bracebridge, and towards herself. In Dorothea Brooke, Nightingale might have seen the rewriting of her own life. Although they met only a few times, there are a series of connections between Eliot and Nightingale that suggest the possibility that the Brooke family in *Middlemarch* was based to some degree on the Nightingale family. As the leading intellectual women of their age, Nightingale and Eliot knew

many of the same people and had met each other before the Crimean War through Nightingale's favorite aunt, Mai Smith. Eliot first encountered Nightingale in 1852. In a letter to Sara Hennell, Eliot writes: "[Mai] Smith *had* called on me before she received your letter of introduction, and Miss Florence Nightingale with her. I like them both . . . They came again last night with Miss Carter, your Hilary—and Madame Mohl . . ." (1954-1978, 2:39). One month later Eliot again writes to Hennell that "my talk the evening Miss Carter was at Mr. Chapman's was chiefly with Miss Nightingale and [Mai] Smith" (1954-1978 2:45).

Aside from many casual mutual acquaintances, five of Eliot's most intimate friends were people who had ties to Nightingale and her family. Sara Sophia Hennell, Eliot's close friend since 1842, had been Hilary Bonham Carter's governess and remained very intimate with her former pupil. Bonham Carter was Nightingale's first cousin and, after Aunt Mai, Nightingale's dearest relative. In 1852, Eliot befriended Barbara Leigh Smith Bodichon, another of Nightingale's first cousins. Although Haight claims that Nightingale and her other cousins ostracized the Leigh Smith cousins because they were illegitimate and therefore the "tabooed family," this doesn't actually seem to be true (Haight 105). Mary Clarke Mohl, less intimate with Eliot than Hennell or Bodichon, was nonetheless a good friend with whom Eliot spent time whenever she was in Paris. Mohl, or "Clarky," was Nightingale's lifelong confidante. Both Eliot and Nightingale were also intimate with Harriet Martineau and Benjamin Jowett, who served as a spiritual advisor to both women. Eliot could have gathered details of Nightingale's early life and family through any of these people.

Eliot and Nightingale also shared another connection—Charles Bracebridge. The Bracebridges were Nightingale's strongest supporters during her rebellious years when she attempted to break from her family and become a nurse and public- health reformer. She traveled with them in Europe and Egypt, and they chaperoned her during the Crimean War. After the publication of *Scenes from Clerical Life* and *Adam Bede,* all of England was speculating on the identity of "George Eliot." Some believed that the real author was an impoverished cleric named Liggins, and no one advocated this more than Bracebridge. Once Eliot's true identity was revealed, however, Bracebridge became even more painfully meddlesome due, in great part, to Nightingale's father William. Although Eliot was born and raised in Warwickshire, Eliot's father and the Nightingale family were from the same part of Derbyshire on the Derwent River, a coincidence that was to have some repercussions in Eliot's life after she wrote *Adam Bede.* While visiting the Nightingales in Derbyshire, Bracebridge (along with William Nightingale) got caught up in tracking down the original models of the *Adam Bede* characters. Among their findings, they decided that William Nightingale's tailor's wife (Eliot's first cousin) was actually a daughter of the "original" Dinah (Eliot's Aunt Elizabeth Evans) and they claimed that Eliot had copied Dinah's sermons out of Elizabeth Evans's papers. Eliot was very disturbed by all of these snoopings. In 1859, she writes of the "prevaricating and low-minded imbecility of Mr. Bracebridge's letters," and characterizes Bracebridge as "so nearly an idiot, that it would not be safe to predict his mental processes" (1954-1978 3:166). Gordon S. Haight asserts that the Evans family maintained close ties to their Derbyshire relatives (4), and here Eliot sets *Adam Bede,* hearing in her head the accents of her father's family: "the dialect of Lisbeth in 'Adam Bede' arose from her occasionally hearing her father when with his brothers revert to the dialect of his native district, Derbyshire" (1954-1978 3:427).

Although Eliot's portrait of Arthur Brooke obviously derives from the cultural and literary stereotype of the dilettante gentleman, there are some specific connections between both Bracebridge and William Nightingale in Mr. Brooke. Haight implies that Eliot based her depiction of Arthur Brooke in part on Bracebridge (284), no doubt for a bit of revenge. Yet there are also connections between Arthur Brooke and William Nightingale. Vicinus and Nergaard describe William Nightingale as a "charming dilettante whose chief interest was in speculative problems" (14). In *Reputation and Power,* F. B. Smith quotes Florence Nightingale's own assessment of her father as, "a man who has never known what struggle is . . . & having never by circumstance been forced to look into anything, to carry it out (19)." Smith posits that had William Nightingale "succeeded in entering Parliament in 1835 he might have found a focus for his abilities" (19). He then notes that Nightingale privately felt her father to be a weak, inexpressive man who felt "utter indifference to me—he never cared *what I was* or *what I might become* (19)." Thereby paralleling Arthur Brooke's indifference to Dorothea's fate.

Further echoes of the Nightingale family come through Dorothea and Celia. Nightingale and her sister Parthenope were not orphans being raised by an uncle, but the configuration of two sisters, one an idealist and the other a pragmatist, also fits the Nightingale family. Nightingale herself characterized Parthenope as being "in unison with her age, her position, her country" and she saw her sister as "a child playing in God's garden & delighting in the happiness of all His works, knowing nothing of human life but the English drawing room" (1990, 47). In 1852, Parthenope writes to Mary Clarke Mohl of Nightingale's relationship with their aunt Mai Smith: "Now Aunt Mai is the person she loves the best in the world, and whose metaphysical mind suits her best . . ." (1990, 56). Like Celia, Parthenope married a wealthy baronet, Sir Harry Verney, who had originally evinced an interest in her sister: "In the summer of 1857 . . . a tall, exceedingly handsome, rich, benevolent, charming and altogether remarkable baronet began to pay frequent calls [on Florence Nightingale]. He was a widower of fifty-six, a Liberal MP, the owner of a large estate in Buckinghamshire where he had built model cottages, founded schools and devoted himself to improving the lot of the rural poor. . . . Sir Harry Verney proposed to Florence [and was rejected]. . . . [Florence Nightingale's mother Fanny] invited him to Embley to console him for his rejection, and he proceeded to transfer his affections to Parthe" (Huxley 168). Verney, like Chettam, remained interested in Nightingale's plans even after his marriage to her sister. Unlike Sir James Chettam, however, Sir Harry was a great deal older than Parthenope and they never had children.

Dorothea shares some obvious traits with Nightingale such as her idealism and interest in architecture and sanitary reform. Commentators today rarely mention Dorothea without comparing her to Nightingale. Nightingale's mother Fanny is known to have said "we are ducks who have hatched a wild swan" (Strachey 141). It is possible that Eliot is remembering this phrase when she characterizes the occurrence of would-be St. Teresas in England as "Here and there a cygnet is reared uneasily among the ducklings in the brown pond" (viii). Although we can never know if the Brooke family is indeed a rewriting of the Nightingales, the parallels are indeed remarkable.

8.   Although *Romola* is considered to be Eliot's only "historical novel," the interval between Scott's Scotland of 1801 and *Waverly*'s setting of 1741 is only sixty years. Indeed, many of the "Waverly" novels are set back by only a generation. Likewise, *Adam Bede* is placed seventy years earlier than the time of its writing, while *Middlemarch* has a gap of forty years. Thus Eliot most likely viewed her novels, with the exception of *Daniel Deronda*, as historical novels. See Semmel 1994, 4.

9.   Most obviously, there was Queen Victorian (1819-1901) who came to the throne in 1837, as well as Elizabeth Fry (1780-1845), Harriet Martineau (1802-76), Mary Wollstonecraft Shelley (1797-1851), Caroline Norton (1808-77), Jane Austen (1775-1817), Elizabeth Inchbald (1753-1821), Maria Edgeworth (1767-1849), Frances Trollope (1780-1863), and many other intellectual, philanthropic, and literary women whose works were familiar to Eliot and could presumably have served as models for Dorothea Brooke. In 1840, for example, Eliot writes to Maria Lewis of visiting the "tasteless monument to the learned and brilliant female pedant of Litchfield [Anna] Seward" (1747-1809) (1954-1978, 1:55). In 1838, she writes to Lewis that she has "highly enjoyed Hannah More's (1745-1833) letters; the contemplation of so blessed a character as hers is very salutary" (1954-1978, 1:7, although Eliot later repudiates More, cf. 1954-1978, 1:245). In another letter to Lewis, while discussing "those purifying fires that burn within," Eliot writes that she "cannot refrain from writing some lines of [the English poet Felicia Dorothea Browne Hemans's (1793-1835)], very pet lines of mine" (1954-1978, 1:75). Dorothea Barrett points out a similar contra-

diction in *Romola* in that Eliot represents Romola's desire to find a heroic vocation as being thwarted by gender prejudices and limitations that seem to make female heroism impossible. Yet simultaneously, the narrator mentions Cassandra Fedele (1465-1558), the distinguished Venetian classical scholar, poet, and philosopher. Barrett notes that by evoking Fedele, Eliot undermines her assertion of Romola's victimization at the hands of history because of her gender: "just as in *Middlemarch* the invisible presence of George Eliot as female vocational success casts doubt on the historical and biological determinism of Dorothea's failure to find a vocation, so in *Romola* the mention of a female historical figure preempts deterministic conclusions" (D. Barrett 88). For more on Fedele (although Eliot spells her name "Fidele" in *Romola,* she is more commonly known as "Cassandra Fedele") see Fedele or Tomasini. Information concerning Fedele is sparse. For example, she is absent from most modern Anglo-American dictionaries, biographies, and encyclopedias, although reference to her can be found in late-nineteenth-century French and Italian encyclopedias.

10. Levine further argues that "the idealists, even in their purest rational ideas of order, become irrational forces of nature. Seeking to impose an idea on the multifariousness of history and experience, they lose control of self and of others." For admission to the realist novel, these "monstrous energies" must be contained (1981, 205).

11. Enthusiasm for Nightingale's heroism was not limited to men. For a literary woman who championed Nightingale's path, see, for example, Elizabeth Gaskell's letters to friends and family extolling Nightingale's nursing (1967, 305-10; 314; 316-21; 327; 358-59; 376-78; 382-83; 402-3; 522; 587-89). See, also, Gaskell's letter where she recounts her response to her daughter's wish to become a nurse, chapter 2 above.

12. Other mid-Victorian moderate-voiced "wisdom writers" include John Stuart Mill, Harriet Martineau, William Thackeray, and Elizabeth Gaskell.

13. Although Nightingale remained a member of the Church of England throughout her life, her evangelical passions were directed after the 1840s towards science's ability to alleviate human suffering and create a utopic society, especially through public-health reform. In this sense, Nightingale's work exemplifies the positivist agenda of a secular humanitarianism coupled with rational, scientific principles. Eliot's relationship with positivism is more enigmatic. Both Eliot and George Henry Lewes were affiliated with the English positivist circle. Indeed, their essays on Comte and their strong friendships with English positivist such as Maria Congreve and Frederic Harrison "led to [them] being identified as Positivist[s] by much of the British public" (Semmel 1994, 10). Semmel notes the contention among commentators "concerning the significance of Eliot's attraction to Comtism," especially the ways in which "Eliot's 'conservative-reforming' impulse has been identi-

fied with that of Comte" (1994, 8-9). However, Semmel points out that Eliot's embracing of Comte's philosophy was highly qualified: [Eliot] was torn between attraction to certain Comtian views . . . and her determined resistance to Comte's authoritarianism and ideological formulas" (1994, 10).

14. Beatrice Webb recounts how in the mid-nineteenth-century England, "the impulse of self-subordinating service was transferred, consciously and overtly, from God to man." Webb traces this shift in the conception of moral duty to the influence of positivism (see Semmel 1994, 10). Indeed, it was above all in Eliot's humanitarianism that she was seen to be most affiliated with positivism. Semmel notes that "Lord Acton . . . insisted that Eliot, unlike Lewes, revered not so much the philosophical Comte but the 'dogmatising and emotional' Comte of the *Politique,* and that this attachment was a 'yoke' that she never shook off," and further that "Herbert Spencer believed that Eliot was especially attached to Comte's religion of humanity" (1994, 9). Indeed, Semmel asserts that "Eliot certainly approved Comte's stress on a sense of moral duty based on feelings of sympathetic altruism" (1994, 10).

15. In November of 1845, Nightingale decided to spend three months training at the Salisbury Infirmary near her Embley Park home. Her parents forbade this plan, plunging Nightingale into a deep depression. On December 5, she recorded in her diary that:

> As for me, all my hopes for this winter are gone & all my plans destroyed. . . . [B]etween the destruction of one idea & the taking up of another I can understand now how a soul can die. . . . God has something for me to do for him—or he would have let me die some time ago. . . . [N]ow I am dust & nothing—worse than nothing—a curse to myself & others. This morning I felt as if my soul would pass away in tears—in utter loneliness. . . . Oh for some great thing to sweep this loathsome life into the past. (1990, 28-30)

16. Nightingale's essay *Cassandra* is a section from the second volume of *Suggestions for Thought.* See Mary Poovey's useful introduction (Poovey 1992).

17. The *Punch* poem "Scutari" characterizes Nightingale as

> A steady radiance: breathing balm . . .
> Investing death with hallowed calm,
> Taking the sting from pain . . .
> God guard thee, noble woman; still
> Wear the saint's glory round thy brow,
> Let bigots call thee as they will,
> What Christ preached, doest thou.

18. See, for example, Nightingale 1860, fn pp. 113-14.

19. For a detailed discussion of Eliot's "politics of compromise," see Semmel 1994, 78-102. Similarly, Semmel charts Eliot's move from "rigid Calvinism to an equally doctrinaire free thought . . . to a species of positivism, primarily in the early 1850s . . . and, finally, to what she probably saw as the nonideological position of the politics of national inheritance" (1994, 11).

20. For example, Bailin writes that "the purity and ease of action in the sickroom is made possible in effect by the passivity of both nurse and patient" (1994, 117) and that both nurse and patient are "outside of or beyond the entanglements of interest and desire which obstruct the moral relations of man to man in the world of the healthy" (1994, 117).

21. Both Agatha in "Agatha," and Janet Dempster in "Janet's Repentance" display their noble or redeemed natures through their nursing, while Romola, a character who prefigures Dorothea in her search for intellectual and spiritual vocation and in her need to "reconcile self-despair with the rapturous consciousness of life beyond the self" (Eliot 1977, 3), finds a path to heroic labor through her nursing of impoverished plague victims.

22. According to Cottom, the "scene of suffering exemplifies Eliot's art as all those involved in it are bound to each other by the mysterious knowledge constituted by pain, which appears as the experience of humanity and thus as the truth of society embedded in culture" (143). Cottom claims that through Eliot's nursing scenes, we can see that "the liberal humanitarianism of her age was a rigorous social law, the promotion of sympathetic feeling an ideological construction, and the observation of individuals the rhetoric of this ideology" (xxiii). See also Cottom 141-60.

23. For example, in the 'Proem' to *Romola*, set in fifteenth-century Florence, the narrator palliates the distance between the modern reader and the narrative's remote setting by remarking that: "The great river-courses which have shaped the lives of men have hardly changed; and those other streams, the life-currents that ebb and flow in human hearts, pulsate to the same great needs, the same great loves and terrors. As our thought follows close in the slow wake of the dawn, we are impressed with the broad sameness of the human lot, which never alters in the main headings of its history—hunger and labour, seed-time and harvest, love and death" (3).

24. Jowett continues: "how they have really been made better by Dinah and Milly and Romola and the Garths and many of our other friends, and how much knowledge of life they have gained from your writings which is one of the best sorts of knowledge. I know that it is not the writer of fiction's direct business to preach morality and truth, but it is a great blessing to the world when he can teach this indirectly by his own natural sense of them pervading his creations."

25. See, also, Dorothea Brooke's explanation for her dislike of her uncle's paintings and sculptures: "I used to come from the village with all that dirt and coarse ugliness like a pain within me, and the simpering pictures in the drawing-room seemed to me like a wicked attempt to find delight in what is false, while we don't mind how hard the truth is for the neighbors outside our walls" (1977, 269).

26. Indeed, Mary Garth is affiliated with the novelistic imagination in a way that none of the other characters are. Along with sharing Eliot's first name, Mary is a voracious reader of fictional narratives. Dorothea reads scientific and religious texts, but not, apparently, novels (the volumes of polite literature in Dorothea's dressing room at Lowick remain "un-read"). Ladislaw is associated much more with poetry than novels, while Lydgate, a passionate reader in his youth, decided by the age of ten that "books were stuff, and that life was stupid" (98) and ceased feeling intellectually connected to anything except medical subjects.

27. Semmel believes that Eliot's own traumatic experiences of disinheritance caused her to endorse the importance of national identity and national inheritance.

28. Semmel points out that Ladislaw's anxieties about the Dunkirk inheritance stem not only from the illegality of the money, but more pointedly from "an anxiety to avoid the inference that his mother was Jewish. To be a pawnbroker and a fence at this time was almost certainly to be thought Jewish, though, of course, there were pawnbroking fences who where not" (1994, 97). Above all, Ladislaw wants to be thought of as "pure" so that he will be worthy of Dorothea. When Raffles tells Will of his mother's past, Will feels "as if he had had dirt cast on him. . . . His mother had braved hardship in order to separate herself from [her dishonourable parents] . . . But if Dorothea's friends had know the story . . . they would have had . . . a welcome ground for thinking him unfit to come near her" (1977, 422-23). Indeed, when news gets out about Ladislaw's maternal grandparents, even the sympathetic and sensitive Rev. Camden Farebrother comments: "so our mercurial Ladislaw has a queer genealogy. A high-spirited young lady and a musical Polish patriot made a likely enough stock for him to spring from, but I should never have suspected a grafting of the Jew pawnbroker. However, there's no knowing what a mixture will turn out beforehand. Some sorts of dirt serve to clarify" (497). It is difficult to know whether Farebrother is making this statement in order to gain sympathy from Hawley, the prejudiced man to whom he is speaking, or if he believes these ideas himself. Further, if Farebrother does endorse this anti-Semitic view, that does not mean that Eliot herself shared in this blind racism; she may be pointing to Farebrother's flaws here. Nonetheless, by emphasizing, and apparently endorsing, the notion that some types of wealth are ill-gotten and tainted and others are "pure," Eliot apparently erases the possibility that the money of the landed gentry is itself based on exploitation.

Hence Dorothea's inheritance is unsullied, while "city money" incurred by speculation and illegal activity, whether the pawnbrokers are Jewish or Calvinist, is tainted.

29. Elsie Michie has argued that during the mid nineteenth century, women were "defined [as being] naturally excluded from the realm of history and politics," while Deirdre David has delineated Eliot's profound sense of her restriction from participation in Victorian masculine "high culture" (E. Michie 146).

30. For this reading, see D. Barrett 88-89 and Lerner 249.

31. Eliot writes to Elizabeth Phelps that "it is perhaps less irrelevant to say, apropos of a distinction you seem to make between my earlier and later works, that though I trust there is some growth in my appreciation of others and in my self-distrust, there has been no change in the point of view from which I regard our life since I wrote my first fiction—the 'Scenes of Clerical Life.' Any apparent change of spirit must be due to something of which I am unconscious. The principles which are at the root of my effort to paint Dinah Morris are equally at the root of my effort to paint Mordecai" (1954-1978, 6:318).

Works Cited

Abel-Smith, Brian. 1960. *A History of the Nursing Profession*. London: Heinemann.

Abrams, M. H. 1971. *Natural Supernaturalism: Tradition and Revolution in Romantic Literature*. New York: W. W. Norton.

Ackroyd, Peter. 1991. *Dickens*. New York: Harper Collins.

Acton, William. 1972. *Prostitution, Considered in its Moral, Social and Sanitary Aspects in London & Other Large Cities & Garrison Towns, with Proposals for the Control & Prevention of its Attendant Evils*. London: Cass.

Alexander, Ziggi and Dewjee, Audrey. 1984. "Editors' Introduction." *Wonderful Adventures of Mrs. Seacole in Many Lands*. By Mary Seacole. Bristol: Falling Wall Press.

Alma-Tadema. 1977. New York: Rizzoli.

Anderson, Amanda. 1993. *Tainted Souls and Painted Faces: the Rhetoric of Fallenness in Victorian Culture*. Reading Women Writing Series, Shari Benstock & Celeste Schenck, eds. Ithaca: Cornell University Press.

Andrews, William L. 1988. "Introduction." *Wonderful Adventures of Mrs. Seacole in Many Lands*. By Mary Seacole. New York: Oxford University Press.

"A Nightingale in the Camp." 1855. *Punch, or the London Charivari* (June 9): 229.

Arac, Jonathan. 1979. *Commissioned Spirits: The Shaping of Social Motion in Dickens, Carlyle, Melville, and Hawthorne*. New Brunswick: Rutgers University Press.

Armstrong, Nancy. 1987. *Desire and Domestic Fiction: A Political History of the Novel*. New York: Oxford University Press.

Austen, Jane. 1984. *Persuasion*. New York: Bantam.

Austin, Anne L. 1957. *History of Nursing Source Book*. New York: Putnam.

The Author of the *Midwife Rightly Instructed*. 1744. *The Nurse's Guide: or Short and Safer Rules for the Management of Women of each Rank and Condition in CHILD-BED with Directions about the Choice of a WET-NURSE. In a DIALOGUE Betwixt a SURGEON and a NURSE*. London: M. Cooper.

Bailey, Wilma R. 1973. "The Geography of Fevers in Early Jamaica." *The Jamaican Historical Review* 10 (Fall): 23-32.

Bailin, Miriam. 1987. "The Consummation of Debility: Illness and Convalescence in Victorian Fiction." Diss. University of California, Berkeley.

———. 1994. *The Sickroom in Victorian Fiction: The Art of Being Ill.* Cambridge Studies in Nineteenth-Century Literature and Culture, Gillian Beer and Catherine Gallagher, gen. eds. Cambridge: Cambridge University Press.

Baker, Tracey Alison. 1985. "The Figure of the Nurse: Struggles for Wholeness in the Novels of Jane Austen, Anne, Charlotte, Emily Brontë, and George Eliot." Diss. Purdue University, Illinois.

Baly, Monica. 1980. *Nursing and Social Change.* 2nd ed. London: Heinemann.

———. 1984. "The Nurse Elite." *Nursing Times* 17 (October): 55-57.

———. 1986. *Florence Nightingale and the Nursing Legacy.* London: Croon Helm.

Barker, Anthony J. 1978. *The African Link: British Attitudes to the Negro in the Era of the Atlantic Slave Trade, 1550-1807.* London: F. Cass.

Barreca, Regina, ed. 1990. *Sex and Death in Victorian Literature.* Bloomington: Indiana University Press.

Barrett, Dorothea. 1989. *Vocation and Desire: George Eliot's Heroines.* London: Routledge.

Barrett, Edwin B. 1970. "*Little Dorrit* and the Disease of Modern Life." *Nineteenth-Century Fiction* 25:2 (September): 199-215.

Barrett Browning, Elizabeth. 1897. *The Letters of Elizabeth Barrett Browning.* Frederic G. Kenyon, ed. 2 vols. New York: Macmillan.

Beer, Gillian. 1983. *Darwin's Plots: Evolutionary Narrative in Darwin, George Eliot, and Nineteenth-Century Fiction.* Boston: Routledge & Kegan Paul.

Bell, Bernard W. 1992. "*Beloved:* A Womanist Neo-Slave Narrative; or Multivocal Remembrances of Things Past." *African American Review* 26:1 (Spring): 7-15.

Bellis, Peter J. 1987. "In the Window-Seat of Power: Vision and Power in Jane Eyre." *ELH* 54 (Fall): 639-52.

Bender, John. 1987. *Imagining the Penitentiary: Fiction and the Architecture of Mind in 18th-Century England.* Chicago: University of Chicago Press.

Benjamin, Walter. 1986. *Illuminations.* Harry Zohn, trans. New York: Harcourt, Brace & World.

Blackwood, Alicia. 1881. *A Narrative of Personal Experiences and Impressions during a Residence on the Bosphorus throughout the Crimean War.* London: Hatchard.

Bodenheimer, Rosemarie. 1987. "Jane Eyre in Search of her Story." *Charlotte Brontë's "Jane Eyre."* Harold Bloom, ed. New York: Chelsea House.

Bolt, Christine. 1971. *Victorian Attitudes to Race.* London: Routledge and K. Paul.

Borroff, Marie. 1980. "William Carlos Williams: The Diagnostic Eye." *Literature and Medicine.* Enid Rhodes Peschel, ed. Intro. by Edmund D. Pellegrino. New York: Neale Watson Academic Pub. Inc.

Briggs, Asa. 1948. "Middlemarch and the Doctors." *Cambridge Journal* 1:12 (September): 749-62.

Brightfield, Myron F. 1961. "The Medical Profession in Early Victorian England as Depicted in the Novels of the Period (1840-1870)." *Bulletin of the History of Medicine* 35 (Fall): 225-37.

Brontë, Charlotte. 1975. *Shirley, A Tale.* Andrew and Judith Hook, eds. New York: Penguin.

———. 1977. *Jane Eyre, An Autobiography.* Richard J. Dunn, ed. New York: Norton.

———. 1980. *Villette.* Mark Lilly, ed. Intro. by Tony Tanner. New York: Penguin.

Brooks, Peter. 1988. "The Tale vs. the Novel." *Novel* 21: 2,3 (Winter/Spring): 285-92.

Brown, Andrew. 1993. Introduction. *Romola.* By George Eliot. Andrew Brown, ed. Oxford: Clarendon Press.

Brown, John Crombie. 1894. *The Ethics of George Eliot.* London: William Blackwood & Sons.

Buckley, Jerome Hamilton. 1951. *The Victorian Temper.* New York: Vintage.

Carlyle, Thomas. 1899. *The Works of Thomas Carlyle in Thirty Volumes.* Centenary Edition. New York: Charles Scribner's Sons.

Casteras, Susan P. 1981. "Virgin Vows: The Early Victorian Artists' Portrayal of Nuns and Novices." *Victorian Studies* 24 (Winter): 157-84.

Césaire, Aimé. 1969. *Return to my Native Land.* John Berger and Anna Bostock, trans. Baltimore: Penguin.

Christ, Carol. 1989. "Aggression and Providential Death in George Eliot's Fiction." *Novel* 9 (Spring): 130-40.

———. 1990. "'The Hero as Man of Letters': Masculinity and Victorian Nonfiction Prose." *Victorian Sages and Cultural Discourse: Renegotiating Gender and Power.* Thaïs E. Morgan, ed. New Brunswick: Rutgers University Press.

Clarke, Bruce and Aycock, Wendell, eds. 1990. *The Body and the Text: Comparative Essays in Literature and Medicine.* Studies in Comparative Literature 22. Lubbock: Texas Tech University Press.

Cohen, Stanley and Scull, Andrew. 1986. Introduction. *Social Control and the State.* Stanley Cohen and Andrew Scull, eds. London: Basil Blackwell.

Compton, Pier. 1970. *The Colonel's Lady and the Camp Follower.* London: Robert Hale.

Cook, Edward. 1913. *The Life of Florence Nightingale*. 2 vols. London: Macmillan.

Cooper, Helen M. et al. 1989. *Arms and the Woman: War, Gender, and Literary Representation*. Chapel Hill: University of North Carolina Press.

Cope, Zachary. 1954. *Florence Nightingale and the Doctors*. London: Museum.

Corbin, Alain. 1986. "Commercial Sexuality in 19th Century France: A System of Images and Regulations." *Representations* 14 (Spring): 209-19.

Cottom, Daniel. 1987. *Social Figures: George Eliot, Social History, and Literary Representation*. Foreword by Terry Eagleton. Theory and History of Literature, vol. 44. Minneapolis: University of Minnesota Press.

Crabbe, George. 1901. *The Life and Poetical Works of George Crabbe*. London: John Murray.

Dale, Peter Alan. 1989. *In Pursuit of a Scientific Culture: Science, Art and Society in the Victorian Age*. Madison: University of Wisconsin Press.

Davidoff, Lenore. 1979."Class and Gender in Victorian England: The Diaries of Arthur J. Munby and Hannah Cullwick." *Feminist Studies* 5 (Spring): 89-141.

Davies, Celia, ed. 1980. *Rewriting Nursing History*. London: Croon Helm.

Dawson, Terence. 1988. "Unexpected Death in Scott, Emily Brontë, and Benjamin Constant." *New Comparison* 6 (Autumn): 83-100.

de Almeida, Hermione. 1991. *Romantic Medicine and John Keats*. New York: Oxford University Press.

Defoe, Daniel. 1960. *A Journal of the Plague Year*. New York: Signet.

Delaporte, François. 1986. *Disease and Civilization: The Cholera in Paris, 1832*. Arthur Goldhammer, trans. Cambridge: MIT Press.

De Quincey, Thomas. 1971. *Confessions of an English Opium Eater*. Alethea Hayter, ed. New York: Penguin Books.

Dickens, Charles. 1967. *Little Dorrit*. John Holloway, ed. New York: Penguin.

———. 1968. *The Life and Adventures of Martin Chuzzlewit*. P. N. Furbank, ed. New York: Penguin.

———. 1977. *Bleak House*. George Ford and Sylvère Monod, eds. New York: W. W. Norton.

Dietz, Lean Dixon R.N. and Lehozky, Aurelia R. R.N. 1963, 1967. *History of Modern Nursing*. 2nd Ed. Philadelphia: F. A. Davis Co.

Dijkstra, Bram. 1986. *Idols of Perversity: Fantasies of Feminine Evil in Fin-de-Siècle Culture*. Oxford: Oxford University Press.

Dingwell, Robert and McIntosh, Jean, eds. 1978. *Readings in the Sociology of Nursing*. Edinburgh: Churchill Livingstone.

Dobson, Jessie. 1969. "Doctors in Literature." *Library Association Record* 121 (May): 272.

Dock, Lavinia L. 1925. *A Short History of Nursing from the Earliest Times to the Present Day*. In collaboration with Isabel Maitland Stewart. New York: G. P. Putnam's Sons.

Donahue, M. Patricia. 1996. *Nursing, the Finest Art: An Illustrated History.* St. Louis: Mosby-Year Books.

Dreyfus, Hubert L. and Paul Rabinow. 1983. *Michel Foucault: Beyond Structuralism and Hermeneutics.* Afterword by Michel Foucault. 2nd Ed. Chicago: University of Chicago Press.

Dryden, John. 1972. *The Works of John Dryden.* H. T. Swedenberg, Jr. et al, eds. 20 vols. Berkeley: University of California Press.

Duberly, Mrs. 1855. *Journal Kept During the Russian War.* London.

Easson, Angus, ed. 1991. *Elizabeth Gaskell: The Critical Heritage.* New York: Routledge.

Eigner, Edward. 1987. "Death and the Gentleman: *David Copperfield* as Elegiac Romance." *Dickens Studies Annual* 16: 39-60.

Eliot, George. 1885. *George Eliot's Life as Related in Her Letters and Journals.* J. W. Cross, ed. 3 vols. Edinburgh: William Blackwood & Sons.

———. 1954-1978. *George Eliot Letters.* Gordon S. Haight, ed. 9 vols. New Haven: Yale University Press.

———. 1975. *Scenes from Clerical Life.* New York: Garland.

———. 1977. *Middlemarch.* Bert G. Hornback, ed. New York: W. W. Norton.

———. 1990. *Selected Essays, Poems and Other Writings.* A. S. Byatt and Nicholas Warren, eds. New York: Penguin.

———. 1993. *Romola.* Introduction by Andrew Brown, ed. Oxford: Clarendon Press.

———. n.d. *Impressions of Theophrastus Such, Essays and Poems.* New York: A. L. Burt Co.

Ellis, [Sarah Stickney]. 1850. *The Women of England, Their Social Duties, and Domestic Habits.* London: Fisher.

Fanon, Franz. 1967. *Black Skin, White Masks.* New York: Grove.

Fedele, Cassandra [Fidele, Alexandra]. 1589. *Epistolae et Orationes.*

Ferguson, Moira. 1992. *Subject to Others: British Women Writers and Colonial Slavery, 1570-1834.* New York: Routledge.

Finer, S. E. 1952. *The Life and Times of Sir Edwin Chadwick.* London: Methuen & Co.

"Florence Nightingale." 1855. *Punch, or the London Charivari* (December 8): 225.

Foucault, Michel. 1965. *Madness and Civilization.* Richard Howard, trans. New York: Vintage.

———. 1975. *The Birth of the Clinic: An Archaeology of Medical Perception.* A. M. Sheridan Smith, trans. New York: Vintage.

———. 1979. *Discipline and Punish: The Birth of the Prison.* Alan Sheridan, trans. New York: Vintage.

———. 1980a. *The History of Sexuality: Volume I, An Introduction.* Robert Hurley, trans. New York: Vintage.

————. 1980b. *Power/Knowledge: Selected Interviews & Other Writings 1972-1977*. Colin Gordon, ed. New York: Pantheon.

Fraiman, Susan. 1996. "Jane Eyre's Fall from Grace." *Jane Eyre*. Beth Newman, ed. Boston: Bedford Books of St. Martin's Press.

Freud, Sigmund. 1963. *Dora: An Analysis of a Case of Hysteria*. Philip Rieff, ed. New York: Macmillan.

Gallagher, Catherine. 1984. "The Politics of Culture and the Debate Over Representation." *Representations* 5 (Winter): 115-47.

————. 1985. *The Industrial Revolution of English Fiction: 1832-1867*. Chicago: Chicago University Press.

————. 1986a. "The Body versus the Social Body in the Works of Thomas Malthus and Henry Mayhew." *Representations* 14 (Spring): 83-106.

————. 1986b. "George Eliot and *Daniel Deronda:* The Prostitute and the Jewish Question." *Sex, Politics and Science in the Nineteenth Century.* Ruth Bernard Yeazell, ed. Baltimore: Johns Hopkins University Press.

————. 1988. "Who Was that Masked Woman? The Prostitute and the Playwright in the Comedies of Aphra Behn." *Women's Studies* 15 (Fall): 23-42.

Gallop, Jane. 1982. *The Daughter's Seduction*. Ithaca: Cornell University Press.

Gamarnikow, Eva. 1978. "Sexual Division of Labour: The Case of Nursing." *Feminism and Materialism: Women and Modes of Production*. Annette Kuhn and AnnMarie Wolpe, eds. London: Routledge & Kegan Paul.

Garber, Marjorie. 1980. "The Healer in Shakespeare." *Medicine and Literature*. Enid Rhodes Peschel, ed. Intro. by Edmund D. Pellegrino. New York: Neale Watson Academic Pub.

Garrett, Elizabeth. 1987. "Hospital Nursing." *Barbara Leigh Smith Bodichon and the Langham Place Group*. Candida Ann Lacey, ed. Women's Source Library Series. New York: Routledge & Kegan Paul.

Gaskell, Elizabeth. 1967. *The Letters of Mrs Gaskell*. J. A. V. Chapple and Arthur Pollard, eds. Cambridge: Harvard University Press.

————. 1975. *The Life of Charlotte Brontë*. Alan Shelston, ed. New York: Penguin.

————. 1985. *Ruth*. Alan Shelston, ed. Oxford: Oxford University Press.

Gates, Henry Louis, Jr. 1980. "James Gronniosaw and the Trope of the Talking Book." *Autobiography: Essays Theoretical and Critical*. James Olney, ed. Princeton: Princeton University Press.

Gay, Peter. 1984. *Education of the Senses: The Bourgeois Experience Victoria to Freud*. Oxford: Oxford University Press.

Gerin, Winifred. 1976. *Elizabeth Gaskell: A Biography*. Oxford: Clarendon Press.

Gernsheim, Helmut and Alison, eds. 1954. *Roger Fenton, Photographer of the Crimean War*. London: Secker and Warburg.

Gibbs, Peter. 1960. *Crimean Blunder: The Story of the War with Russia a Hundred Years Ago*. New York: Holt, Rinehart & Wilson.

Gilbert, Sandra and Gubar, Susan. 1979. *The Madwoman in the Attic: The Woman Writer and the 19th Century Literary Imagination*. New Haven: Yale University Press.

Goellnicht, Donald C. 1984. *The Poet-Physician: Keats and Medical Science*. Pittsburgh: University of Pittsburgh Press.

Goldie, Sue M. Introduction. 1987. *"I Have Done My Duty": Florence Nightingale in the Crimean War 1854-1856*. By Florence Nightingale. Iowa City: Iowa University Press.

[Gowing, T.]. 1895. *A Soldier's Experience or A Voice from the Ranks: Showing the Cost of War in Blood and Treasure, A Personal Narrative of the Crimean Campaign, from the Standpoint of the Ranks; The Indian Mutiny, and some of its Atrocities; the Afghan Campaigns of 1863. Also Sketches of the Lives and Deaths of Sir H. Havelock, K. C. B., and Captain Hedley Vicars, Together with Some Things Not Generally Known*. By One of the Royal Fusiliers. Nottingham: Thomas Forman & Sons.

Gregory, Brendan. 1991. "Mock Blacks and Racial Mockery: the 'Nigger' Minstrel and British Imperialism." *Acts of Supremacy: the British Empire and the Stage, 1790-1930*. J. S. Bratton, ed. New York: St. Martin's Press.

Gurney, Michael S. 1990. "Disease as Device: The Role of Smallpox in *Bleak House*." *Literature and Medicine* 9: 79-92.

Haight, Gordon S. 1968. *George Eliot: A Biography*. New York: Oxford University Press.

Haley, Bruce. 1978. *The Healthy Body and Victorian Culture*. Cambridge: Harvard University Press.

Hawthorne, Nathaniel. 1983. *The Scarlet Letter: A Romance*. Intro. by Nina Baym. New York: Penguin.

Hayter, Althea. 1968. *Opium and the Romantic Imagination*. London: Faber & Faber.

———. 1971. Introduction. *Confessions of an English Opium Eater*. By Thomas De Quincey. Althea Hayter, ed. New York: Penguin Books.

Heidegger, Martin. 1962. *Being and Time*. New York: Harper & Row.

Hellerstein, Erna O. Hume, Leslie P. and Offen, Karen M. 1981. *Victorian Women: A Documentary Account of Women's Lives in 19th-Century England, France and the U.S*. Stanford: Stanford University Press.

Herstein, Sheila R. 1985. *A Mid-Victorian Feminist: Barbara Leigh Smith Bodichon*. New Haven: Yale University Press.

Heuman, Gad J. 1981. *Between Black and White: Race Politics and the Free Coloreds in Jamaica, 1792-1865*. Westport: Greenwood Press.

Himmelfarb, Gertrude. 1984. *The Idea of Poverty: England in the Early Industrial Age*. New York: Knopf.

Hine, Darlene Clark. 1989. *Black Women in White: Racial Conflict and Cooperation in the Nursing Profession, 1890-1950*. Bloomington: Indiana University Press.

Hobsbawn, E. J. 1975. *The Age of Capital: 1848-1875*. New York: Mentor.

Holstein, Michael E. 1987. "Keats: The Poet-Healer and the Problem of Pain." *Keats-Shelley Journal* 36: 32-49.

Holton, Sandra. 1984. "Feminine Authority and Social Order: Florence Nightingale's Conception of Nursing and Care." *Social Analysis* 15 (Fall): 59-72.

Homans, Margaret. 1987. "Dreaming of Children: Literalization in *Jane Eyre*." *Charlotte Brontë's "Jane Eyre"*. Harold Bloom, ed. New York: Chelsea House.

Homer. *The Odyssey*. 1963. Robert Fitzgerald, trans. Garden City: Anchor.

Horkheimer, Max and Adorno, Theodor W. 1982. *The Dialectic of Enlightenment*. John Cumming, trans. New York: Continuum.

"The Hospital Nurse.—An Episode of the War Founded on Fact." 1855. *Fraser's Magazine* 52 (January): 96-105.

Houghton, Walter Edwards. 1957. *The Victorian Frame of Mind*. New Haven: Yale University Press.

House, Humphrey. 1942. *The Dickens World*. Oxford: Oxford University Press.

Hughes, H. Stuart. 1958. *Consciousness and Society*. New York: Random House.

Hughes, Winifred. 1980. *The Maniac in the Cellar: Sensation Novels of the 1860s*. Princeton: Princeton University Press.

Humphreys, James. 1767. *The Nurse's Guide, or Companion for a Sick Chamber*. London.

Hurwitz, Samuel Justin and Edith F. 1971. *Jamaica: A Historical Portrait*. New York: Praeger.

Huxley, Elspeth. 1975. *Florence Nightingale*. London: Weidenfeld & Nicolson.

Jameson, Anna. 1855. *Sisters of Charity Catholic and Protestant, Abroad and at Home*. London: Longmans.

———. 1856. *The Communion of Labour: A Second Lecture on the Social Employments of Women*. London: Longmans.

Jameson, Fredric. 1981. *The Political Unconscious: Narrative as a Socially Symbolic Act*. Ithaca: Cornell University Press.

Jay, Martin. 1984. *Marxism and Totality: The Adventures of a Concept from Lukács to Habermas*. Berkeley: University of California Press.

Johnson, Robert Wallace. 1767. *Some Friendly Cautions to the Heads of Families: Containing Ample Directions to Nurses who Attend the Sick, and Women in Child-bed, &c*. London: David Wilson.

Jones, Anne Hudson, ed. 1988. *Images of Nurses: Perspectives from History, Art, and Literature*. Philadelphia: University of Pennsylvania Press.

Jordanova, Ludmilla J. Introduction. 1986. *Languages of Nature: Critical Essays on Science and Literature.* New Brunswick: Rutgers University Press.

Joseph, Gerhard. 1992. *Tennyson and the Text: the Weaver's Shuttle.* Cambridge: Cambridge University Press.

Jowett, Benjamin. 1987. *Dear Miss Nightingale: A Selection of Benjamin Jowett's Letters to Florence Nightingale 1860-1893.* Vincent Quinn and John Prest, eds. Oxford: Clarendon Press.

Kestner, Joseph A. 1989. *Mythology and Misogyny: The Social Discourse of Nineteenth-Century British Classical Subject Painting.* Madison: University of Wisconsin Press.

Kingsley, Charles. 1887. *Health and Education.* London: Macmillan.

———. 1889. *Sanitary and Social Lectures and Essays.* London: Macmillan.

Lagemann, Ellen Condliffe, ed. 1983. *Nursing History: New Perspective, New Possibilities.* New York: Teachers College Press.

Lamming, George. 1991. *In the castle of my skin.* Intro. by Sandra Pouchet Paquet. Ann Arbor: University of Michigan Press.

Landow, George P. 1990. "Aggressive (Re)interpretations of the Female Sage: Florence Nightingale's *Cassandra.*" *Victorian Sages and Cultural Discourse: Renegotiating Gender and Power.* Thaïs E. Morgan, ed. New Brunswick: Rutgers University Press.

Langland, Elizabeth. 1995. *Nobody's Angels: Middle-Class Women and Domestic Ideology in Victorian Culture.* Ithaca: Cornell University Press.

Laqueur, Thomas. 1990. *Making Sex: Body and Gender from the Greeks to Freud.* Cambridge: Harvard University Press.

"The Laureate's View of the War." 1855. *Punch, or the London Charivari* (August 18): 69.

Lawson, George. 1968. *Surgeon in the Crimea: The Experiences of George Lawson Recorded in Letters to his Family 1854-1855.* Victor Bonham-Carter, ed. with Monica Lawson. London: Constable.

Lawson, Kate. 1992. "Madness and Grace: Grace Poole's Name and her Role in *Jane Eyre.*" *English Language Notes* 30:1 (Sept.): 46-50.

Leavis, F. R. and Q. D. 1970. *Dickens the Novelist.* London: Chatto & Windus.

Lerner, Laurence. 1973. *The Truthtellers: Jane Austen, George Eliot, D. H. Lawrence.* London: Chatto & Windus.

Levine, George Lewis. 1980. "The Hero as Dilettante: *Middlemarch* and *Nostromo.*" *George Eliot: Centenary Essays and an Unpublished Fragment.* Anne Smith, ed. Totowa: Barnes & Noble.

———. 1981. *The Realistic Imagination: English Fiction from Frankenstein to Lady Chatterley.* Chicago: Chicago University Press.

"London, Saturday, December 31, 1831." 1831. *The Lancet:* 479.

Longfellow, Henry Wadsworth. 1857. "Santa Filomena." *The Atlantic Monthly* 1 (November): 22-23.

Lonsdale, Margaret. 1880. *Sister Dora: A Biography.* Boston: Roberts.

McCarthy, Patrick J. 1970. "Lydgate, 'The New Young Surgeon' of *Middlemarch.*" *Studies in English Literature* 10:4 (Autumn): 805-16.

Maggs, Christopher. 1984. "Made, not born." *Nursing Times* 19 (September): 31-34.

Marcus, Steven. 1966. *The Other Victorians: A Study of Sexuality and Pornography in Mid-Nineteenth Century England.* Studies in Sex and Society, no. 1. New York: Basic Books.

Marcuse, Herbert. 1960. *Reason & Revolution: Hegel and the Rise of Social Theory.* Boston: Beacon Press.

Marsh, Jan. 1985. *The Pre-Raphaelite Sisterhood.* New York: St. Martin's Press.

Matus, Jill L. 1995. *Unstable Bodies: Victorian Representations of Sexuality and Maternity.* Manchester: Manchester University Press.

Mayhew, Henry. 1968. *London Labour and the London Poor.* Intro. by John D. Rosenberg. 4 vol. New York: Dover Press.

Maynard, John. 1984. *Charlotte Brontë and Sexuality.* Cambridge: Cambridge University Press.

Meredith, George. 1865. *Rhoda Fleming.* London: Tinslay.

Meyers, Jeffrey. 1985. *Disease and the Novel, 1880-1960.* New York: St. Martin's Press.

Michie, Elsie B. 1993. *Outside the Pale: Cultural Exclusion, Gender Difference, and the Victorian Woman Writer.* Reading Women Writing Series, Shari Benstock and Celeste Schenck, eds. Ithaca: Cornell University Press.

Michie, Helena. 1987. *The Flesh Made Word: Female Figures and Women's Bodies.* Oxford: Oxford University Press.

Miller, D. A. 1988. *The Novel and the Police.* Berkeley: University of California Press.

Miller, Richard. 1975. A Note on the Text. *The Pleasure of the Text.* By Roland Barthes. Richard Miller, trans. New York: Hill & Wang.

Moglen, Helene. 1987. "The End of *Jane Eyre* and the Creation of a Feminist Myth." *Charlotte Brontë's "Jane Eyre".* Harold Bloom, ed. New York: Chelsea House.

Montandon, Alain. 1982. "Ann: de Thomas de Quincey à Alfred de Musset." In *Romantisme Anglais et Eros.* Christian La Cassagnere, ed. Centre Du Romantisme Anglais Nouvelle Serie 3, Fascicule 14.

Moore, Judith. 1988. *A Zeal for Responsibility: The Struggle for Professional Nursing in Victorian England, 1868-1883.* Athens: University of Georgia Press.

Morris, James. 1973. *Heaven's Command: An Imperial Progress.* New York: Harecourt, Brace, Jovanovich.

Morrison, Toni. 1987. *Beloved: A Novel.* New York: Knopf.

Mort, Frank. 1987. *Dangerous Sexualities: Medico-Moral Politics in England Since 1830.* London: Routledge & Kegan Paul.

Naipaul, V. S. 1984. *Finding the Center: Two Narratives*. New York: Knopf.

Nerlich, Michael. 1987. *Ideology of Adventure: Studies in Modern Consciousness 1100-1750*. Ruth Crowley, trans. Foreword by Wlad Godzich. Minneapolis: University of Minnesota Press.

Newman, Beth. 1990. "'The Situation of the Looker-On': Gender, Narration, and Gaze in *Wuthering Heights*." *PMLA* 105:5 (October): 1029-41.

Nightingale, Florence. 1858. *Subsidiary Notes as to the Introduction of Female Nursing into Military Hospitals in Peace and in War*. London: Harrison & Sons.

———. 1860. *Notes on Nursing: What It Is and What It Is Not*. London: Harrison.

———. 1873. "A 'Note' of Interrogation." *Fraser's Magazine* 87:7 (May): 567-77.

———. 1934. "Letters of Florence Nightingale." Laura E. Richards, ed. *The Yale Review* 24 (December): 326-47.

———. 1954. *Selected Writings of Florence Nightingale*. Lucy Ridgely Seymer, ed. New York: Macmillan.

———. 1974. *Letters of Florence Nightingale in the History of Nursing Archive, Special Collections, Boston University Libraries*. Lois A. Monteiro, ed. Intro. by S. Palmer. Boston: Boston University Mugar Memorial Library Nursing Archive.

———.1979. *Cassandra: An Essay*. Myra Stark and Cynthia MacDonald, eds. Old Westbury: Feminist Press.

———.1987a. *Letters from Egypt: A Journey on the Nile, 1849-1850*. Intro. by Anthony Sattin, ed. New York: Weidenfeld & Nicolson.

———. 1987b. *"I Have Done My Duty": Florence Nightingale in the Crimean War 1854-56*. Sue M. Goldie, ed. Iowa City: University of Iowa Press.

———. 1990. *Ever Yours, Florence Nightingale: Selected Letters*. Martha Vicinus and Bea Nergaard, eds. Cambridge: Harvard University Press.

Norris, John. 1986. "'Sam is Only a Surgeon, You Know.'" *Persuasions: the Jane Austen Society of North America* 8 (December 16): 92-95.

"One Who Has Walked a Good Many Hospitals." 1857. *Times* (London), April 15, 10.

Paget, Francis Edward. 1868. *Lucretia, or the Heroine of the Nineteenth Century: A Correspondence Sensational and Sentimental*. London: 1868.

Paquet, Sandra Pouchet. 1992. "The Enigma of Arrival: *The Wonderful Adventures of Mrs. Seacole in Many Lands*." *African American Review* 26:4: 651-63.

Paris, Bernard J. 1970. "George Eliot's Religion of Humanity." *George Eliot: A Collection of Critical Essays*. George R. Creeger, ed. Englewood Cliffs: Prentice-Hall.

Patmore, Coventry. 1909. *Poems*. London: George Bell & Sons.

Paxton, Nancy L. 1992. "Mobilizing Chivalry: Rape in British Novels About the Indian Uprising of 1857." *Victorian Studies* 36:1 (Fall): 5-30.

Pellegrino, Edmund D. 1980. "Introduction." *Medicine and Literature*. Enid Rhodes Peschel, ed. New York: Neale Watson Academic Pub. Inc.

Perkin, Harold. 1969. *Origins of Modern English Society*. London: Ark.

Peschel, Enid Rhodes. 1980. "Richard Selzer and the Sacraments of Surgery." *Medicine and Literature*. Enid Rhodes Peschel, ed. Intro. by Edmund D. Pellegrino. New York: Neale Watson Academic Pub. Inc.

Peters, Margot. 1974. *Unquiet Soul: A Biography of Charlotte Brontë*. New York: Atheneum.

Poovey, Mary. 1988. *Uneven Developments: The Ideological Work of Gender in Mid-Victorian England*. Chicago: University of Chicago Press.

———. 1992. Introduction. *Cassandra*. By Florence Nightingale. Mary Poovey, ed. New York: New York University Press.

———. 1995. *Making a Social Body: British Cultural Formation 1830-1864*. Chicago: Chicago University Press.

Prince, Mary. 1989. "History of Mary Prince, a West Indian Slave." *Six Women's Slave Narratives*. Intro. by William L. Andrews. The Schomburg Library of Nineteenth-Century Black Women Writers, Henry Louis Gates, Jr., gen. ed. New York: Oxford University Press.

Prince, Nancy. 1988. "A Narrative of the Life and Travels of Mrs. Nancy Prince." *Collected Black Women's Narratives*. Intro. by Anthony G. Barthelemy. The Schomburg Library of Nineteenth-Century Black Women Writers, Henry Louis Gates, Jr., gen. ed. New York: Oxford University Press.

Pryor, Elizabeth Brown. 1990. *Clara Barton: Professional Angel*. Philadelphia: University of Pennsylvania Press.

Quinn, Vincent and Prest, John. 1987. Introduction. *Dear Miss Nightingale: A Selection of Benjamin Jowett's Letters to Florence Nightingale 1860-1893*. By Benjamin Jowett. Vincent Quinn and John Prest, eds. Oxford: Clarendon Press.

Rappe, Emmy Carolina. 1977. *"God Bless you my Dear Miss Nightingale": Letters from Emmy Carolina Rappe to Florence Nightingale 1867-1870*. Intro. by Bertil Johansson, ed. Stockholm: Almqvist & Wiksell International.

"Real Nurses Protest Sexy 'Nightingales.'" 1989. *San Francisco Chronicle*, March 15.

Reed, John. 1975. *Victorian Conventions*. Athens: Ohio University Press.

Reichler, Claude. 1987. *L'age libertin*. Paris: Minuit.

Reverby, Susan M. 1987. *Ordered to Care: The Dilemma of American Nursing, 1850-1945*. Cambridge: Cambridge University Press.

Rivers, Christopher. 1995. "Safe Sex: The Prophylactic Walls of the Cloister in the French Libertine Convent Novel of the Eighteenth Century." *Journal of the History of Sexuality* vol. 5:3 (January): 381-402.

Roach, John Peter Charles. 1978. *Social Reform in England 1780-1880.* New York: St. Martin's Press.

Robbins, Bruce. 1993. *The Servant's Hand: English Fiction from Below.* Durham: Duke University Press.

Rosenberg, Charles E. 1979. "Florence Nightingale on Contagion: The Hospital as Moral Universe." *Healing and History.* Charles E. Rosenberg, ed. New York: Dawson.

———. 1987. *The Care of Strangers: The Rise of America's Hospital System.* New York: Basic Books.

Rothfield, Lawrence. 1992. *Vital Signs: Medical Realism in Nineteenth-Century Fiction.* Princeton: Princeton University Press.

Rousseau, G. S. 1981. "Literature and Medicine: The State of the Field." *Isis* 72:263: 406-24.

Ruskin, John. 1871. *Sesame and Lilies: Three Lectures.* New York: Hurst & Co.

———. 1900. "Fiction—Fair and Foul." *Ruskin's Works.* Boston: Dana Estes & Co.

Russell, J[ohn] Rutherfurd M.D. 1861. *The History and the Heros of the Art of Medicine.* London: John Murray.

Russell, William Howard. 1858. *The British Expedition to the Crimea.* London: G. Routledge.

———. 1966. *Russell's Despatches from the Crimea: 1854-1856.* Nicholas Bentley, ed. New York: Hill & Wang.

Sabatini, Rafael. 1934. *Heroic Lives: Richard I; Saint Francis of Assisi; Joan of Arc; Sir Walter Raleigh; Lord Nelson; Florence Nightingale.* Boston: Houghton Mifflin Co.

Sanders, Valerie. 1983. "'No Ordinary Case of a Village Apothecary': The Doctor as Hero in Harriet Martineau's *Deerbrook.*" *Notes and Queries.* 30:40 (August): 293-94.

Savulêscu, Constantin. 1973. "The First War Photographic Reportage." *Image* 16:13-16.

Scarry, Elaine. 1983. "Work and the Body in Hardy and Other Nineteenth-Century Novelists." *Representations* 3 (Summer): 90-123.

———. 1987. *The Body in Pain: The Making and Unmaking of the World.* Oxford: Oxford University Press.

Schor, Hilary M. 1992. *Scheherezade in the Marketplace: Elizabeth Gaskell and the Victorian Novel.* New York: Oxford University Press.

"Scutari." 1855. *Punch, or the London Charivari* 28 (Feburary 10): 61.

Seacole, Mary. 1988. *Wonderful Adventures of Mrs. Seacole in Many Lands.* Introduction by William L. Andrews. The Schomburg Library of

Nineteenth-Century Black Women Writers. Henry Louis Gates, Jr., gen. ed. Oxford: Oxford University Press.

Selzer, Richard. 1976. *Mortal Lessons: Notes on the Art of Surgery.* New York: Simon & Schuster.

Semmel, Bernard. 1963. *Jamaican Blood and Victorian Conscience: The Governor Eyre Controversy.* Boston: Houghton Mifflin.

———. 1994. *George Eliot and the Politics of National Inheritance.* Oxford: Oxford University Press.

Showalter, Elaine. 1977. *A Literature of Their Own.* Princeton: Princeton University Press.

———. 1985. *The Female Malady: Women, Madness, and English Culture, 1830-1980.* New York: Penguin.

Simon, Walter Michael. 1983. *European Positivism in the Nineteenth Century: An Essay in Intellectual History.* Ithaca: Cornell University Press.

Sio, Arnold A. 1987. "Marginality and Free Coloured Identity in Caribbean Slave Society." *Slavery and Abolition* 8:2 (Fall): 166-82.

Smith, F[rancis] B[arrymore]. 1979. *The People's Health 1830-1910.* New York: Holmes & Meier.

———. 1982. *Florence Nightingale: Reputation and Power.* London: Croom Helm.

Sobal, Nancy Lee. 1984. "Curing and Caring: A Literary View of Professional Medical Women." Diss. University of Cincinnati.

Sollors, Werner, ed. 1993. *The Return of Thematic Criticism.* Cambridge: Harvard University Press.

Sontag, Susan. 1978. *Illness as Metaphor.* New York: Farrar, Straus, Giroux.

Southey, Charles Cuthbert. 1850. *The Life and Correspondence of the Late Robert Southey.* 6 vols. London: Longman.

Southey, Robert. 1829. *Sir Thomas More; or Colloquies on the Progress and Prospects of Society.* 2 vols. London: J. Murray.

Soyer, Alexis. 1859. *Memoirs of Alexis Soyer: With Unpublished Receipts & Odds & Ends of Gastronomy.* Compiled by F. Volannt and J. R. Warren, eds. London: W. Kent & Co.

Spears, Richard A. 1981. *Slang and Euphemism.* Middle Village: Jonathan David Pub.

Sprague, Rosemary. 1968. *George Eliot: A Biography.* Philadelphia: Chilton.

Stallybrass, Peter and White, Allon. 1986. *The Politics and Poetics of Transgression.* Ithaca: Cornell University Press.

Steiner, George. 1991. "Mars." *New Yorker.* (March 11): 88-92.

Sterne, Laurence. 1983. *The Life and Opinions of Tristram Shandy, Gentleman.* Ian Campbell Ross, ed. Oxford: Oxford University Press.

Stewart, Garrett. 1974. *Dickens and the Trials of Imagination.* Cambridge: Harvard University Press.

Stoneman, Patsy. 1987. *Elizabeth Gaskell.* Bloomington: Indiana University Press.

Strachey, Lytton. 1918. *Eminent Victorians: Cardinal Manning, Florence Nightingale, Dr. Arnold, General Gordon.* New York: G. P. Putnam's Sons.

Summers, Anne. 1988. *Angels and Citizens: British Women as Military Nurses, 1854-1914.* New York: Routledge & Kegan Paul.

———. 1989. "The Mysterious Demise of Sarah Gamp: The Domiciliary Nurse and her Detractors, c. 1830-1860." *Victorian Studies* (Spring): 365-86.

Taylor, Frances Margaret. 1856. *Eastern Hospitals and English Nurses.* London.

Tennyson, Alfred. 1893. *Life and Works of Alfred Lord Tennyson.* Hallam Tennyson, ed. 10 vols. New York: Macmillan.

———. 1971. *Tennyson's Poetry.* Robert W. Hill, Jr., ed. New York: W. W. Norton.

Thackeray, William Makepeace. 1912. *The Newcomes.* London: Dent.

Thompson, E. P. 1966. *The Making of the English Working Class.* New York: Vintage.

Thompson, Roger. 1979. *Unfit for Modest Ears: A Study of Pornographic, Obscene and Bawdy Works Written or Published in England in the Second Half of the Seventeenth Century.* London: Macmillan.

Tomasini, F. 1636. *Vita della Signora C. Fedele.*

Tooley, Sarah. 1906. *The History of Nursing in the British Empire.* London: S. H. Bousfield.

Traumann, Joanna and Carol Pollard. 1982. *Literature and Medicine: An Annotated Bibliography.* Revised Edition. Pittsburgh: University of Pittsburgh Press.

Valverde, Mariana. 1989. "The Love of Finery: Fashion and the Fallen Woman in Nineteenth-Century Social Discourse." *Victorian Studies* 32:2 (Winter): 169-88.

Vicinus, Martha. 1985. *Independent Women: Work and Community for Single Women 1850-1920.* Chicago: Chicago University Press.

Vicinus, Martha and Bea Nergaard. 1990. Introduction. *Ever Yours, Florence Nightingale: Selected Letters.* By Florence Nightingale. Martha Vicinus and Bea Nergaard, eds. Cambridge: Harvard University Press.

Vincent, Thomas. 1668. *God's Terrible Voice in the City of London: wherein you have the narration of the two late dreadful judgements of plague and fire, inflicted by the Lord upon that city; the former in the year 1665. the latter in the year 1666.* Cambridge: Marmaduke Johnson.

Vrettos, Athena. 1990. "From Neurosis to Narrative: The Private Life of the Nerves in *Villette* and *Daniel Deronda.*" *Victorian Studies* 33 (Summer): 551-79.

———. 1995. *Somatic Fictions: Imagining Illness in Victorian Culture.* Palo Alto: Stanford University Press.

Walkowitz, Judith R. 1980. *Prostitution and Victorian Society: Women, Class and the State.* Cambridge: Cambridge University Press.

Ward, Samuel Ringgold. *Autobiography of a Fugitive Negro.* 1856. New York: Arno Press, 1968.

Watt, George. 1984. *The Fallen Woman in Nineteenth Century Fiction.* Ottowa: Barnes and Noble.

Webb, Igor. *From Custom to Capital: The English Novel and the Industrial Revolution.* Ithaca: Cornell University Press.

Weintraub, Stanley. 1991. "Victorian Poets and Physicians." *Literature and Medicine.* 10: 86-97.

Wells, Ruth Gilpin. 1988. *A Woman of Her Time and Ours: Mary Magdalen Taylor, SMG.* Charlotte: Laney-Smith.

Welsh, Alexander. 1971. *The City of Dickens.* Oxford: Oxford University Press.

Williams, A. Susan. 1987. *The Rich Man and the Diseased Poor in Early Victorian Literature.* Atlantic Highlands: Humanities Press.

Williams, Guy. 1987. *The Age of Miracles: Medicine and Surgery in the 19th Century.* Chicago: Academy Chicago Pub.

Williams, Raymond. 1958. *Culture and Society, 1780-1950.* New York: Columbia University Press.

———. 1984. *The English Novel: From Dickens to Lawrence.* London: The Hogarth Press.

———. 1986. Foreword. *Languages of Nature: Critical Essays on Science and Literature.* Ludmilla J. Jordanova, ed. New Brunswick: Rutgers University Press.

Woodham-Smith, Cecil. 1951. *Florence Nightingale, 1820-1910.* London: Constable.

———. 1972. *Queen Victoria: From Her Birth to the Death of the Prince Consort.* New York: Dell.

Woolf, Virginia. 1929. *A Room of One's Own.* New York: Harcourt, Brace & Co.

Young, G. M. 1977. *Portrait of an Age: Victorian England.* Oxford: Oxford University Press.

Zweig, Paul. 1974. *The Adventurer.* New York: Basic Books, Inc.

Index